April 1984

Love Sharon.

The Book of Canadians

Carlotta Hacker

The Book of Canadians

An Illustrated Guide to Who Did What

Hurtig Publishers
Edmonton

Hurtig Publishers Ltd.
10560–105 Street
Edmonton, Alberta

Canadian Cataloguing in Publication Data

Hacker, Carlotta, 1931–
The book of Canadians

ISBN 0-88830-243-6

1. Canada—Biography—Dictionaries, Juvenile.
I. Title.
FC25.H33 j920'.071 C83-091231-2
F1005.H33

Design/David Shaw & Associates Ltd.
Cover illustration/David Chang
Printed and bound in Canada
by Ashton-Potter Ltd.

Acknowledgements

Firstly, I wish to acknowledge my debt to all those who have written full-length biographies about many of the people who appear in this book. Without their years of dedicated research, *The Book of Canadians* could not have been written.

I am also greatly indebted to a wide range of reference works and to numerous histories of Canadian achievement in particular areas. Of special value were the University of Toronto Press's multivolume *Dictionary of Canadian Biography* and the wonderfully detailed *Encyclopedia of Music in Canada*; also *The Oxford Companion to Canadian History and Literature* by Norah Story; *Canada's Sporting Heroes* by S. F. Wise and Douglas Fisher; and *Canadian Aviation Pioneers* by Alice Sutherland.

The following people have taken the time and trouble to read portions of the manuscript and to offer criticism and suggestions: Professor David Bentley, Department of English, University of Western Ontario; Professor F. A. De Lory, Faculty of Applied Science and Engineering, University of Toronto; Hugh A. Dempsey, Assistant Director (Collections), Glenbow Museum, Calgary; Professor D. M. L. Farr, Department of History, Carleton University; Professor Carl Morey, Faculty of Music, University of Toronto; Cheryl A. Rielly, Assistant Curator, Canada's Sports Hall of Fame; and Dr. Helen Evans Reid, former Director of Medical Publications, The Hospital for Sick Children, Toronto. Their advice and comments were of great value, and I am most appreciative, but I should like to stress that I alone bear all responsibility for content and accuracy.

Many archivists and librarians across Canada have, as usual, taken infinite pains to answer my questions and to check out obscure details for me. Special thanks go to the staff of London Public Library, and particularly to Cheryl Froud, Alastair Neely, Mariko Obokata, and Helen Stephenson, who have co-operated so energetically in my search for information, sometimes spending a whole afternoon helping me discover which of two conflicting dates is the correct one. Among others who have helped search out details, I am especially grateful to José Druker and Andrea Lemieux.

Many thanks go to J. Harrison Shannon, Dagmar Stegelmann, and Susan Hedley of David Shaw & Associates Ltd. for their enthusiastic work in the production of the book. And, above all, I wish to express my appreciation to David Shaw for his great contribution as the book's designer and picture editor. The sources of the pictures are acknowledged in the Credits on p.232.

Carlotta Hacker

How to Use This Book

If you want to read about a particular person, turn first to the index. Some of the people included in the book do not have entries of their own, but the index will direct you to the pages on which they are featured. The index also gives full names and titles, including Orders of Canada. In most cases, honours and titles are not mentioned in the actual entries.

Rather than looking up a particular person, you may prefer to browse through the book. This could be very rewarding, as you will find some fascinating Canadians here. There are villains as well as heroes and heroines, little-known inventors as well as famous pop stars, and a wide variety of men and women who set out to do something—and did it.

In many of the biographies, there is an asterisk (*) against a name. This means that there is a separate entry on that person. You will find it worth following up these cross references and reading the related biography, as it often gives another aspect of the same story.

This book covers almost a thousand years of achievement—from the early Norse explorers to the latest sports champions. We hope you will enjoy sharing their adventures.

How to Find Out More

Further information is readily available on most of the people in this book. Some have had individual biographies written about them in such series as "The Canadians" (published by Fitzhenry & Whiteside). In other cases, you would do best to look under subject headings and consult books on hockey players, painters, and so on. *The Heroes* by Stephen Franklin and *The Inventors* by J. J. Brown (both published by McClelland and Stewart) are especially recommended.

There are also numerous collections of general biography. These include Terry Angus and Shirley White's *Canadians All* (Methuen), Pierre Berton's *My Country* and *The Wild Frontier* (McClelland and Stewart), George Lonn's *Faces of Canada* (Pitt Publishing), Grant MacEwan's *Fifty Mighty Men* and *And Mighty Women Too* (Prairie Books), and George Woodcock's *Faces from History* (Hurtig Publishers). Although most of these books were written for adults, they tell interesting stories and can be enjoyed by young people too.

In addition, brief biographies of Canadians who have won bravery awards may be obtained by writing to: The Chancellery of Canadian Orders and Decorations, Government House, Ottawa, K1A 0A1 (or phone: (613) 993-9395).

Francis Abbott
Drowned 1831
Francis Abbott was called the Hermit of Niagara. For two years he lived on Goat Island between the two falls, his only companions being his dog, his books, and his musical instruments. Fascinated by the terrifying grandeur of Niagara, he used to play his violin to the accompanying roar of the falls. At other times he would hang by his hands or feet from a timber that projected over the precipice.

Abbott was the son of English Quakers and was said to have travelled widely. But he was a bit of a mystery figure and little was known about his background. His death, though, was fully recorded. He often swam at the base of the falls, and one day he was sucked into the Great Whirlpool. For several days, his body was carried round in the whirlpool, horrifying all who saw it, before the waters finally released their victim.

John J. C. Abbott
Born 1821, St.Andrews, Que.
Died 1893
John J. C. Abbott was Canada's third prime minister. He took over when Sir John A. Macdonald* died in 1891 and was in office just over a year. Very much the elder statesman, Abbott was the most suitable Conservative available, a respectable and respected figure, leader of the Conservatives in the Senate and a former dean of law at McGill University. Although he had been involved in the Pacific Scandal, that was far in the past by the time he became prime minister.

Abbott had, in fact, been at the very centre of the scandal. As lawyer to the businessman Sir Hugh Allan,* he had arranged for vast sums of money to be given to Macdonald and other leading Conservatives. He also handled the details of the Pacific Railway contract, which Macdonald and his ministers awarded to Sir Hugh Allan. All the wheeling and dealing came to light when some business correspondence was stolen from Abbott's law office—and then printed in the newspapers for all to read. And so began the great Pacific Scandal of 1873. Yet Abbott suffered little long-term harm. He was tough and very shrewd, and he went on to be made not only prime minister but a knight. He was Sir John Abbott when he died.

Maude Abbott
Born 1869, St.Andrews, Que.
Died 1940
One of Canada's early women doctors, Maude Abbott was also one of the most impressive. She had tremendous energy and enthusiasm. As a child, she longed to learn "exciting subjects" such as Latin and German. Later, her great ambition was to study medicine at McGill, her favourite university. McGill would not accept women as medical students in those days, but it did take Dr. Abbott on staff—after she had become highly qualified at other universities.

Maude Abbott spent most of her working life at McGill. She ran the medical museum and catalogued all the specimens in it. She taught, researched, wrote countless medical papers, and became famous throughout the world as *the* expert on congenital heart disease. Some people at that time thought women had no place in medicine, but Dr. Maude Abbott proved them wrong.

Lord Aberdeen
Born 1847, Scotland
Died 1934
The Governor General of Canada for most of the 1890s was Lord Aberdeen, and to some extent Lady Aberdeen. She was such a powerful character that she was sometimes referred to as the Governess General.

Both the Aberdeens were keen social reformers. At home in Scotland they had established hospitals, schools, and clubs, and they continued their good work in Canada. Lady Aberdeen helped to form the National Council of Women and served as its first president. And in 1897 she founded the Victorian Order of Nurses, which still provides nursing care to the sick in their own homes.

William Aberhart
Born 1878, nr.Kippen, Ont.
Died 1943
William Aberhart was well known in the West long before he was premier of Alberta. A Calgary school principal and fire-and-brimstone preacher, he broadcast a radio program called *Back to the Bible Hour*. There were few Albertans who hadn't heard Bible Bill's voice thundering into their homes. Then, during the Great Depression, he began to thunder about a new type of political party —Social Credit. Aberhart said that a Social Credit government would give each Albertan, every month, a dividend worth $25.

Times were bad and Bible Bill sounded good, so Albertans voted for Social Credit in the 1935 provincial election. William Aberhart became premier of Alberta and head of the first Social Credit government anywhere in the world. But when he tried to give Albertans the various benefits he had promised, the federal government ruled some of them improper and wouldn't allow them. Even so, Social Credit was regularly voted back into power right up to the 1970s. And Bible Bill is still remembered for his "funny money."

Carl Agar
Born 1901, Lion's Head, Ont.
Died 1968

Carl Agar was Mr. Helicopter. By his daring experimental flights, he gave the helicopter a new and immensely useful purpose. This was in the years following World War II, in which Agar had served in the RCAF.

Although helicopters had been flown in the war, they were considered too frail for many purposes, and their use had been very limited. But Agar believed they were just the machines for rugged country, for they could land where fixed-wing aircraft couldn't; for instance, on small mountain plateaus. At the time, nobody knew how a helicopter would stand up to mountain flying. Would the blades bite at heights of 2,000 metres or so? Would the helicopter fall out of the sky? Agar proved it wouldn't, as month after month he made his trial flights among the British Columbian mountains.

His experiments attracted wide notice, and he soon had the chance to prove how useful the machine could be as an aerial packhorse. All the material for building B.C.'s Palisade Lake Dam was humped in by helicopter. This involved 1,000 trips, with Agar himself flying 250 of them. Thanks to Carl Agar, helicopters are now used throughout the world to take people and equipment into rough terrain.

Robert Aitken
Born 1939, Kentville, N.S.

Robert Aitken learned to play the flute as a child, and when he was 19 he became principal flutist in the Vancouver Symphony Orchestra. He was the youngest flute player ever to hold this position. Since then, he has performed with many orchestras, both in Canada and abroad, as well as playing in a trio he formed.

Aitken is also known as a composer, the writer of experimental works. Sometimes he uses drawings instead of notes and then leaves it to the performers to decide what to play.

Emma Albani
Born 1847, Chambly, Que.
Died 1930

Hailed as the "queen of song," soprano Madame Albani won the hearts of the whole world with her beautiful voice. She first sang in public aged nine at the Mechanics' Hall in Montreal. Half a century later, she was still delighting her audiences. She was so famous that when Queen Victoria died, Albani was asked to sing at the private funeral service at Windsor Castle.

Like many later Canadian singers, Emma Albani gained her fame abroad. She left Canada when she was 18, studied in the United States, France, and Italy, and then settled in England as the star of Covent Garden opera house. There she married the manager's son, Ernest Gye. This kept her based in England, though she went on singing tours throughout the world and came several times to Canada.

Her real name was not Albani (she decided on that when studying in Italy). She was born Marie Lajeunesse, a French Canadian girl without much money but with a lot of talent. And she became one of the greatest superstars of her time.

Viscount Alexander of Tunis
Born 1891, Ireland
Died 1969

One of the great Allied commanders of World War II, Alexander was appointed Governor General of Canada soon after the war. He was one of the most popular men ever to hold this position. During most of the war years, the Earl of Athlone had been Governor General. He was a member of the British royal family, and he too had served as an army officer.

Andrew Allan
Born 1907, Scotland
Died 1974
Andrew Allan was one of the key figures who gave CBC radio such a fine reputation during its early years. He is especially associated with *CBC Stage*, the long-running program of plays which he masterminded and often acted in.

Allan was a stickler for perfection, though he had rather a gentle air of wise melancholy. A graduate of the University of Toronto, he first worked in radio with CFRB in Toronto, moving to the CBC in 1939. Over the years, he was involved in live theatre as well as radio and TV, and was a writer as well as an actor and producer. He also gave radio talks, some of which were printed in the book *Andrew Allan: A Self-Portrait*, which was published after his death.

Henry Alline
Born 1748, U.S.A.
Died 1784
Henry Alline started a religious revival in the Maritimes during the early years of settlement—the New Light movement. He was the son of a New England couple who had moved to Falmouth, N.S., when he was a child. Like most settlers at Falmouth, they were deeply religious, and Alline was encouraged to read his Bible from an early age.

In 1775 he experienced a "conversion," a personal call from God to go out and convert others so that they too would see the New Light and be saved. So he became a travelling preacher, moving from village to village, holding services and writing hymns for his followers to sing. Although most clergy disapproved, the New Light movement was extremely popular. But it lost its impetus when, at the age of 36, Alline died of tuberculosis.

Hugh Allan
Born 1810, Scotland
Died 1882
The son of a Glasgow shipowner, Hugh Allan came to Canada as a young man and soon made a fortune. He ran a shipping line and a bank—he was into every type of business—and he became so important that he was awarded a knighthood.

When plans were afoot to build the Canadian Pacific Railway, Prime Minister John A. Macdonald* gave the contract for the job to Sir Hugh Allan. This may or may not have been because Allan gave a total of $350,000 to Macdonald and other leading Conservatives to help them campaign for the forthcoming federal election. Although such campaign funds were legal, Canadians were horrified when they learned what had been going on. Some said Allan had bribed Macdonald. Even worse, Allan was backed by American businessmen who wanted to control Canada's railway. The whole thing was a scandal!

As a result of the Pacific Scandal of 1873, John A. Macdonald lost his job as prime minister and Hugh Allan lost the railway contract. But that was all Allan lost. He lived on in splendour in his Montreal mansion, growing richer and more powerful each year.

Almighty Voice
Born 1874, nr.Batoche, Sask.
Killed 1897
Almighty Voice only lived 23 years, yet he lives on in legend because of the way he died. He was a Cree from One Arrow Reserve near Batoche, and in 1895 he was arrested for stealing a steer. This was not a serious offence. But he then escaped and shot the Mountie who came after him—and that was a very serious offence.

The Mounties were determined to "get their man," even if it took a year or more. Eventually, they traced Almighty Voice to a small poplar wood near his reserve. But he would not surrender. Along with two relatives (one of whom was only 13 years old), he determinedly held out, firing at all who approached. The Mounties then brought in reinforcements: more than a hundred men and two cannons. And they pounded the wood with shells for four hours. All three Indians were killed in the bombardment.

Doris Anderson
Born 1925, Calgary, Alta.
As editor of *Chatelaine* from 1958 to 1977, Doris Anderson transformed the magazine. It used to be a docile journal for housewives. She turned it into a vigorous publication that questioned women's traditional roles and specialized in topical (and often controversial) articles. In the process, she boosted the magazine's circulation from 46,000 to more than one million.

Raised in Alberta, where she briefly taught school, she had a number of copywriting and editing jobs before she took over *Chatelaine*. She has long been a champion of the women's movement, constantly speaking out for women's rights and serving on committees to help improve conditions for women. In recent years, she has also written novels, and they too carry a strong message about the problems women face.

Brother André
Born 1845, St.Grégoire, Que.
Died 1937
In 1982 the Pope beatified Brother André (declared him blessed). Beatification is the second of three steps towards being made a saint.

Brother André was born Alfred Bessette, the son of a very poor family. Poor in health too, he could seldom keep a job for long. But he was so devout that the Holy Cross Brothers took him into their community and gave him the job of doorkeeper at their school for boys in Montreal.

Whenever the boys or the priests were sick, Brother André visited them and prayed to St. Joseph, and around 1877 he prayed in a ward of smallpox victims. Some of the patients in the ward had already died of smallpox, but the remainder all recovered. This was attributed to Brother André's prayers.

Word of his faith-healing soon spread, and people came flocking to him for cures. He built a small wooden chapel on Mount Royal so that he could pray for the sick there. This tiny chapel grew to become St. Joseph's Oratory. Today, millions of pilgrims from all over the world visit Brother André's shrine in St. Joseph's Oratory, and many swear that they have come away cured.

Margaret Anglin
Born 1876, Ottawa, Ont.
Died 1958
For many years, the most famous leading lady on the American stage was Canadian actress Margaret Anglin. Born in the Parliament Buildings, Ottawa (where her father was speaker of the House of Commons), she grew up in eastern Canada and then went to New York to train for the theatre. There, at the age of 22, she had her first big success in the play *Cyrano de Bergerac*. Her stage career spread over more than 50 years, from the 1890s to the 1940s. Meanwhile, her fame spread throughout the world. She was hailed as one of the greatest dramatic actresses of her day.

Paul Anka

Born 1941, Ottawa, Ont.

Paul Anka became a star overnight when at the age of 15 he recorded *Diana*, one of the most successful pop records ever. It sold more than 5 million copies. At the time, Anka was already a practised musician. As well as having sung on radio, he had written songs and recorded one of them in Hollywood. He had also performed on television in the CBC's *Pick the Stars* and *Cross-Canada Hit Parade*.

As a teen idol during the 1950s and early 1960s, Anka toured the world to the accompaniment of screaming audiences. He made record after record, had hit after hit, and also wrote a number of hits for other singers, such as "My Way," which he composed for Frank Sinatra. Since his rise to stardom, Paul Anka has lived mostly in the United States, though he has given numerous concerts in Canada. In 1982-83 he hosted his own show on CBC television.

Franklin Arbuckle

Born 1909, Toronto, Ont.

Some of the pictures in this book were painted by Franklin Arbuckle, one of Canada's best-known illustrators. He is especially famous for his historical illustrations, which capture the character of early Canadians as well as their appearance.

Arbuckle grew up in Toronto, graduating from the Ontario College of Art, and over the years he has produced many types of art: paintings, book illustrations, tapestry designs . . . everything from covers for *Maclean's* magazine to a huge mural in Hamilton City Hall. A prominent figure in the art world, he was president of the Royal Canadian Academy 1960-64. (See Credits on p.232 for his illustrations in this book.)

Violet Archer

Born 1913, Montreal, Que.

Violet Archer has devoted her whole life to music and is among Canada's most celebrated composers. She was born Violet Balestreri, the daughter of Italian Canadians, and grew up in Montreal, where she studied the piano and later graduated in music from McGill. During the following years, she studied under two of the world's leading composers, Bela Bartok and Paul Hindemith. She has written a wide range of compositions, from religious works to a comic opera, and has also held several university positions. Since 1962 she has been on the staff of the University of Alberta.

Canada has many very talented composers, and a large number of them are women. They include Norma Beecroft of Ontario, Barbara Pentland of British Columbia, and Micheline Saint-Marcoux of Quebec.

Adams George Archibald
Born 1814, Truro, N.S.
Died 1892

A level-headed Nova Scotian who spoke fluent French, Adams Archibald was made the first lieutenant governor of Manitoba in 1870. Being a Maritimer, he was considered acceptable both to the Métis and the English-speaking settlers. A lieutenant governor from Quebec or Ontario would have been thought biased, and probably would have been, because of the way the two provinces had taken different sides over the Red River Rebellion.

Archibald was a good choice in other ways too, for he was tactful and understanding. Unfortunately, he arrived at the Red River just after Colonel Wolseley's* army, which was bent on wreaking vengeance on the Métis. But he worked hard to lessen the tensions and gradually established order in Manitoba.

Archibald had a long experience in politics (he had been a Father of Confederation), and he later served as lieutenant governor of Nova Scotia.

Elizabeth Arden
Born 1884, Woodbridge, Ont.
Died 1966

Elizabeth Arden's real name was Florence Nightingale Graham, and at first she intended to be a nurse like her namesake. But after a year's training she realized that she "not only wanted to make people well, but she wanted to make them beautiful."

Moving to the U.S. when she was 25, she took a job as a secretary in a cosmetics firm and learned how to give massages and facial treatments. She then borrowed some money from a relative and set up her own beauty salon. This was when she took the name Elizabeth Arden. Her salon was a success from the start, partly because she hired chemists to make new and improved skin creams. It grew into a world-famous beauty empire.

The queen of this empire had an equally successful sideline career. Under the name Elizabeth Graham, she was known as a "leading lady of the turf," owner of a string of racehorses (which gained her more than $2 million in prize money). Her personal life was less successful. She married twice and divorced twice, first to an American silk manufacturer and then to a Russian prince.

Margaret Atwood
Born 1939, Ottawa, Ont.

Margaret Atwood was an author at a very young age. From early childhood, she composed stories for her brother, setting them out in comic-book manner. Intent on being a writer, she avoided career jobs when she grew up. Although she was a university graduate, she took casual work (such as being a waitress) so that she would have the time to think and to put her thoughts down.

She first gained fame in her late twenties, when her poetry book *The Circle Game* won a Governor General's Award. A few years later, in 1969, she published her first novel, *The Edible Woman*. Since then, Margaret Atwood has written other widely praised novels, as well as more very fine poetry. Her works include a controversial book called *Survival*, which discusses themes in Canadian Literature. One of Canada's leading contemporary writers, Margaret Atwood has sold more than 2 million copies of her books throughout the world.

Philippe-Joseph Aubert de Gaspé
Born 1786, Quebec, Que.
Died 1871

Philippe Aubert de Gaspé wrote the classic historical novel *Les Anciens Canadiens*, which was translated into English as *The Canadians of Old*. It was published when he was 77.

Gaspé was a lawyer by training and a former sheriff of Quebec, but he had gone bankrupt and been imprisoned for debt. Shortly before he was thrown in prison, his son Philippe-Ignace Aubert de Gaspé wrote what was the first French Canadian novel, *L'Influence d'un Livre*. It did very badly, partly because it came out in 1837, the year Lower Canada was in a turmoil of rebellion. Young Philippe-Ignace died a few years later, so the father was continuing the son's work when, after his release from prison, he settled down to write his historical epic. It took him many years to write and gives a great fund of information on social customs and folklore.

William Baffin
Born c.1584, England
Died 1622

Sailing with Captain Robert Bylot, William Baffin made two Arctic voyages in search of the Northwest Passage, hoping to find a sea route to the Pacific and the rich markets of China. Baffin was Bylot's pilot, and he was a first-rate navigator. During his explorations in 1615, he concluded that Hudson Bay was indeed a bay, rather than a passageway westward. The following year, he sailed through Davis Strait and explored Baffin Bay, getting farther north than anyone else was to do for more than 200 years.

Among the other British seamen who searched for the Northwest Passage in the early 1600s were Henry Hudson,* Thomas Button, Thomas James, and Luke Foxe.

Charles Baillairgé
Born 1825, Quebec, Que.
Died 1906

The architect Charles Baillairgé designed Laval University and numerous other buildings in Quebec. For many years he was the city engineer of Quebec. In addition, he designed buildings in Ottawa and was one of the architects who worked on the design of the original Parliament Buildings.

Baillairgé was a member of an outstanding family who for four generations produced some of Quebec's leading artisans, sculptors, and architects.

Carroll Baker
Born 1949, Bridgewater, N.S.

Singer and songwriter Carroll Baker was raised in Port Medway, N.S., and moved to Toronto when she was 16. For several years she sang at country fairs and in Ontario clubs, making her first record in 1970. In 1975 she made her breakthrough with her recording of "I've Never Been This Far Before." By the following year she was a star, one of Canada's most popular country singers.

Edwin Baker
Born 1893, Collins Bay, Ont.
Died 1968

The Canadian National Institute for the Blind was established and built up by Edwin Baker, an engineering graduate of Queen's University who had enlisted in World War I—and was blinded by a sniper's bullet at the age of 22. He thought that was the end of everything, that he would have no chance of a career. But after a readjustment course in England, he realized that blind people could live purposeful, happy lives, provided they were given the necessary training and help.

On returning to Canada, Baker started a small centre for blinded war veterans in Toronto, and before long he was planning a centre for all blind Canadians. With other enthusiasts, he formed the CNIB in 1918, which grew into a large and vigorous organization under his management.

Baker worked to prevent blindness as well as helping those who had already lost their sight, and in 1954 he was elected first president of the World Council for the Welfare of the Blind.

Meanwhile, Charles Frederick Fraser (1850-1925) had been knighted for his work for the blind. He was the Nova Scotian pioneer, head of the School for the Blind in Halifax for 50 years—from 1873 almost until his death. He too had been blinded in his youth.

Casey Baldwin
Born 1882, Toronto, Ont.
Died 1948
Casey Baldwin was the first Canadian to fly an airplane and the seventh person in the world to do so. His historic flight took place on March 12, 1908, when he piloted the *Red Wing* 97 metres over the ice of Lake Keuka at Hammondsport, New York.

Baldwin was 26 years old at the time, and he had already gained a name as a football star, captaining the University of Toronto's team. A graduate in engineering, he was one of the aircraft pioneers working in Alexander Graham Bell's* Aerial Experiment Association. His college friend J. A. D. McCurdy* was also on this team, and he too achieved a "first." It was McCurdy who made the first flight in Canada (in 1909).

Casey Baldwin pioneered with watercraft as well as aircraft, and he became a world-famous expert on hydrofoils.

Karen Baldwin
Born 1963, London, Ont.
Miss Universe 1982 was 18-year-old Karen Baldwin. She was the first Canadian ever to win the world beauty contest.

Karen started on her road to success while still a secondary school student. She took a course at the Elegance School of Self-improvement and Modelling in Lambeth, Ont., and had her first modelling assignments before she had even finished the course. In September 1981 she was selected Miss London, winning the Miss Canada title two months later. And in July 1982, with the world's cameras focused on her, the chestnut-haired beauty gained her crowning glory at the Miss Universe contest in Peru.

Robert Baldwin
Born 1804, York (Toronto), Ont.
Died 1858
Robert Baldwin was one of the men who paved the way for the system of government we have today. Soon after the Province of Canada was formed in 1841, he became leader of the Reform party in Canada West, and he formed an alliance with Louis-Hippolyte La Fontaine,* who was leader of the Reformers in Canada East. Together these two men worked to bring responsible government to the Province of Canada. And together they achieved it when they led the government known as the Great Ministry (1848-51).

Baldwin's father had also been a prominent Reform leader: William Warren Baldwin. Indeed, it was he who first suggested, in a letter to the Duke of Wellington, that the colonies of British North America should be given responsible government.

(For an explanation of responsible government, see J. B. Uniacke.*)

Frederick Banting
Born 1891, Alliston, Ont.
Died 1941

Dr. Banting offered life to the dying with his discovery of insulin as a treatment for diabetes. The disease used to kill millions of people.

Banting made his great breakthrough in the summer of 1921—a young researcher with a ridiculous theory, working on sufferance at first in Professor J. Macleod's physiology laboratories at the University of Toronto. Banting's enthusiastic assistant was Charles Best, a 22-year-old medical student who had already graduated in physiology. James Collip, a biochemist from the University of Alberta, joined the team later in the year, as did several others. Their work won a Nobel Prize, which was awarded jointly to Banting and Macleod, much to Banting's fury. He felt that Best, not Macleod, deserved the honour.

The three young researchers all made further contributions to medicine. Collip did major work on hormones, and Best's many research projects included the production of heparin, a substance which prevents blood from clotting (and makes open-heart surgery possible). As for Banting, he led a wide-ranging program of medical research at the Banting Institute, which was founded in his honour. He was killed in a plane crash while on a military mission in Newfoundland during World War II.

Marius Barbeau
Born 1883, Ste.Marie, Que.
Died 1969

The first person to collect Canadian folk songs in a scientific and organized manner was Marius Barbeau, an anthropologist with the National Museum in Ottawa.

Starting in 1911 with a research trip to a Huron reserve, Barbeau travelled far across Canada, eagerly studying folklore and folk songs. He copied down the tunes, noting where he had discovered each song and who had sung it to him. He also recorded many of the songs, no easy task before the days of tape recorders. During his early trips, Barbeau had to make his recordings on Edison wax cylinders. In all, he documented about 8,000 tunes and 13,000 texts (some of them different versions of the same songs).

Billy Barker
Born c.1820, England
Died 1894

Billy Barker was a boisterous sailor who jumped ship in Victoria so that he could join the gold rush. He knew very little about prospecting, and the experienced miners laughed at him when in 1862 he began to dig far up Williams Creek in the Cariboo. They were already mining the promising parts of the creek. They stopped laughing when, in only two days, Billy dug up $1,000 worth of gold. His claim eventually yielded $600,000.

The town of Barkerville quickly sprang up in the area—a rip-roaring mining town. One of the attractions was Billy himself, who used to dance on the tavern tables and sing this song:

I'm English Bill,
Never worked, never will.
Get away, girls,
Or I'll tousle your curls.

But Billy was too free and easy. His money went as quickly as it came. Having been fabulously rich, he died desperately poor.

William Barker
Born 1894, Dauphin, Man.
Died 1930
One of the greatest fighter pilots of World War I, Billy Barker shot down 53 enemy aircraft. He used different tactics from most pilots. Instead of diving on the enemy from above, he flew close to the ground, luring the enemy down to his level. At low altitudes, with little air space to manoeuvre in, his agile Sopwith Camel had an advantage over the faster German planes.

Barker spent part of the war in northern Italy, where he and his squadron conducted such daring attacks on enemy air bases that they virtually grounded the Austrian air force. His most outstanding achievement was in the last month of the war, during what was expected to be a non-combat flight to England. All on his own, Barker took on about 60 enemy aircraft and succeeded in downing five of them before he went crashing to the ground. He not only received the Victoria Cross for this incredible air battle; he also survived it. Barker was not so lucky after the war when his plane crashed at Rockcliffe air station, Ottawa.

Isaac Barr
Born 1847, nr.Hornby, Ont.
Died 1937
The Barr Colony in northwest Saskatchewan was established in 1903 by Isaac Barr, an Anglican clergyman with great dreams of empire, very little organizing ability, and a talent for causing offence. Barr was in fact more or less an ex-clergyman by 1903, for he had made himself unpopular with the church authorities. Not only had he preached against church doctrines, but he had divorced and remarried. He married four different women during the course of his life.

Although Barr was no angel, he did dare to rush in where angels feared to tread. Believing that the prairies ought to be populated by British settlers, he formed his own colonization scheme, set up an office in England, and almost single-handedly brought 2,000 British settlers to Canada. This was far too much for one man to cope with, even with government co-operation, and inevitably there was

muddle, lost luggage . . . any amount of trouble.

Barr's autocratic manner didn't help matters, and most of the colonists turned against him during the voyage across the Atlantic. Another clergyman, George E. Lloyd, emerged as the group's leader. Barr was obliged to pull out of the enterprise soon after he had established the settlers on their land. Their town, Lloydminster, was named after his rival, who later became bishop of Saskatchewan. As for Barr, he lost his money, his colony, his dream, and his reputation. He eventually emigrated to Australia.

James Barry
Born c.1795, England
Died 1865
James Miranda Stuart Barry was a woman who disguised herself as a man so that she could study medicine and be a doctor. This was in the days when women were not even allowed into university. She joined the British army, became a first-rate surgeon, and proved so good at her job that in 1857 she was appointed inspector general of all military hospitals in the Province of Canada.

Dr. Barry was the first woman to work as a doctor in Canada, but nobody realized this. She was still thought to be a man, though a very odd one. She was tiny, with a slim figure, and no hair on her face. And she used to drive round Montreal in

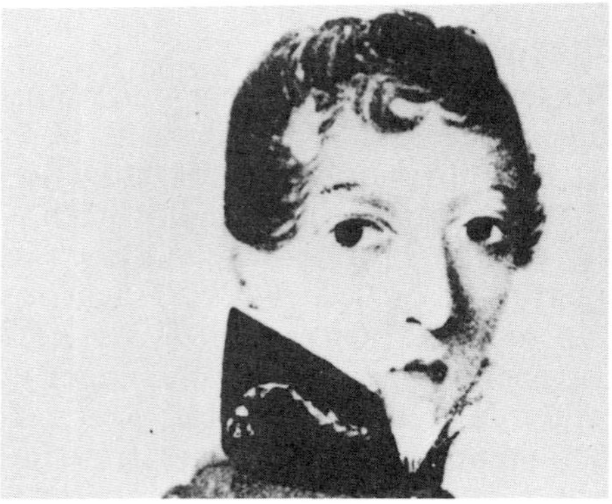

a scarlet sleigh, accompanied by a large black manservant and a small white dog.

When, on her death, Barry was found to have a woman's body, there was a terrific fuss. A woman surgeon! A woman army officer! Dr. Barry passed from this world in a blaze of publicity.

Bob Bartlett

Born 1875, Brigus, Nfld.
Died 1946

The first expedition ever to reach the North Pole was led by the American, Robert E. Peary. But it was guided by the Newfoundlander, Robert A. Bartlett.

Bob Bartlett was an experienced seaman who had twice taken Peary on Arctic voyages, and he was again captaining the ship when in 1908 Peary made his final and successful attempt to get to the Pole. After sailing north as far as they could go, the explorers spent the winter in the Arctic, resuming their journey by sled early in 1909. Bartlett went ahead across the ice, breaking the trail for the others. But when he was at 87°47′ N (less than three degrees from the top of the world) he was ordered to return to the ship. Peary had decided to do the final lap accompanied only by his servant and four Inuit.

It was a bitter blow, but Bartlett obeyed orders. He had at least been the first to get so far north. He later went on many more Arctic explorations, often as head of his own expeditions.

Alex Baumann

Born 1964, Czechoslovakia

In 1981 Alex Baumann of Sudbury, Ont., was hailed as the fastest swimmer in the world. He had come to Canada with his family in 1969 and since the age of nine had taken special coaching in swimming. In 1981 he set four Canadian records in freestyle events, as well as setting a new world record for the 200-metre individual medley. The following year, at the 1982 Commonwealth Games, he broke his own world record in the 200-metre race, carrying off the gold medal in the process. He also won a gold in the men's 400-metre individual medley. The year 1983 brought him more gold medals.

Lord Beaverbrook

Born 1879, Maple, Ont.
Died 1964

The Beaverbrook newspaper empire, the Beaverbrook Art Gallery in Fredericton, and many other enterprises were all founded by the man who was born William Maxwell Aitken, the son of a Presbyterian minister. Raised in Newcastle, N.B., he showed a flair for business even as a young man, progressing from rookie insurance agent in Saint John to master financier in Montreal. Before he was 30 he had made his first million.

Beaverbrook's success was due to his bubbling enthusiasm as much as his organizing ability. Moving to England in 1910, he was taken up by the Conservative party, and in World War I (during which he was made a lord) he served as minister of information. In World War II, as the minister in charge of aircraft production, he got the planes built that won the Battle of Britain. However many British fighter planes were shot down, his ministry always had others ready to replace them, so that the pilots could go up night after night to fight off the German bombers.

Of all Beaverbrook's achievements, this was probably the greatest. But he was most widely known as a newspaper baron, owner of the London *Daily Express* (which he took over in 1917) and other highly successful papers.

Adam Beck
Born 1857, Baden, Ont.
Died 1925

Ontario Hydro owes its origins to the provincial cabinet minister Adam Beck, who started his career in a very different line of business—running the family cigar-box factory in London, Ont.

"Power for the people" was Beck's slogan. Electric power. In 1906 he introduced a bill into the Ontario legislature which created the Hydro-Electric Power Commission of Ontario (Ontario Hydro) so that Niagara Falls could be used to produce cheap electricity. Beck served as chairman of the commission until his death, overseeing the development of the project. Under his guidance, Ontario Hydro grew into one of the largest energy producers in the world. Meanwhile, industry grew throughout Ontario because of the electricity supplied by Hydro.

Abigail Becker
Born 1830, Portland Twp., Ont.
Died 1905

Abigail Becker was the Heroine of Long Point, Lake Erie. When she was 24, she saved the lives of seven seamen whose ship was wrecked offshore in a raging storm. The men were clinging to the rigging, with no hope of getting to the beach. But she shouted to them to swim for it—one by one. And as each man plunged into the lashing waves, she struggled out to meet him and help him ashore.

Later in life, Abigail Becker again rescued people in distress. She saved 12 lives all told. She also brought up 17 children, most of them step-children for she was married twice, each time to a widower with a family.

William George Beers
Born 1843, Montreal, Que.
Died 1900

William Beers caused lacrosse to become a popular, organized sport. He wrote the book of standard rules and promoted the game vigorously. He is called "the father of modern lacrosse." He might also be called "the father of dental journals" because he started Canada's first magazine for dentists. (He earned his living in Montreal as a dentist.) Beers also helped to make snowshoeing and tobogganing into popular sports.

Matthew Baillie Begbie
Born 1819, Indian Ocean
Died 1894

Matthew Baillie Begbie was called "the hanging judge" because of his reputation for sentencing people to death. He once told a jury that he would like to see them all hanged, each and every one of them, for finding a murderer guilty only of manslaughter. Such ferocious pronouncements added strength to the Begbie legend, though in fact his words were often harsher than his actions.

The son of army parents (who were on their way to Mauritius when he was born), Begbie had trained as a lawyer in Britain. He was sent to British Columbia to keep order in the colony when gold was discovered on the Fraser River in 1858. This was a tough job, because many of the men who came to pan for gold were adventurers who cared little for the law. They met their match in Begbie. He was a huge man, and he looked especially stern when dressed in his judge's wig and robes. When he rode into a mining settlement, it was obvious that the law had arrived. Because of his courage and firmness, order was maintained even in the wildest days of the gold rush. And long after. Begbie served as a judge in British Columbia for 36 years.

Jean Béliveau
Born 1931, Trois Rivières, Que.
Hockey players who tried to check Jean Béliveau said it was like running into the side of an oak tree. They just bounced off him. Big Jean played for the Montreal Canadiens from 1953 to 1971, their team captain for the last ten years and one of their all-time stars. In his day, he was the highest-scoring centre in NHL history, with 507 regular season goals and 79 more in playoffs. In total, he played in well over 1,000 NHL games.

Alexander Graham Bell
Born 1847, Scotland
Died 1922
The telephone was invented by Alexander Bell, whose family settled in Brantford, Ont., and whose father had developed a way of teaching the deaf to talk. Bell taught his father's speech methods at Boston University, and it was his interest in voice that led him to try and transmit speech by wire. He worked on the invention every spare minute, at home in Brantford and in his boarding house in Boston.

Bell rigged up a transmitter and receiver in the attic of the Boston house, and while trying to make them function one evening in 1876, he accidentally spilled some acid he was using. The acid began to burn a hole in his trousers. "Watson, come here! I want you!" he shouted in alarm to his assistant Thomas Watson. Watson was in the neighbouring attic room, and he heard Bell's words through the receiver. They were the first words ever heard down the phone. Later that year, the two young men made the world's first long-distance phone call—from Brantford to Paris, Ont.

In the course of his life, Bell was responsible for many other inventions, including flying machines. Although he lived in the United States, he bought a summer estate on Cape Breton Island. There he ran his Aerial Experiment Association, experimenting with giant kites and then airplanes and hydrofoils. Casey Baldwin* and J. A. D. McCurdy* were two of the pioneers associated with him in these projects.

Marilyn Bell

Born 1937, Toronto, Ont.

Sixteen-year-old Marilyn Bell was the first person to swim across Lake Ontario. She waded into the water in Youngstown, N.Y., at midnight on September 8, 1954. On the evening of the next day, she struggled ashore at the CNE grounds in Toronto. Much to her surprise, an enormous crowd had come to cheer her arrival. All day the excitement had been building as the radio broadcast news of her swim. For years, both Americans and Canadians had tried to swim the lake, and now a Canadian girl had done it.

The following year Marilyn again made history when she was the youngest person ever to swim the English Channel. The year after that she crossed the Strait of Juan de Fuca. Then she gave up marathon swimming and married her American boyfriend. Her awards included the Lou Marsh Trophy (1954) as outstanding Canadian athlete of the year.

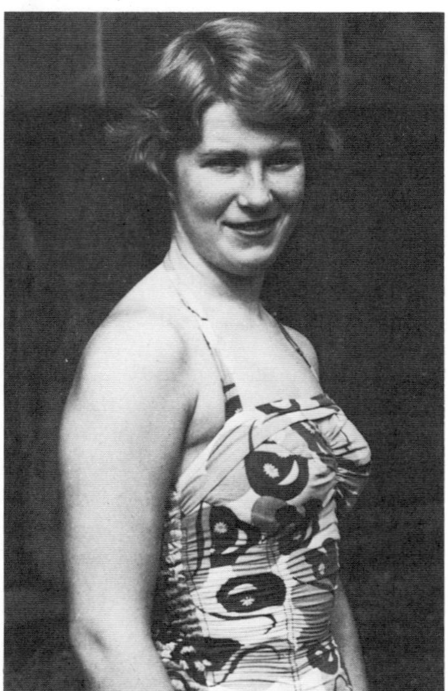

Margrét Benedictsson

Born 1866, Iceland

Died 1956

When Margrét Benedictsson was in her twenties she immigrated to Manitoba, and there she spearheaded the campaign to get women the vote. In 1898 she founded Canada's first suffragette newspaper (which was written in Icelandic); and she organized Winnipeg's first suffragette society (also Icelandic).

Immigrants from Iceland were often ardent suffragettes, for women were permitted to vote in Iceland. When they settled in Canada, they no longer had this right. It was partly because of their efforts that, in January 1916, Manitoba became the first Canadian province to give women the vote.

R. B. Bennett

Born 1870, Hopewell Hill, N.B.

Died 1947

Of the many Bennetts who have been politicians, one of the best known was Richard Bedford Bennett (always called R. B. Bennett). He was Conservative prime minister of Canada 1930-35, during the Great Depression.

Although Bennett had all sorts of plans to cope with the Depression, he was not a popular prime minister. He seemed out of touch with ordinary people. He was too rich, a millionaire, having made his money as a lawyer in Calgary. In Ottawa, he lived at the Chateau Laurier Hotel, and he liked to dress in top hat and tail coat. Such splendours did not go down well with the poor and jobless, especially as Bennett's anti-Depression measures were having little effect. Bitterly, prairie farmers called their horse-drawn automobiles "Bennett buggies." (They had to pull their cars with horses, since they couldn't afford to buy gas.)

Bennett suffered a crushing defeat in the 1935 elections, even though no one else could find a solution to the Depression either. A few years later he retired from politics and went off to England, where he was made a lord and lived in a lordly manner until his death.

John Wilson Bengough

Born 1851, Toronto, Ont.

Died 1923

J. W. Bengough was the first of the great Canadian cartoonists, best known for his scrawny caricatures of John A. Macdonald.* He ran a humorous paper called *Grip*, which specialized in political cartoons and satirical verse.

Bengough started *Grip* at the age of 22, in 1873. Fortunately for him (and unfortunately for Macdonald) this was the same year the Pacific Scandal rocked Canada (see Hugh Allan*). The scandal was a gift for any satirist, and *Grip* quickly gained a big circulation. It continued to do well for more than 20 years.

W. A. C. Bennett
Born 1900, Hastings, N.B.
Died 1979
Premier of British Columbia for 20 years (1952-72), W. A. C. Bennett was affectionately known as "Wacky" Bennett. This was not just because of his initials. He was a loud, rumbumptious man who said what he thought and had grand schemes for British Columbia.

Bennett spent his childhood in the Maritimes and went west as a young man, settling eventually in Kelowna, where he ran a hardware business and winery. On entering politics, he was at first a Conservative but in 1951 joined B.C.'s newly formed Social Credit party. From then on, Wacky Bennett was the shining knight of Social Credit. As premier, he took over B.C. Electric, launched huge hydro-electric projects on the Peace and Columbia rivers, built dams and railways, and worked to build British Columbia into a prosperous, go-ahead province.

William R. Bennett
Born 1932, Kelowna, B.C.
Bill Bennett, the son of W. A. C. Bennett,* succeeded his father as leader of the B.C. Social Credit party and in 1975 was elected premier of the province. He had previously worked as a businessman. While being a strong promotor of Social Credit policies in provincial affairs, Bennett has gained increasing attention in national affairs. He played a leading role at the 1981 meetings of the premiers, when they were negotiating with Prime Minister Trudeau* on how to bring the constitution home to Canada.

Jehane Benoit
Born 1904, Montreal, Que.
Madame Benoit has had a love of cooking since early childhood, when she used to pore over her grandmother's handwritten recipes. She studied in Paris and then ran her own cooking school in Montreal during the 1930s. She has since become Canada's most famous cook, the host of radio and TV cooking programs, and the author of numerous cookbooks. Whether using modern microwave techniques or age-old family recipes, she has shown that Canadian food need never be dull and can be delicious.

William Berczy
Born 1748, Germany
Died 1813
Artist, architect, and colonizer, William Berczy brought a group of German settlers to Upper Canada in 1794 and established them at Markham. They completed the building of Yonge Street from York to Markham, which had been started by Governor Simcoe's* soldiers. Meanwhile, Berczy designed some of York's first buildings. He later moved to Montreal, where he also designed buildings and worked as a portrait painter. His best-known paintings are his portrait of Joseph Brant* and his group portrait of the Woolsey family.

Mario Bernardi
Born 1930, Kirkland Lake, Ont.
In 1972 conductor Mario Bernardi was made a Companion of the Order of Canada for his great contribution to the development of Canadian music. Of Italian origin, he had been sent to Italy as a child so that he could grow up in the Italian culture. There he studied the piano, and he was already a fine pianist when he came home at the age of 17.

After completing his studies at the Royal Conservatory of Music in Toronto, Bernardi worked as an opera coach and then as an opera conductor. He then spent several years in England with the famous Sadler's Wells opera. He returned to Canada in 1968 to form an orchestra for the new arts centre in Ottawa, and he was conductor of the National Arts Centre Orchestra until 1982.

Joseph-Elzéar Bernier
Born 1852, L'Islet, Que.
Died 1934

Captain Bernier claimed the Arctic Archipelago for Canada. Although the region had been officially ceded to Canada by Britain in 1880, some of the islands had not been explored or even located. If other nations got there first, Canada could lose its rights to the territory. Bernier prevented this happening. Early in the 1900s he sailed again and again to the Arctic, holding ceremonies, firing 20-gun salutes, and informing the Inuit that they were Canadians. By 1909 he had established Canada's right to our entire Arctic Archipelago up to 90°N.

Bernier had been bred on the high seas. He went on his first voyage when he was two and was in charge of his own ship when he was 17. During his life, he made 260 voyages throughout the world. He married twice, the second time to a girl called Alma Lemieux. He named Lemieux Island (east of Baffin) after his nephew Romeo Lemieux, who accompanied him on one of his voyages of exploration.

Pierre Berton
Born 1920, Whitehorse, Yukon
Pierre Berton is one of the few writers anywhere in the world who has become a millionaire. Through his many books, he has brought Canadian history to a wide audience by making it a "popular read," lively, stirring, jostling with characters. Two of his most famous books are *The National Dream* and *The Last Spike*, which together tell the story of how the CPR was built.

Berton spent his early years in the Yukon, moving to British Columbia when he was 12. As a young man, he worked as a journalist, at first in Vancouver and later in Toronto. Since those early days, he has also had a prominent career in television through such programs as *The Pierre Berton Show* and *Front Page Challenge*. He is now as well known a figure as the Canadian beaver and twice as busy, bringing out a book each year in addition to his many other activities. He has won the Governor General's Award three times.

Lord Bessborough

Born 1880, England
Died 1956

Lord Bessborough's full name was Vere Brabazon Ponsonby, ninth Earl of Bessborough. He was Governor General from 1931 to 1935, during the desperate years of the Great Depression. R. B. Bennett* was prime minister at this time.

Gérard Bessette

Born 1920, Ste.Anne de Sabrevois, Que.

Gérard Bessette has twice won the Governor General's Award, for his novels *L'Incubation* and *Le Cycle*. He is one of French Canada's leading writers, author of poetry books and literary criticism as well as novels. Several of his novels have been translated into English and most are strong satires dealing with social problems. Bessette himself is a graduate of the University of Montreal, and he has had a number of teaching positions in universities across Canada.

Norman Bethune

Born 1890, Gravenhurst, Ont.
Died 1939

Dr. Norman Bethune was a born crusader, a man who believed passionately in causes. As a medical student he served as a stretcher bearer in World War I, and after gaining his degree he worked among the poor in Detroit. There he caught TB, which at the time was incurable. As Bethune had nothing to lose, he volunteered to try a new form of treatment, which involved collapsing the diseased lung. It cured him, and he returned to Canada determined to save the lives of others by this method.

During the early 1930s Bethune worked in Montreal, a leading surgeon in the fight against tuberculosis. But though he earned the gratitude of his patients, he was not popular with his colleagues. He was too outspoken and too ardently left wing.

In 1936 he went off to the Spanish Civil War, where he ran the first mobile blood-transfusion service ever used in a war. It saved thousands of lives. A few years later he was in China, serving as chief medical officer in Mao Tse-tung's Red Army during the Japanese invasion. He died there, of blood poisoning, having cut his finger during an operation. The Chinese have never forgotten Bethune's sacrifice, and they honour him as one of their greatest heroes.

Buzz Beurling

Born 1921, Verdun, Que.
Died 1948

One of the most brilliant fighter pilots of World War II, Buzz Beurling first flew a plane when he was 14 and won an aerobatic competition when he was 17. Yet he couldn't get into the RCAF. He didn't have enough education.

Eager to join the war effort, Beurling applied to the RAF in Britain. They were glad to accept him and then glad they had, for he became one of their star pilots. He played a key role in the successful defence of Malta in 1942; during the massive German and Italian assault on the island, he shot down 27 enemy aircraft in less than five months.

As one of the heroes of the siege of Malta, Beurling transferred to the RCAF, but he was not happy there.

He was too much of a loner, better at making decisions than taking orders. He resigned in 1944 and four years later offered his services to Israel in its war against the Arabs. He died on the way to Israel, aged 26, when his plane caught fire over Urbe Airfield on the outskirts of Rome.

Big Bear

Born c.1825, nr. Fort Carlton, Sask.
Died 1888

Big Bear was regarded as a bloodthirsty villain by nineteenth-century Canadians, but he was simply a brave man who wanted to remain free. He wanted to ride after the buffalo as his ancestors had done; but there were fewer and fewer buffalo in the West, and more and more settlers. Big Bear was the first major chief who refused to sign a treaty with the government, remaining aloof when other Cree chiefs signed Treaty No. 6. He believed that the government was not offering a good enough deal in exchange for the Indians' lands, and that it was not living up to the promises made to Indians in other treaty areas.

Big Bear met with Louis Riel* when in 1884 Riel came to the Saskatchewan country to champion the rights of the people. But Riel's intervention led to the Northwest Rebellion, during which Big Bear's followers attacked the mission at Frog Lake, killing nine men, including two priests. Big Bear was held responsible, though he had tried to prevent the bloodshed. After the rebellion, he was imprisoned for two years and his hair was cut off—a great indignity. Broken in spirit, he died shortly after his release.

Wilfred Bigelow

Born 1913, Brandon, Man.

One of the world's leading heart surgeons, Dr. Wilfred Bigelow invented the pacemaker, a small electrical device which can start a stopped heart and then keep it beating regularly. Pacemakers have saved thousands of lives since they were first implanted in patients early in the 1960s. Working with Bigelow on the invention was John Callaghan, his research fellow at Toronto General Hospital, and J. A. Hopps of the National Research Council in Ottawa.

Dr. Bigelow headed the division of heart surgery at Toronto General Hospital for more than 20 years, and there he trained and inspired many younger men who in turn became leading cardiac surgeons. Meanwhile, he led the medical world into a new type of Ice Age by developing the procedure called hypothermia. This is a system of making a patient's body very cold before an operation in order to reduce the amount of oxygen required. One of the advantages of hypothermia is that it makes long and complex operations far safer. It has led to great advances in heart and brain surgery.

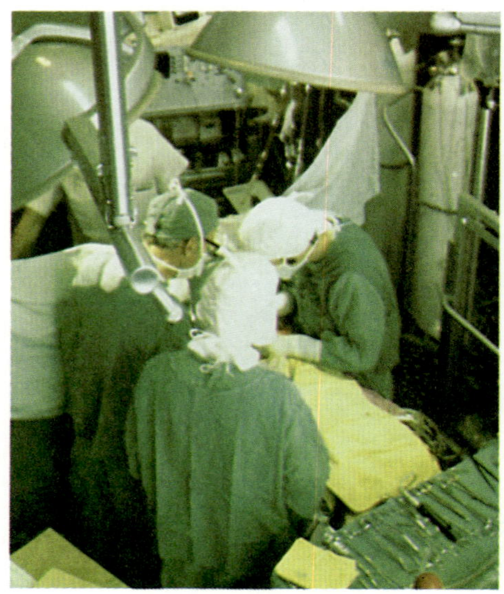

François Bigot
Born 1703, France
Died 1778

François Bigot was the last intendant of New France (1748-60), an efficient administrator but notoriously corrupt. He forced the people of New France to sell their goods very cheaply to the various companies he controlled. He then sold the same goods at very high prices to the French government. By such practices he made a huge private fortune—and also helped bring on a serious financial crisis in New France.

After the battle of the Plains of Abraham and the British conquest, Bigot returned to France, where he was given a very cold reception. Having lost Canada, the French were looking for a scapegoat, and Bigot fitted the part perfectly. He was thrown in the Bastille and when brought to trial was heavily fined and then banished. He spent his last years in Switzerland.

Billy Bishop
Born 1894, Owen Sound, Ont.
Died 1956

Billy Bishop went to war and gained a chestful of medals, including the Victoria Cross. He was one of the most celebrated air aces of World War I, shooting down a phenomenal score of 72 enemy planes. Often he went out alone, far behind enemy lines, to make surprise attacks on German air bases. It was said of him that he had that most difficult type of courage, "the courage of the early morning."

Billy Bishop married Timothy Eaton's* granddaughter, and after the war he had a successful business career. For a time he ran a small aviation firm, in partnership with William Barker* who had also won the VC. But then Bishop gave up regular flying and became an oil company executive. During World War II, as an honorary air marshal, he was in charge of recruiting and gave a tremendous boost to the war effort.

Earle Birney
Born 1904, Calgary, Alta.

In 1942 Earle Birney published his first book of poems, and it won a Governor General's Award. His second collection in 1945 also won a Governor General's Award. He has long been recognized as one of Canada's leading poets, a man who moves with the times, vigorously experimenting with new forms and styles.

Raised as a farm boy in western Canada, Birney had a wide range of jobs in his youth, everything from selling *Maclean's* subscriptions to serving in World War II. Soon after the war, he became a professor at the University of British Columbia, and he has since taught at universities across Canada. He has written fiction and criticism as well as poetry, and has been awarded the Lorne Pierce Medal for distinguished service to Canadian literature.

Earle Birney's generation produced many other fine poets. The year 1909 alone saw the birth of Dorothy Livesay,* Malcolm Lowry, and A. M. Klein; and also John Glassco, who made a great contribution by translating French Canadian poetry into English.

Martha Louise Black

Born 1866, U.S.A.
Died 1957

She was known as the "queen of the Yukon" and the "lady sourdough" —a spunky young woman from Chicago who joined the Klondike gold rush in 1898, trekking across the dangerous Chilkoot Pass dressed in ankle-length skirt and high Victorian collar.

The lady sourdough struck gold on her claim and settled in Dawson, setting up a sawmill there; and in 1904 she married a Dawson lawyer, George Black. He was made commissioner of the Yukon in 1912, so the couple moved into Government House, where Martha grew her own flowers and vegetables. George later served as MP for the Yukon and was made speaker of the House of Commons in Ottawa. In 1935, when he was too sick to run for Parliament, Martha campaigned in his place. She was elected and became the second woman ever to sit in the House of Commons. She was 70 at the time. She lived another 21 years, tirelessly working for her beloved Yukon. Her book, *My Ninety Years,* tells the fascinating story of her life.

Marie-Claire Blais

Born 1939, Quebec, Que.

Marie-Claire Blais wrote her first novel when she was 19. Called *Mad Shadows* in its English translation, the book caused horror as well as praise. It was a grim story, loaded with hatred, not at all the type of book expected from an innocent young girl. But Marie-Claire Blais had no reason to write a light-hearted book. Her childhood had been overshadowed by poverty and unhappiness; she had grown up in a crowded three-room apartment, miserable at home and miserable at her strict convent school.

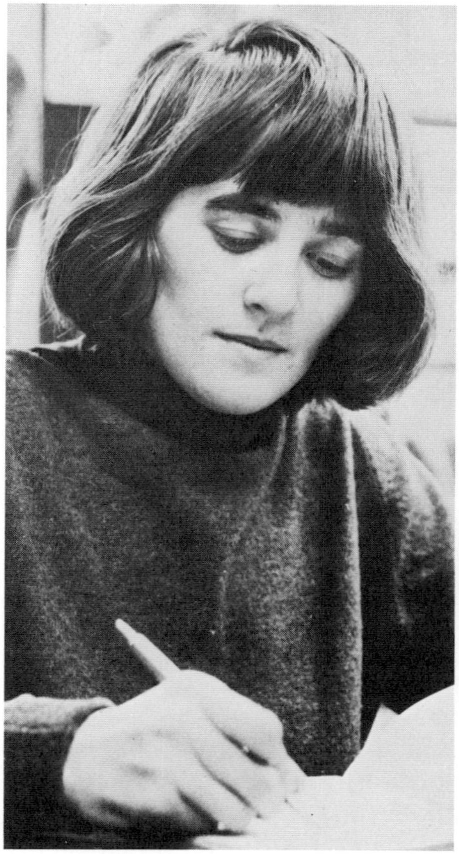

Many of Marie-Claire Blais's books hark back to her childhood, and all are stark, gaunt, very powerful. One of Canada's best-known novelists, she has twice won the Governor General's Award.

Ann Blades

Born 1947, Vancouver, B.C.

Mary of Mile 18 was written and illustrated by Ann Blades when she was teaching in a school in northern British Columbia. The story was based on one of her students, and purposely so, for the children had very few books that they could relate to. Most story books were set in southern Canada. Ann Blades's second book, *A Boy of Taché*, was also based on a student—an Indian boy she taught on the Taché Reserve near Fort St. James. Although Ann Blades gave up teaching in 1971, she continues to write and, above all, to illustrate books for young readers.

Another well-known illustrator-author of children's books is Elizabeth Cleaver (born 1939, Montreal), who is known for her puppet shows and animated TV stories, as well as her books.

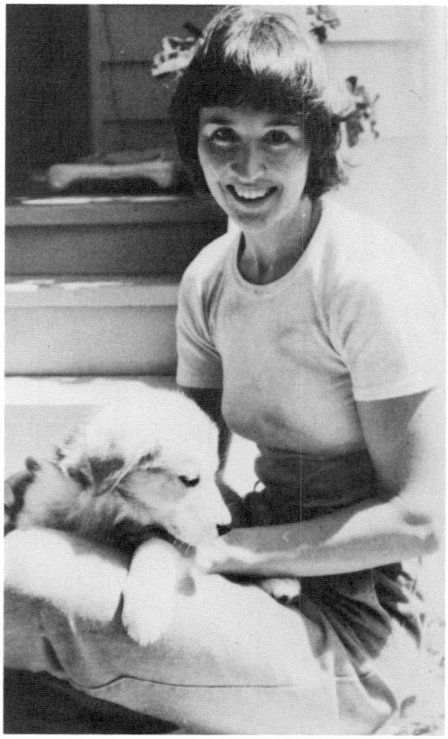

Edward Blake

Born 1833, Adelaide, Ont.
Died 1912

Edward Blake was one of the most formidable Liberals in Parliament during the years following Confederation. A man of wide knowledge and great ability, he was particularly respected for his speeches. Standing at his desk in the House of Commons, he would build up his arguments point by point, exploring every detail. But Blake had an aloof, cold manner. He spoke in a flat, dull voice. Sometimes he spoke for five hours or more. He bored his listeners, even while he impressed them.

Blake's whole life was like this: though extremely capable, he never fully succeeded in his aims. He should have been prime minister in 1873 when the Liberals took over the government after the Pacific Scandal (he was the obvious person for the job). But he was not leader of the Liberal party just then. Later, when he did serve as leader, the Liberals couldn't win an election. Eventually, Blake left Canada and became an MP in Britain. But he didn't top the heights there either.

Allan Blakeney

Born 1925, Bridgewater, N.S.

Allan Blakeney, who was NDP premier of Saskatchewan 1971-82, grew up in Nova Scotia and graduated from Dalhousie University. He won a Rhodes Scholarship to Oxford, where he was secretary of his college's labour club and also a member of the university hockey team. Moving to Saskatchewan in 1950, he worked as a lawyer until he was elected to the legislature in 1960.

In the early 1960s, as minister of health in the provincial government, Blakeney was in charge of Saskatchewan's medical insurance scheme, guiding it through its difficult early stages. This was the first government medicare in Canada.

During Blakeney's years as premier, Saskatchewan changed substantially from a "have not" to a "have" province. There was a greatly improved standard of living, an enlargement of medicare, and the introduction of other social democratic policies. But after 11 years in power, Blakeney's government was defeated by the Conservatives under their new provincial leader, Grant Devine.*

Salem Bland

Born 1859, Lachute, Que.
Died 1950

Salem Bland was one of the most controversial churchmen of his day, an ardent reformer and a powerful public speaker. He supported labour unions and other workers' organizations, and called for a New Christianity in which the church would take an active part in politics in order to make life better on earth.

Ordained into the Methodist church, Bland was appointed in 1903 to Wesley College in Winnipeg. In the West he became very involved in farming and labour movements, and he was dismissed from the college in 1917. Returning to eastern Canada, he wrote a book on the New Christianity and embarked on a 20-year career as a journalist with the Toronto *Star*. Meanwhile, he continued to preach his "social gospel" in every way possible, expressing his views vigorously in speeches as well as in print.

Armand Bombardier
Born 1907, Valcourt, Que.
Died 1964

The snowmobile was invented by Armand Bombardier, who started his career operating a small garage in Valcourt, Que. There in 1926 he built his first snowmobile, and by the late 1930s he was producing the vehicles commercially. This was the beginning of a huge family business which pioneered many other off-the-road vehicles, including the Bombardier muskeg tractor and the ski-doo.

Meanwhile, another type of winter vehicle, the snowblower, had been invented by Arthur Sicard. The son of a Quebec farmer, Sicard got the idea by watching threshers at work. The first of his machines came into operation in 1925—a strange-looking motor truck with rotating blades which scooped up the snow. Improved models were brought out over the years, and today snowblowers are used throughout the world. As for Bombardier's company, it now makes many types of vehicles, including subway cars for New York and other large cities.

William Carpenter Bompas
Born 1834, England
Died 1906

William Bompas went to the Northwest as a missionary in 1865, and nine years later he was appointed the first Anglican bishop of Athabasca. This was an arduous job, involving long journeys by dog sled or on horseback. Year after year, Bompas travelled round his huge diocese, ministering to the few traders there and to the many Indians and Inuit, some of whom had never seen a white man before.

Bompas often found himself acting as teacher or doctor as well as priest, and he later wrote two books about his unusual experiences. His wife Charlotte, who accompanied him to the Northwest, also wrote about her life there. Her book *Owindia* tells the story of an Indian orphan to whom she gave a home.

Robert Laird Borden
Born 1854, Grand Pré, N.S.
Died 1937

The prime minister of Canada from 1911 to 1920 was Robert Borden, a lawyer and long-time Conservative politician. His period in office covered the troubled years of World War I and the Winnipeg General Strike.

After visiting the battlefields of Europe in 1917, Borden was convinced that many more troops were needed and he brought in conscription (compulsory military service). This caused an outcry in Quebec. Most French Canadians felt that World War I was "Britain's war" and they didn't see why they should get killed for a cause that did not concern them. The bitterness aroused by Borden's conscription law carried on for years.

During the war, Borden gave Canadian women the right to vote in federal elections, a measure which suffragettes had long been calling for. And after the war, he helped to get Canada made a member of the League of Nations.

This gave Canada a new status in the world, for previously the dominion had been treated as an arm of Britain, rather than as a separate country. It was a significant step towards Canada's emergence as an independent nation that could decide its own policies, abroad as well as at home.

Paul-Émile Borduas

Born 1905, St. Hilaire, Que.
Died 1960

Paul-Émile Borduas and his contemporary Alfred Pellan* are key figures in the story of Canadian art. They broke with tradition and introduced Surrealist painting to Canada. Instead of painting what they saw, they used shapes and forms to convey deeper meanings.

Borduas started his career as an apprentice to Ozias Leduc,* and for the first part of his life he attracted little attention as he painted traditional murals in churches, studied art and taught it. He did not exhibit a painting until he was 32. A few years later, in 1942, he caused a sensation with his one-man show of Surrealist paintings, which won excited praise from the critics. At the time, Borduas was teaching at the École du Meuble in Montreal, and there he became the leader of a group of experimental young artists called the Automatists. Their 1946 exhibition was the first group show of abstract paintings ever held in Canada.

But Borduas wanted to reform society as well as art, and in 1948 he and his followers published a statement of their revolutionary beliefs, *Refus Global*. This pamphlet caused such an uproar that Borduas was fired from the École du Meuble. He had a tough time for a while, but by the end of his life his paintings had brought him a worldwide reputation. Meanwhile, *Refus Global* inspired many young French Canadians with a renewed sense of nationalism. It was, in a way, the opening chord of the Quebec separatist movement.

Marie Bottrell

Born 1961, London, Ont.

One of the best-selling country singers in Canada, Marie Bottrell started writing songs when she was seven. But she was a rather shy little girl and few people took her ambitions seriously. But her family did, and when she was a teenager her brother sent out tapes of her songs to various country and western groups. As a result, Marie Bottrell was hired as a songwriter and then as a recording artist. Her first album, *Just Reach Out and Touch Me*, was recorded when she was 17.

Henri Bourassa

Born 1868, Montreal, Que.
Died 1952

The fiery Henri Bourassa was a dedicated French Canadian nationalist. He wanted more power for Canada's French-speaking people so that the "two founding nations" could play an equal role in the country's affairs. By profession he was a politician and journalist, editor of the newspaper *Le Devoir*, which he founded in 1910 with Olivar Asselin, a fellow nationalist.

Devoir means "duty," and Bourassa had a strong sense of duty, especially to the people of French Canada. He was their hero, their champion, their eloquent spokesman. On their behalf in World War I, he waged an all-out campaign against compulsory service in the forces. Although many French Canadians (including Olivar Asselin) volunteered for military service, Bourassa felt they should not be forced to fight in "Britain's war." Some people said he was a traitor like his rebel grandfather Papineau.* This was unfair to both men. Bourassa was a loyal Canadian, but he felt that Canada should decide its own foreign policy, instead of doing whatever Britain asked.

Marguerite Bourgeoys
Born 1620, France
Died 1700

In 1982, Marguerite Bourgeoys was made a saint of the Roman Catholic church. Besides being the most recent Canadian saint, she was also one of Canada's earliest social workers.

More than three centuries ago, in the 1650s, Marguerite Bourgeoys came to the tiny settlement of Montreal, wanting to do good and eager to take on any job. She was given every job. She acted as nurse, social worker, missionary; she started the first schools in Montreal and even ran a marriage bureau, for she looked after the orphan girls who were sent from France to be wives of the settlers; and she personally interviewed each courting settler to make sure he would treat his wife well.

Although deeply religious, Marguerite Bourgeoys was not a nun in the convent-trained meaning. But in Canada she founded a religious order, the Congrégation de Notre Dame de Montreal. This brought some raised eyebrows among the clergy, for her sisters didn't confine themselves demurely in a convent; they worked in the community and taught in the bark cabins of Montagnais Indians.

Marguerite Bourgeoys's *congrégation* was the first truly Canadian religious order. Others were formed later, including the celebrated Grey Nuns, which was founded in the 1740s by a widow who was also called Marguerite: Marguerite d'Youville.

Liona Boyd
Born 1950, England

The well-known guitarist was brought to Canada as a child and was a student at the University of Toronto. She gained wide fame in 1976 when she toured North America with Gordon Lightfoot,* playing classical guitar pieces at the beginning of his concerts. Since then, she has performed throughout Canada, as well as touring in Australia, the United States, and South America.

Mackenzie Bowell
Born 1823, England
Died 1917

Of all our prime ministers, Sir Mackenzie Bowell is the most forgettable. He was a fussy, pompous man, good-hearted but no good as a leader. Before taking up politics, he had been a newspaperman in Belleville, Ont., and he was far better at behind-the-scenes work than at public affairs.

Bowell was one of the four Conservatives who served as prime minister during the five years after Sir John A. Macdonald* died and before Sir Wilfrid Laurier* brought the Liberals to power. He was in office 1894-96, which some of his cabinet ministers considered quite long enough. Half of them resigned because they thought he was running the country so badly. And then he resigned too.

Cavendish Boyle
Born 1849, Barbados
Died 1916

The provincial anthem "Ode to Newfoundland" was written by Sir Cavendish Boyle, the British aristocrat who was governor of Newfoundland 1901-04. He wrote the words soon after his arrival in St. John's, and the ode was first sung publicly in the Total Abstinence Hall during a theatrical performance in January 1902.

Boyle was also the man who gave Newfoundland its famous hockey trophy, the Boyle Challenge Cup. Designed by his niece, the cup was first presented in 1904.

Joe Boyle
Born 1867, Toronto, Ont.
Died 1923
Joe Boyle was known as "the king of the Klondike" and "the saviour of Romania." Above all, he was an adventurer, a man who lived his life to the full, partly because he was always prepared to risk it.

Raised in Woodstock, Ont., Boyle ran away to sea when he was 17 and saw the world. During the Klondike gold rush he saw the Yukon, stayed there for 18 years and made a million. During World War I he acted as a type of agent, making the Russian railways run efficiently. And when the Russian Revolution broke out, he acted as a "knight errant," rescuing about 50 important Romanians who were being held hostage by the Communists. Queen Marie of Romania considered him her dearest friend. On his death, she had his tombstone inscribed with the following words, based on a Robert Service* poem: "Man with the heart of a Viking and the simple faith of a child."

Joseph Brant
Born 1742, U.S.A.
Died 1807
Brantford, Ont., is named after the Mohawk chief Joseph Brant, who became principal chief of the Six Nations (the Iroquois Confederacy).

Brant was a strong supporter of the British, and so was his sister Molly who was married to a senior official, Sir William Johnson. Between them, brother and sister had great influence in keeping many of the Iroquois loyal to Great Britain during the eighteenth-century wars. Brant led his followers on the British side in the Seven Years' War, and again in the American Revolutionary War. Then, like other Loyalists, he moved north to Canada, where he was given a large tract of land.

A well-educated man, Brant was an author as well as a soldier, and he translated parts of the Bible into Mohawk. He lived for many years in a large house on Burlington Bay.

Jean de Brébeuf
Born 1593, France
Martyred 1649
The Jesuit priest Jean de Brébeuf worked among the Huron people near Georgian Bay during the early days of the fur trade. His mission was one long ordeal against impossible odds. He had great difficulty in making any converts, and some of those he did convert later returned to their own religion. Stricken by smallpox and harried by the Iroquois, they blamed their misfortunes on the missionaries.

As the Iroquois gradually fought their way into the heart of Huron territory, Brébeuf continued his mission. He would not flee. Some historians believe that he wanted to be a martyr. He certainly became one. Captured by the Iroquois, he was tortured to death. A fellow missionary, Gabriel Lalemant, died with him. In all, eight Jesuits were martyred during the Iroquois wars. A shrine near Midland, Ont., honours their memory.

Yet Brébeuf has a more widespread memorial. Every Christmas, thousands of Canadians sing the beautiful Huron Carol, which he wrote for his little band of Indian followers. In 1940 the Pope proclaimed Brébeuf patron saint of Canada, along with his fellow martyrs.

Ed Broadbent
Born 1936, Oshawa, Ont.
The leader of the New Democratic Party was a university professor before he took up politics. Having graduated in Toronto and then gained a doctorate in England at the London School of Economics, Ed Broadbent taught political science at York University in Toronto.

He was first elected to Parliament in 1968 and three years later ran for the leadership of the NDP. Though he lost to David Lewis,* he was the obvious choice when Lewis resigned, and in 1975 Ed Broadbent was elected leader of Canada's NDP. He has since become well known throughout the country, a firm spokesman for Canadian working people.

Dave Broadfoot
Born 1925, North Vancouver, B.C.
Dave Broadfoot believes that people need laughter, that it really is the best medicine, and he ladles out big doses of it in *The Royal Canadian Air Farce*, playing such characters as Sergeant Renfrew, the Mountie who never gets his man. First broadcast on radio, and then on television, *Air Farce* has been one of the CBC's most popular programs since it was first heard in 1973.

But long before that, Broadfoot was making audiences laugh. Though he started his career in his father's clothing business, he soon realized that he wanted to act and joined the North Vancouver Community Players. In 1952 he moved to Toronto, where he appeared year after year in the popular annual revue *Spring Thaw*. Besides his CBC programs, Broadfoot performs at conventions, banquets, and in hockey rinks . . . and also at RCMP socials.

Isaac Brock
Born 1769, Guernsey
Killed 1812
General Brock is remembered as the hero of the War of 1812—the daring military commander who halted the American invasion with his lightning victories.

Brock was a career soldier in the British army, a courteous, popular officer, who was serving as administrator of Upper Canada when the war started. Quickly, he moved against the enemy. First, his forces captured the American post at Michilimackinac. Then, in alliance with Tecumseh* and the Shawnee Indians, he captured Detroit. This victory brought Brock a knighthood, though he died before the news came through. He was killed at Queenston Heights while repelling an American advance across the Niagara River.

Although the war dragged on until the end of 1814, Brock's early victories put heart into the Canadian people and inspired them to rally to repel the invaders.

Steve Brodie

Born 1912, Scotland

During the Great Depression, Steve Brodie organized a sit-in for jobless men in Vancouver which ended in violence on Bloody Sunday—June 19, 1938.

Orphaned when he was seven, Brodie had been brought to Canada by the Salvation Army, and he worked as a farm boy until the Depression hit and jobs became scarce. Like many other homeless unemployed, he eventually wound up in Vancouver, where the climate was comfortably mild. These "transients" received no relief payments. They begged in the streets in the daytime and slept on the streets at night. Brodie turned to the Communist party for help and gradually gathered a large following among the unemployed.

In an effort to force the government to provide welfare, he organized a march of jobless men, who occupied three Vancouver buildings, including the post office. There the men stayed for 30 days—peaceful, orderly, and fed by many sympathetic citizens. The government would not arrest them, since imprisonment would mean feeding and housing the men, which was just what they were demanding.

Finally, the police were called in to clear the post office with tear gas, whips, and truncheons. As Brodie's followers streamed from the building gasping for air, they were attacked so viciously that some went on the rampage, breaking shop windows. Others were hospitalized, including Brodie who suffered a permanent eye injury. Bloody Sunday raised a storm of protest, but it did not bring either jobs or relief payments.

Samuel Bronfman

Born 1889, Atlantic Ocean
Died 1971

Samuel Bronfman, the whisky billionaire, was born on board a ship as his parents were immigrating to Canada. As a youth, he peddled fish and firewood round Manitoba villages, making such a profit that he and his family were able to buy a few hotels. This led them into the whisky trade, at first in Canada and then with the United States.

By the 1920s Sam Bronfman, his brothers, and brothers-in-law were operating a huge network, mixing concoctions of liquor and selling it to Americans, who drove across the border into Saskatchewan. This was during the American prohibition era when the sale of liquor was outlawed in the United States, though it was no longer illegal in Canada.

As the Bronfmans' business prospered, they opened a distillery in Montreal to make quality whisky and then went into partnership with other distillers, acquiring a small company called Seagram. They adopted the name of Seagram for their corporation, which became one of the richest in the world, dealing in oil and real estate, as well as liquor.

A. Roy Brown

Born 1893, Carleton Place, Ont.
Died 1944

During World War I, A. Roy Brown gained great renown as the fighter pilot who shot down Germany's greatest air ace, the famous Red Baron, Manfred von Richthofen. At the time, the Red Baron was on the tail of Wop May, a greenhorn from Carberry, Man., who was on one of his first combat flights. It looked as if it would also be May's last flight, but Brown gave chase and stitched the Red Baron's plane with a long burst of fire. Meanwhile, Australian machine-gunners were blazing away from the ground. They too hit the German plane, and just who shot the Baron from the sky has long been a matter of dispute. Brown was certain he had done so, but it now seems likely that it was an Australian rather than Canadian bullet that actually killed the German air ace.

At all events, Wop May's life was saved, and after the war he continued flying and was one of the bush pilots who opened up the North. A seasoned pilot by then, he flew the first official mail service to the Arctic coast, helped track down the Mad Trapper, Albert Johnson,* and performed many other legendary exploits.

As for Brown, the war took its toll. Suffering from battle fatigue, he fainted while flying and crashed. He was not expected to live, but he pulled through and went into business after the war; and in 1934 he organized his own air service, General Airways.

Alan Brown
Born 1887, Toronto, Ont.
Died 1960

Dr. Alan Brown was responsible for a revolution in the care of infants in Canada that saved thousands of young lives. This was while he was physician-in-chief at the Hospital for Sick Children in Toronto (1919-51).

In the days before antibiotics were in general use, Dr. Brown insisted on scrupulous cleanliness to prevent infection; he introduced fluid replacement therapy; he educated the public and the parents of his patients in proper diet and nutrition; and he educated many of the pediatricians who went to work throughout Canada. In addition, it was during his tenure as chief that the world's first precooked baby cereal (Pablum) was developed at the hospital. The main work on this project was done by Dr. Frederick Tisdall and Dr. Theodore Drake.

George Brown
Born 1818, Scotland
Assassinated 1880

A huge man with an impressive mind and tremendous energy, George Brown was known by his enemies as the Tsar of King Street. He was one of the most powerful men of his time: founder and publisher of the influential Toronto *Globe* (with offices in King Street) and one of Canada's major politicians. As leader of the Liberals in the pre-Confederation years, Brown headed our shortest-ever ministry, the Two-Day Government. Even when not serving in Parliament, he was the "power behind the throne" of the Liberal party.

George Brown's greatest role was as a Father of Confederation. It was he who suggested that the Province of Canada's Liberals and Conservatives should form a joint government so that they could concentrate on building a federal nation in British North America. This meant overcoming personal as well as political differences, for Brown hated John A. Macdonald* —thought him a wily trickster— and Macdonald thought Brown a resentful bully. But they worked together at the Charlottetown and Quebec conferences, though Brown pulled out in offence before Confederation.

Forceful in character, Brown died through force. He was shot in his office by a man who had been dismissed from the *Globe*.

Kootenay Brown
Born 1839, Scotland
Died 1916

Kootenay Brown was a born adventurer, one of the bold and brave spirits who built the West. His real name was John George Brown and he had a privileged upbringing—educated at Eton and Oxford. As a young man, he was posted to India as an officer in the British army, but a regimental life was not for him. By 1862 he was in British Columbia, digging for gold in the Cariboo.

Over the years, Kootenay Brown was in on just about everything that happened in the West. He married a Métis woman, went on buffalo hunts with her family, served as a guide for the Mounties, and during the Northwest Rebellion was a scout for the Rocky Mountain Rangers. He finally settled down in southern Alberta at Kootenay Lakes (now called Waterton Lakes) and ended his days as superintendent of the national park that was established there.

Étienne Brûlé

Born c.1592, France
Killed 1633

Young Étienne Brûlé was a footloose adventurer as much as an explorer—game for anything, especially if it offered excitement. He came to Canada very early, probably with Champlain,* and went to live among the Indian people. Travelling with them, he visited all the Great Lakes except Michigan. He was the first European to see these lakes.

Because of his first-hand knowledge, Brûlé was a great help to Champlain as guide and interpreter, though he deserted Champlain when the British captured Quebec in 1629. He was denounced as a traitor and took refuge among his Huron friends. But this ended badly too, for he was killed in a brawl.

Geneviève Bujold

Born 1942, Montreal, Que.

One of filmdom's most celebrated stars is the convent-educated Montrealer, Geneviève Bujold. She began by acting on the stage, but her talent soon attracted the attention of a film director, and he signed her up to play in a movie with the well-known French actor Yves Montand.

This led to many more roles and launched Geneviève Bujold on her successful career. She has won several best actress awards, both at home and abroad, including the Earle Grey Award in 1972 as "most outstanding performer in Canada." One of her most famous films is *Anne of the Thousand Days*, in which she co-starred with Richard Burton.

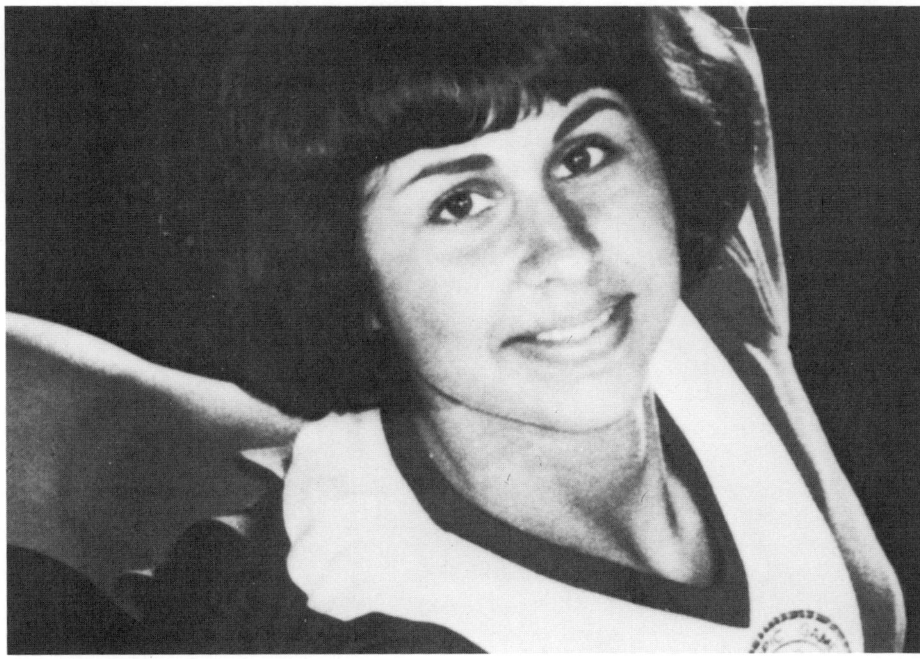

Petra Burka

Born 1946, Holland

Petra Burka, the champion figure-skater, came to Canada when she was four and started skating a couple of years later. Coached by her mother (the former Dutch champion Ellen Burka), Petra won the Canadian junior championship in 1961 and the senior a few years later.

She then began to stack up international awards: a bronze medal in 1964 at the world championships as well as at the Olympics, and in 1965 a gold at the world championships. That was her most successful year, when she won every title going and was awarded the Lou Marsh Trophy as Canada's outstanding athlete of the year. She later turned professional, skating in ice shows, and in recent years has taken a wide range of jobs, from film researcher to sports consultant.

John Buchanan

Born 1931, Sydney, N.S.

The Conservative premier of Nova Scotia since 1978, John Buchanan has a degree in engineering from Mount Allison University and a degree in law from Dalhousie. He practised law in Halifax for several years and was first elected to the Nova Scotia legislature in 1967.

In addition to his political work, Premier Buchanan is an active member of many societies, including the Boy Scouts Association. He is also on the board of directors of the oldest Scottish society in the world—the Buchanan Society of Glasgow, Scotland.

E. L. M. Burns

Born 1897, Montreal, Que.

Canada's fine reputation as the world's peacekeeper owes a lot to General Burns, a career soldier who first gained prominence in war, rather than peace. He won the Military Cross in World War I, and in World War II he commanded the 1st Canadian Corps in its advance through Italy. But his most celebrated role was after the war, in the 1950s, when he served as head of the United Nations peacekeeping force in the Middle East.

Tough as iron and bluntly straightforward, Burns succeeded in keeping the peace in this troubled region. He was respected both by Israelis and Arabs, for he was not only firm, he was determinedly fair. He even learned Arabic in his efforts to be impartial. Although the Middle East has since been scarred by war, Burns kept it stable during the most difficult years—the years when Israel was a newly formed nation. Burns later served as Canada's spokesman at conferences on disarmament.

Tommy Burns

Born 1881, Hanover, Ont.
Died 1955

Tommy Burns was the first and only Canadian to hold the world heavyweight boxing title. He won it in 1906 and defended it successfully 11 times before losing to the huge American champion, Jack Johnson, in 1908. That was a remarkable fight, since Burns was one of the smallest heavyweights ever. During his career, he never weighed more than 80 kg.

He was of German descent, born Noah Brusso, but he called himself Tommy Burns after taking up boxing, because his Methodist parents did not want the family name associated with the sport. In later life he became a minister.

Pat Burns

Born 1856, Oshawa, Ont.
Died 1937

Pat Burns, the Cattle King of the West, built up one of the world's largest meat-packing businesses, dealing in bacon and other products as well as beef. Burns had moved west as a young man, intending to homestead, but found he could do better as a cattle dealer. He supplied beef to the railway crews who were building branch lines in the West, and during the Klondike gold rush of 1898 he achieved the near-impossible feat of providing the miners in the Yukon with fresh beef.

By 1912 Burns was running six huge ranches in Alberta. He was one of the "big four" cattlemen who that same year put up the money to launch the first Calgary Stampede. Known for his generosity, he threw an enormous party on his 75th birthday, complete with a cake big enough to provide 15,000 slices. During his last years, he served as a senator in Ottawa.

William Francis Butler
Born 1838, Ireland
Died 1910

During the 1870s, Captain William Butler fired the imagination of Canadians with his dramatic book *The Great Lone Land*. It told the story of a 4400-km journey he made through the prairies during the winter of 1870-71. An army intelligence officer, Butler had been sent from Fort Garry, after the Red River Rebellion, to find out what conditions were like in the Saskatchewan country.

His book was such a success that he set out on another winter journey the following year and wrote a book about that too, *The Wild North Land*. Then he left Canada for warmer climes. He spent most of the rest of his life serving in Egypt and South Africa.

John By
Born 1781, England
Died 1836

Colonel John By of the Royal Engineers was sent to Upper Canada in 1826 to build the Rideau Canal as a new supply route. The War of 1812 had revealed the hazards of using the St. Lawrence as a supply route along that part of the river which was also a border with the United States. So a new waterway was needed, comfortably distant from the American border.

The Rideau Canal provided this waterway—a connecting system of canals, lakes, and rivers that linked the Ottawa River with Kingston on Lake Ontario. Although this canal system was built for military purposes, it opened up a large area for settlement.

Colonel By spent six years building the Rideau Canal. During this time, a village called Bytown grew up around his headquarters at the junction of the Ottawa and Rideau rivers. This little town was renamed Ottawa in 1855, and in 1857 Queen Victoria chose it as the capital of the Province of Canada. In 1865 the government departments were located there. And at Confederation in 1867, Ottawa became the capital city of the Dominion of Canada.

Lord Byng
Born 1862, England
Died 1935

Lieutenant General Sir Julian Byng commanded the Canadian Corps at the battle of Vimy Ridge, one of the most heroic battles of World War I and a great victory for the Canadian forces. In reward for his war service, he was made a lord, Baron Byng of Vimy, and in 1921 he was sent to Canada to be Governor General.

Byng had been a popular officer, and many Canadians welcomed his appointment. But he was far from popular during his last year in Canada (1926) when he refused to dissolve Parliament and hold new elections as Prime Minister Mackenzie King* requested. Byng had good reasons for his refusal, since Mackenzie King wanted Parliament dissolved so that he would avoid a vote of censure about a scandal that had erupted (which would have caused his resignation). As it was, Byng took matters into his own hands and asked Arthur Meighen* to form a government—thereby putting Mackenzie King out of office.

This caused a great outcry, with accusations that Byng had exceeded his powers as Governor General. The Meighen government was soon defeated in Parliament; and in the elections that followed, the Canadian people voted Mackenzie King back into office, thereby showing their disapproval of Byng's actions.

John Cabot
Born Italy (date unknown)
Died c.1498
Cabot is known as the "discoverer" of North America, though Leif Ericsson* and others had been here before him. Sailing on behalf of Henry VII of England, Cabot crossed the Atlantic in 1497, hoping to find Asia, and arrived off our eastern coast. He went ashore (probably in Newfoundland, but perhaps Cape Breton Island) and claimed the territory for Henry VII. Then he returned to England, full of stories about the teeming fishing grounds on the far side of the ocean.

Cabot set out again the next year and was never seen again. But his son Sebastian made further explorations and may even have sailed our Arctic waters early in the 1500s, looking for a way through to the Pacific. Sebastian Cabot was one of the first to believe in the Northwest Passage, and the maps he drew always showed a nice broad seaway connecting the Atlantic and Pacific.

Morley Callaghan
Born 1903, Toronto, Ont.
Novelist, short-story writer, and playwright, Morley Callaghan has lived most of his life in Toronto, and it was there as a student that he first met Ernest Hemingway. Callaghan had taken a summer job with the Toronto *Star*, and Hemingway was also working for the paper. During the friendship which developed, the young American gave Callaghan heartening encouragement with his writing—he was the first to recognize Callaghan's talent. Consequently, Callaghan not only wrote with renewed confidence, but followed Hemingway to Paris and lived there for eight months. Meanwhile, he had already published his first novel, *Strange Fugitive*.

Since then, Callaghan has written more than 20 books, which have brought him great stature as a writer and won him the Governor General's Award and other honours. One of his most celebrated works is *They Shall Inherit the Earth*.

Cariboo Cameron
Born 1820, Lancaster, Ont.
Died 1888
John Alexander Cameron made a huge fortune during the Cariboo gold rush of the 1860s. He was the richest miner in all British Columbia. But he was not the luckiest, for his wife died of typhoid in the Cariboo Mountains.

Sophia Cameron's death produced one of the strangest sagas of the gold rush, because she wanted to be buried at home in eastern Canada. So Cameron placed her body in a metal coffin, which he filled up with liquor. With the body thus preserved, he set off homeward. After a long journey via the jungles of Panama (and trouble with the customs officers when passing through New York), he eventually laid his wife to rest in her family plot in Cornwall, Ont. He then settled down to spend his fortune. Like many another successful miner, Cariboo Cameron died poor.

Réal Caouette
Born 1917, Amos, Que.
Died 1976
Réal Caouette was leader of the Créditistes, the Quebec wing of the Social Credit party. A superb orator, he was chosen as leader in 1958, and in the 1962 federal elections he and his followers were successful in gaining 26 seats in the House of Commons. From then until his death, Réal Caouette was re-elected at every federal election, and in 1971 he was chosen leader of the national Social Credit party.

Jean Carignan
Born 1916, Lévis, Que.
At festivals and concerts in Europe as well as North America, one of the great attractions used to be Jean Carignan, the Quebec fiddler, who displayed such amazing virtuosity with his playing of jigs and reels. The son of a bricklayer who was an amateur fiddler, Carignan had borrowed his father's violin as a child and learned the tunes his father could play. By the age of five, he was playing on street corners in Lévis. There he was heard by bandleader George Wade, who took him on in 1931, featuring him as The Kid Fiddler.

Carignan later performed with other oldtime bands, but could not make a living from his music. He supported himself with labouring jobs and by driving a taxi. Meanwhile, he gained increasing fame as a fiddle player—had a film made about him, a concerto written for him, and in 1974 was made a Member of the Order of Canada. But Carignan's work on noisy construction sites had affected his hearing, and he suffered from deafness as he grew older. Today, he hardly ever performs in public.

Guy Carleton
Born 1724, Ireland
Died 1808
Sir Guy Carleton was the second governor of Quebec after the British conquest of Canada. Kind and thoughtful, and sympathetic to the French population, he helped arrange for the Quebec Act of 1774, which permitted the French to keep their laws, their seigniorial system, and many other rights. The British had taken away these rights in 1763, and this had caused a lot of resentment.

Although the Quebec Act pleased the French, it infuriated many English colonists and in fact was one of the causes of the American Revolution. During the revolution, Carleton was in Montreal when it was captured by the Americans. But he escaped in a canoe and made for Quebec, where he rallied his troops and then defeated an American attack on the city. He was later made governor-in-chief of British North America.

Bliss Carman
Born 1861, Fredericton, N.B.
Died 1929
"Low Tide on Grand Pré" is the most famous of Bliss Carman's many fine poems. He was one of the earliest Canadian poets to gain an international reputation.

A cousin of Charles G. D. Roberts,* Carman was one of the group called the Confederation Poets. He was less consciously Canadian than the others in the group, even though many of his verses are about Canadian scenes. Although he grew up in the Maritimes, he lived most of his life in the United States, where he worked as a literary journalist.

Emily Carr

Born 1871, Victoria, B.C.
Died 1945

One of the greatest of all Canadian artists, Emily Carr was 70 before her talent was widely recognized. For much of her life she was thought of (by those who knew her at all) as a batty eccentric who ran a boarding house in Victoria and kept a menagerie of dogs and assorted animals. Taking easel and paints, she used to go off alone into the forests, returning with strange pictures of the Indian villages she had visited. Her style was far in advance of her times and not at all popular. Instead of making careful reproductions of what she saw, she painted what she felt about what she saw.

It seemed that only the Coast Indians appreciated Emily Carr or her work. To them, she was Klee Wyck, "the laughing one," a friendly woman who showed great interest in their culture. They hung her paintings in their houses, and this attracted the attention of anthropologist Marius Barbeau,* who arranged for an exhibition of her work in Ottawa.

Well into her fifties by this time, Emily Carr was introduced to members of the Group of Seven and at last praised by fellow artists. She gained national attention in 1941 when she won a Governor General's Award for her book *Klee Wyck*. The first of several books, it made the Canadian public aware of Emily Carr and her powerful paintings.

William Carson

Born 1770, Scotland
Died 1843

Dr. William Carson was the great figure of early nineteenth-century Newfoundland, the man who took the colony out of its fishing-station serfdom and set it on the road to becoming a free and self-governing society. From the moment he arrived there in 1808 until the time of his death, he was the leading mover and shaker.

Carson was hated fiercely by the big merchants and British governors, by all who held sway, for he worked to remove the power from such overlords. He got the system of justice improved and the land laws reformed, and it was mainly because of his efforts that Newfoundland was given representative government in 1832. Carson was elected to the Legislative Assembly, and in 1837 he became speaker of the assembly.

Roch Carrier

Born 1937, Ste. Justine de Dorchester, Que.

Roch Carrier, one of Quebec's leading novelists, earned his living as a university teacher while first making his way as a writer. His best-known book is *La Guerre, Yes Sir!*, a story set in a Quebec village during World War II. The novel has been adapted for the stage and performed in both English and French. It is the first part of a trilogy, the other two books being *Floralie, Where Are You?* and *Is It the Sun, Philibert?* Much of Carrier's work can be read in English, and he can be heard in English too, for he makes frequent lecture tours across Canada.

Wilf Carter

Born 1904, Port Hilford, N.S.

Wilf Carter, the yodelling cowboy, was one of the most popular country and western singers of the 1930s and 1940s. Of Swiss ancestry, he taught himself to yodel during his childhood in Nova Scotia and then got plenty of practice as an adult while working as a cowboy in the West. He developed his famous echo yodel in the Rockies.

Carter first performed as a singer in Alberta, on radio and at rodeos, but could not make a living from it. For several years he worked as a trail rider, escorting tourists and singing to them around the campfire. Then, in 1932, he made his first record, and a few years later CBS radio gave him a regular morning show. This brought him fame throughout North America. He was immensely popular—a real cowboy who yodelled magnificently and sang his own songs. His greatest hit was "There's a Love Knot in My Lariat."

Wilf Carter and another Nova Scotian, Hank Snow (born 1914), were the first to make Canadian country music popular. Hank Snow's records first began to top the charts regularly in the 1950s, and he hasn't looked back since. Both singers have sold literally millions of records.

George-Étienne Cartier

Born 1814, St. Antoine sur Richelieu, Que.
Died 1873

George-Étienne Cartier was one of the leading Fathers of Confederation, involved in the plans from the beginning and present at all three conferences. He convinced his fellow French Canadians that they would benefit from Confederation—and made sure they would by seeing that Quebec (and all the provinces) had a good deal of power within the federal system.

Cartier had long been a champion of the French cause. He fought for the Patriotes during the Rebellion of 1837 and was later one of the most prominent French Canadians in the Province of Canada's legislature, heading the government for some years. After Confederation, he was John A. Macdonald's* second-in-command, acting as prime minister whenever John A., for various reasons, was unable to function. It was Cartier who arranged for Canada to buy all the Hudson's Bay Company lands, and Cartier who made arrangements for the building of the CPR—shouting "All aboard for the West!" when he introduced the railway bill in Parliament.

But it was also Cartier who gave the railway contract to Hugh Allan* and personally received $85,000 in campaign funds from Allan. The whole business looked so much like a deal that it brought on the Pacific Scandal, which in turn brought down the government. Cartier did not live to see this. Desperately ill with Bright's disease, he died before the scandal really broke.

Jacques Cartier
Born 1491, France
Died 1557

Jacques Cartier was the first European to explore the Gulf of St. Lawrence and make his way inland. Hoping to find a seaway to the Pacific Ocean (and also to find plenty of gold and diamonds), Cartier came three times to Canada. He found no riches, but he opened up a whole new world.

Cartier's first voyage was in 1534, when he sailed round the Gulf of St. Lawrence, discovered Prince Edward Island and other islands, and erected a large cross on the Gaspé Peninsula to signify that this new world belonged to France. On his next voyage, in 1535, the sons of the Iroquois chief Donnacona* showed Cartier the way into the St. Lawrence River. Thinking this must be the great seaway to the Pacific, Cartier sailed up the river until stopped by the rapids at Hochelaga (Montreal). On his third voyage, in 1541, he made no new discoveries and he lost the friendship of the Iroquois. He sailed home in a hurry the following summer, not staying to help a Frenchman called Roberval* who had just arrived to try and set up a colony.

But Cartier had already done more than any before him. He had found a way into the heart of Canada.

Richard Cartwright
Born 1835, Kingston, Ont.
Died 1912

Richard Cartwright was one of the most prominent politicians in the post-Confederation period, but not one of the most cheerful. He so often warned of doom and disaster that he was nicknamed Blue Ruin.

Cartwright started out as a Conservative, but he grew bitter when John A. Macdonald* would not make him finance minister. Nursing his grudge, Cartwright campaigned against John A. during the Pacific Scandal and joined the Liberals. He was rewarded by being made finance minister in Alexander Mackenzie's* Liberal government of 1873-78. But Cartwright was not a success in this longed-for portfolio. His outlook was too negative. He was far more effective in the years that followed, when he shone as a cut-and-thrust Opposition MP, striking at the vices of the Conservatives, and especially at those of their leader. He never forgave John A.

Thérèse Casgrain
Born 1896, Montreal, Que.
Died 1981

In 1940 Quebec women at last gained the right to vote in provincial elections, thanks largely to the efforts of Thérèse Casgrain.

As daughter of the wealthy Sir Rodolphe Forget, and as the wife of politician Pierre Casgrain, Mme. Casgrain could have enjoyed a leisurely life. Instead, she chose to battle against social injustices. For almost 20 years she campaigned to get Quebec women the provincial vote. She was also active in health and welfare programs, and in 1951 was elected leader of Quebec's socialist CCF party (a forerunner of the NDP). During these years, Thérèse Casgrain faced a lot of criticism, some of it from family friends. Yet she kept firm to her beliefs, earning the gratitude of many Quebeckers, as well as women throughout Canada. In 1970 she was appointed to the Senate.

A. J. Casson
Born 1898, Toronto, Ont.

For many years now, A. J. Casson has been an influential figure in the art world. He was a later member of the Group of Seven (see J. E. H. MacDonald*), joining the group in 1926 when Frank Johnston left to go his own way.

Casson worked in the art department of Rous and Mann, where several of the Group of Seven painters worked after leaving Grip Ltd. Unlike the others, Casson continued as a commercial artist, and he became vice-president of the printing firm Sampson Matthews. He was president of the Royal Canadian Academy from 1948 until 1952.

Samuel de Champlain
Born c.1570, France
Died 1635

The founder of Quebec was a good-natured, jovial man, a type of laughing cavalier who preferred to cajole people into doing his will, rather than forcing them with punishments. But he was very firm in his purpose.

Champlain founded Quebec in 1608, having earlier helped set up the short-lived trading post at Port Royal (in today's Nova Scotia). Quebec also began as a trading post, but Champlain built it into France's first permanent settlement in the New World. He encouraged farming as well as trading, passed laws to establish order, and brought in priests to start missions. Meanwhile, he explored and mapped the neighbouring territory, and made friends with the Hurons and their allies. And he fought their opponents, the Iroquois, who became bitter enemies of the French.

The British were also the enemy, and in 1629 David Kirke* blockaded Quebec, captured Champlain and took him to England. But Champlain returned to rebuild his

settlement. Though there were only 150 settlers by the time he died, Champlain had established a colony which would grow into a great French empire—and eventually into a nation called Canada.

Thomas Chapais
Born 1858, St.Denis de Kamouraska, Que.
Died 1946

The frail and scholarly Thomas Chapais played a remarkably vigorous role in bringing Canada's "two founding nations" closer together. For he explained Canada to Canadians.

The author of numerous history books, he was also a journalist, a professor at Laval, and for many years a senator. In his writings and speeches, he looked back to the past to explain the present. He helped English Canadians to see why French Canadians felt they had a raw deal. And he helped French Canadians to see how they could benefit by remaining part of Canada. He gave both groups a better understanding of themselves and one another.

Fluently bilingual, Chapais was a complete Canadian, at home in both cultures. His father and father-in-law had both been Fathers of Confederation (Jean Chapais and Hector Langevin).

Robert Charlebois
Born 1945, Montreal, Que.

With his Montreal Canadiens hockey sweater and Afro hair style, pop singer Robert Charlebois took Quebec by storm in the late 1960s, belting out his songs in *joual*. A graduate of Montreal's National Theatre School, he was named "discovery of the year" in 1965 in CBC TV's *Jeunesse Oblige*. Three years later, he was chosen to represent Quebec at the International Festival of French Song, where he won the grand prize with his song "Lindberg."

Charlebois has been a hit in many countries, especially in France where his shows have been a riotous success. With his electrifying performances and electric guitar, he has had great impact on fellow Quebeckers, inspiring singers and songwriters to take a new, vigorous approach in their music.

Brock Chisholm
Born 1896, Oakville, Ont.
Died 1971

The World Health Organization performs its vital role throughout the world partly because of the vision of Dr. Brock Chisholm. Working on behalf of the Canadian government, Chisholm helped set up WHO and served as its first director general (1948-53). He set the pattern which the organization has since followed, fighting not only disease, but poverty, hunger, ignorance, and other conditions which lead to ill health and early death.

A psychiatrist by profession, Chisholm had served in both world wars and was head of the Canadian medical services in World War II. Known for his outspokenness, he once had half of Canada on his back because he said that Santa Claus was bad for children. Yet "the man who wanted to ban Santa Claus" gave more than presents to millions of children throughout the world. He gave them the chance of surviving to be adults.

George Chuvalo
Born 1937, Toronto, Ont.
Heavyweight boxer George Chuvalo fought Muhammad Ali, George Foreman, and other world champs —and in all his fights he was never knocked down. He began boxing when he was 10, in St. Mary's Catholic Church Hall, Toronto, later moving on to the East York Arena and the Palace Pier. In 1955 he won the Canadian amateur heavyweight title and in 1958 won the Canadian professional title. Though he lost the title in 1960, he regained it twice more and then defended it successfully from 1968 to 1976. Since laying down his gloves, Chuvalo has been a boxing commentator on television.

Joe Clark
Born 1939, High River, Alta.
On June 4, 1979, the day before his fortieth birthday, Charles Joseph Clark was sworn into office as prime minister of Canada—the youngest person ever to hold the position. Two weeks earlier, he had led the Conservatives to their first federal election victory in 17 years.

A graduate of the University of Alberta, Clark had begun his career as a journalist, but was soon devoting his full time to politics. He worked for both the provincial and federal Conservatives, and for a while was executive assistant to Robert Stanfield.* First elected to Parliament in 1972, he succeeded Stanfield in 1976 as leader of the Conservative party. He remained Conservative leader until 1983.

Clark's period as prime minister (1979-80) lasted less than a year, for his government was defeated in a House of Commons vote on the budget. During his few months in office, he and his ministers handled the Iranian hostage escape (see Ken Taylor*) and also the Boat People crisis, when thousands of Indo-chinese refugees were offered a new life in Canada. Clark is married to Maureen McTeer, a graduate in law and a published author.

King Clancy
Born 1903, Ottawa, Ont.
King Clancy has been a central figure in professional hockey ever since 1921, when he joined the Ottawa Senators as an 18-year-old defenceman. After starring with the Senators for nine years, he was bought by the Toronto Maple Leafs, who paid the then unheard-of sum of $35,000 (plus two players) to acquire Clancy from the Ottawa club. In the 1931-32 season he led the Leafs to their first Stanley Cup victory. In later life he was the Leafs' coach, and in 1967 he was appointed vice-president of the club. Not only his career but his whole life has been dedicated to hockey.

Adrienne Clarkson
Born 1939, Hong Kong
For 17 years, Adrienne Clarkson was one of the best-known personalities on the CBC, a TV journalist who investigated controversial subjects and was prepared to speak out boldly about them. She gained particular acclaim as co-host of the current affairs show *The Fifth Estate*, for which she travelled the world, interviewing such titans as the Shah of Iran.

She was raised in Ottawa, having been brought to Canada by her parents as a small child. In addition to working in television, she has written a couple of novels, and she taught at the University of Toronto before joining the CBC in 1965. Adrienne Clarkson left the CBC in 1982 to take on another challenging job—Ontario's agent general in France, representing the province's trade and cultural interests.

Bruce Cockburn
Born 1945, Ottawa, Ont.

When he was a child, his parents said he could learn the guitar as long as he didn't wear a black leather jacket. Then his mother suggested that, as a guitarist, he should also sing. So began the career of Bruce Cockburn, from soft-voiced folksinger to rock superstar—and from Cowichan sweaters to black leather jackets.

In his early years, Cockburn worked as a street musician in Paris. He then studied music in Boston and by the late 1960s was singing in Ottawa coffee houses. In 1970 he gained national attention with his theme song for the film *Goin' Down the Road*. He has since gained a large international audience and has had successful overseas tours. Many of his songs reflect his strong Christian beliefs. It has been said that while others sing of Saturday night, Bruce Cockburn sings of eternity.

Leonard Cohen
Born 1934, Montreal, Que.

Leonard Cohen is a rare combination—a serious poet who became a pop star. His poetry has won him great literary acclaim, while his concerts and record albums have won him applause across the world.

Cohen grew up in Montreal, and during his student years at McGill he played the guitar in a country and western band. He first read his poems to the accompaniment of jazz in a Montreal nightclub. Some years later, at a poetry reading in New York, he sang two of his poems, one of them being "Suzanne." By the late 1960s, Cohen's readings had developed into rock-type concerts. Meanwhile, he was writing novels as well as poetry. He lived abroad for many years, mainly on the Greek island of Hydra, but then returned to Montreal, where he has continued his work as a writer, and at times as a performer.

Two-Gun Cohen
Born 1887, England
Died 1970
Young Morris Cohen was such a handful that his family sent him to Canada at the age of 16 to work as a ranch hand on the prairies. In the West, Cohen learned to handle cards as well as cattle, and he was soon doing very well for himself as a gambler and land speculator in Edmonton. Always ready to rush into the fray, he became a hero to Chinese Canadians by knocking out a burglar who was robbing a Chinese restaurant. When in 1911 the Chinese leader Dr. Sun Yat-sen toured North America, he hired Two-Gun Cohen as his personal bodyguard.

In 1922 Cohen joined Sun Yat-sen in China and was appointed colonel (later promoted to general) in the Chinese Nationalist army. He was captured by the Japanese during World War II but survived the ordeal and eventually returned to Canada, where he continued to work ardently for the Chinese cause.

Kit Coleman
Born 1864, Ireland
Died 1915
Long before Ann Landers or Dear Abby sold their columns to our newspapers, Canada had its own columnist—Kit of the *Mail*. From 1889 to 1911 she wrote a weekly page for the Toronto paper. Called "Woman's Kingdom," it was immensely popular, containing book reviews, poems, and a wide range of features, as well as giving advice to people with personal problems.

Kit had plenty of experience of personal problems. Married at 16 to a man called Willis, she was widowed at 20. After immigrating to Canada, she married a man called Watkins and was again widowed. She took her time about marrying her third husband, Dr. Theobald Coleman. Meanwhile, she wrote for the *Mail*, delighting and outraging her readers with her outspoken comments. She was one of the first women to have a regular newspaper job in Canada. And she was the first woman in the world to be a war correspondent. This was in 1898 when she was sent to Cuba to report on the Spanish-American War.

John Colicos
Born 1928, Toronto, Ont.
The celebrated actor grew up in Montreal, and it was there he first performed on the stage. By his early twenties, the young Colicos was making his mark in Shakespeare plays at the Old Vic in England, and he later performed to great acclaim at Shakespeare festivals in Stratford, Conn., and Stratford, Ont.

Although Colicos made his name as a Shakespearean actor, he has also had many film and TV roles, performing in such shows as *General Hospital* and *Star Trek*. But the main star of *Star Trek* was not Colicos but William Shatner (born 1931, Montreal) who played the intrepid Captain Kirk.

John Robert Colombo
Born 1936, Kitchener, Ont.
John Robert Colombo has no connection whatever with Lieutenant Columbo of TV fame. But he is, in his own way, a detective. He is Canada's most energetic seeker-out of facts, jokes, folklore, spooky stories, science fiction, and a wide range of out-of-the-way Canadiana. His findings have been published in such books as *Colombo's Canadian Quotations* and *Colombo's Book of Marvels*.

Colombo also writes poetry, and from time to time he teaches or appears on radio and television. But he is happiest when researching Canadiana. Of his more than 60 books, two of the most recent are *Colombo's Canadiana Quiz Book* and *René Lévesque Buys Canada Savings Bonds*.

Alex Colville
Born 1920, Toronto, Ont.
In 1981 Alex Colville was made a Companion of the Order of Canada for his great contribution to Canadian art. He paints in the realist style, with careful attention to detail, producing very powerful pictures. Many of his paintings have an eerie quality, so that one wonders "What is happening? Why does this picture make me feel uneasy?"

Colville was raised in the Maritimes and studied art at Mount Allison University in New Brunswick. After serving as a war artist in World War II, he returned to Mount Allison where he taught art until 1963. Now a full-time painter, he has a waiting list of customers, who gladly pay many thousands of dollars for a picture almost as soon as the paint is dry.

Charles Comfort
Born 1900, Scotland
Charles Comfort has long been a leading figure in the art world. He started his career at the age of 14, working for a commercial art firm in Winnipeg, and then studied art in Winnipeg and New York. Settling in Toronto, he taught art for many years at the University of Toronto. From 1960 to 1965 he was director of the National Gallery in Ottawa.

One of Comfort's best-known paintings is *Young Canadian*, a portrait of the artist Carl Schaefer (born 1903). Schaefer is especially noted for his landscapes of the Ontario countryside.

Lionel Conacher
Born 1902, Toronto, Ont.
Died 1954
Nobody was surprised when the Canadian Press poll of 1950 selected Lionel Conacher as Canada's outstanding athlete of the half-century. Known as "the Big Train," he was the most amazing all-rounder. By the time he was 18 he had already won an Ontario wrestling title and the Canadian light-heavyweight boxing title. He went on to star in four different sports: football, lacrosse, baseball, and hockey.

Playing for the Toronto Argos in their 1921 Grey Cup win, Conacher scored three touchdowns. The following year he was on the Toronto Maitlands team which won the Ontario Amateur Lacrosse League championship. In 1926 he was a member of the Toronto Maple Leafs baseball team which won the Triple A championship. And he was playing for the Chicago Black Hawks when they won the Stanley Cup in 1934.

On retiring from professional sport, Conacher became a Liberal MP. He died of a heart attack while playing in a softball game against the parliamentary press corps. His brother Charlie was also a well-known hockey player.

Duke of Connaught
Born 1850, England
Died 1942
The Duke of Connaught was Governor General of Canada 1911-16. He was the third son of Queen Victoria. A famous regiment, the Princess Patricia's Canadian Light Infantry, was named after his daughter. He was followed as Governor General by another duke, the Duke of Devonshire.

Ralph Connor
Born 1860, Glengarry County, Ont.
Died 1937
Ralph Connor was the pen name of the Rev. Charles Gordon, who wrote almost 30 books which were very popular in the early 1900s. The best known is *Glengarry School Days*, which is based on memories of his childhood. In all, he sold more than 3 million copies of his books. Yet writing was only a sideline. First and foremost, Gordon was a Presbyterian minister. He was located in Winnipeg for many years and in 1922 was elected moderator of the Presbyterian Church in Canada.

Stompin' Tom Connors
Born 1936, Saint John, N.B.

Tom Connors wrote his first song when he was 11. Since then, he has written more than 500 songs, made more than 30 LPs, and had a couple of films made about him. He is one of Canada's most popular country singers, but he had a hard time getting to the top. Brought up in an orphanage and then in a foster home, he was out on his own as a teenager, working as a labourer. Then for about ten years he hitchhiked round Canada, living rough, taking odd jobs, and trying without success to interest radio stations in the songs he wrote.

His big break came in 1964, when he began to sing regularly at the Maple Leaf Hotel in Timmins, Ont. There he became known as Stompin' Tom because he pounded the floor with his foot to emphasize the rhythm. To save the carpet, he then took to using a "stomping board." His first big hit came a few years later with his record *Bud the Spud*. Part of Stompin' Tom's appeal is that he sings about working Canadians from all provinces. He has said that he wants "to sing Canada to the world."

James Cook
Born 1728, England
Killed 1779

Captain Cook and his sailors were the first Europeans to set foot on Canada's West Coast. This was in 1778 when they landed at Nootka Sound, Vancouver Island. Cook was on his third voyage round the world at the time; and though he died before the end of the voyage, his sailors returned to Britain to tell of the furs which they had obtained from the Nootka Indians and then sold at great profit in China. Before long, dozens of trading ships were beating a path to Vancouver Island.

Cook left his mark on eastern Canada too. As a young navigator in the British navy, he spent several years surveying and mapping the coast of Newfoundland. He met his death in Hawaii, where he was attacked by the islanders.

Edward Cornwallis

Born 1713, England
Died 1776

In 1749 the newly appointed governor of Nova Scotia, Edward Cornwallis, arrived in Chebucto Bay with about 2,500 settlers. He chose a fine hill on the west side of the bay, and on it he built the town of Halifax. This marked the beginning of the first large-scale British settlement of Nova Scotia, and from then on the colony grew rapidly. But Cornwallis did not stay long as governor. He resigned three years later, with a good deal of anger, because of a quarrel with his superiors in Britain, who said he was spending too much money.

Cornwallis's career didn't suffer, for he was the son of a lord (he and his twin brother had been pages to the king as children). Although he had a rather stormy life, he was always promoted. He ended up as a lieutenant-general, and his twin brother became archbishop of Canterbury.

William Epps Cormack

Born 1796, St. John's, Nfld.
Died 1868

William Cormack was the first European to cross Newfoundland and explore the interior of the island. He did this exhausting expedition on foot in 1822, accompanied by a young Micmac hunter, Joseph Sylvester.

On their way across the island, the two men met up with several groups of Micmacs and Montagnais, but they found no Beothuk Indians. Cormack had been hoping to contact the remaining Beothuks, and he tried to do so again on a later expedition. He wanted to save them from extinction. He failed. The most he could do was befriend Shawnawdithit,* the last of the Beothuks, when she was brought to St. John's. Much of our knowledge of the Beothuk culture is based on what Cormack learned from Shawnawdithit.

Toller Cranston

Born 1949, Hamilton, Ont.

Toller Cranston is known throughout the world for his dramatic, balletlike skating. He first performed in public when he was eight, giving an impromptu Cossack-style dance on skates at the Kirkland Lake carnival. Although Cranston lived in several different towns as a child, he always found his way to the nearest rink, and in 1964 he won the Canadian junior figure-skating championship. He first won the senior title in 1971 and went on to win the bronze medal at the 1974 world championships. After gaining the bronze at the 1976 Olympics, he gave up competitive skating and turned his talents to ice shows.

Cranston is also known as a painter, and here too he has his own original style. But though his skating style is unique, his success is part of a long Canadian tradition. Back in 1890, Louis Rubenstein of Montreal won the world figure-skating championship, having held the Canadian title for many years. More recently, both Donald Jackson and Donald McPherson have won the world championship, Jackson gaining his gold medal in 1962, and McPherson in 1963.

Marie-Josephte Corriveau

Born 1733, St. Vallier, Que.
Hanged 1763

She has gone down in legend as a witch, a chain-rattling ghost who waylays travellers on lonely Quebec roads. There are any amount of scary tales about La Corriveau—the woman who took an axe and gave her husband two great whacks. (This was her second husband. Her first husband had died unexpectedly too.)

La Corriveau was hanged for murder and then, as a warning to others, her body was displayed in an iron cage at Lauzon, near Lévis, Que. The ghost stories began about a century later when the cage, with some bones in it, was found in Lauzon cemetery. La Corriveau has been haunting people's imagination ever since.

Isabella Valancy Crawford

Born 1850, Ireland
Died 1887

The poet Isabella Valancy Crawford was the daughter of Irish immigrants who brought her to Canada when she was eight. They were desperately poor, and when Isabella grew up she struggled to support herself and her widowed mother by writing short stories and articles.

When she was 33, she published a book of poems at her own expense, but she only sold 50 copies. The collection included "Malcolm's Katie," a narrative poem which many people now consider to be her best work. Recognition finally came about 20 years after her death, when the editor and publisher John Garvin brought out a collected edition of her poems.

Donald Creighton

Born 1902, Toronto, Ont.
Died 1979

Donald Creighton was one of Canada's most distinguished historians, the author of scholarly books and articles which were widely read and widely acclaimed. He treated the writing of history as an art, weaving his facts into an interesting and often intriguing story.

Brought up in Toronto, Creighton taught for many years at the University of Toronto, where he was chairman of the history department 1955-59. Among his many honours, he received two Governor General's Awards (for his masterly two-volume biography of John A. Macdonald*) and in 1967 was named a Companion of the Order of Canada. He was married to Luella Creighton, the author of historical novels and several popular children's books, as well as numerous short stories.

Octave Crémazie

Born 1827, Quebec, Que.
Died 1879

Called "the father of French Canadian poetry," Octave Crémazie wrote stirring patriotic poems, many of which had historical themes. During the 1850s he ran a bookshop in Quebec City, which became a meeting place for writers and the centre of a vigorous literary group.

Crémazie's fame increased year by year, but he got in a desperate muddle with his bookshop, buying far more stock than he could sell, or even pay for. By 1862 he owed about $100,000. To escape imprisonment, he fled to France, where he lived in poverty, too depressed to write poetry. Although friends sent him money, he could never return home. He died a lonely exile, even while his work was being honoured in Quebec.

Thomas Alexander Crerar
Born 1876, Molesworth, Ont.
Died 1975

The Progressive Party was formed in 1920 by T. A. Crerar and other MPs who supported the interests of Canadian farmers. For a few years, this party was a strong power in Parliament, though it split up around 1926.

Crerar had long been involved in the problems of farmers. He had grown up on a Manitoba farm and then worked as a grain elevator agent, and he was made manager in 1907 of the company which later became known as United Grain Growers. He was president of UGG until 1929. Meanwhile, he held several cabinet positions in Ottawa, serving in Robert Borden's* wartime coalition government (before forming the Progressive Party) and later joining Mackenzie King's* Liberal government. He ended his career as a senator. Whatever his position, Crerar continually strove to get the farmers of western Canada a fairer system of marketing the grain they grew.

Crowfoot
Born c.1830, nr. Belly River, Alta.
Died 1890

The celebrated Blackfoot chief gained renown at an early age by his outstanding bravery during the guerrilla warfare on the prairies. Crowfoot was a teenager when he was first the hero of a battle. But gradually he realized that the Plains Indians would do better if they stopped fighting one another, so he made peace with the Cree and other traditional enemies, and spent the rest of his life working for peace.

When the Mounted Police came west in 1874, Crowfoot used his influence to make them welcome. Later, he played a key role in the signing of Treaty No. 7 and in the peaceful construction of the CPR. Most important, he prevented the Blackfoot from joining the Northwest Rebellion. Although his sympathies were with the rebels, Crowfoot guessed that a full-scale war would only bring disaster.

Red Crow, the shrewd head chief of the Bloods, also remained neutral during the rebellion. Both these men were skilled diplomats, and their wise leadership brought their people safely through the desperate years of change, when the buffalo vanished from the prairies and settlers moved in.

Maurice Cullen
Born 1866, St. John's, Nfld.
Died 1934
Maurice Cullen was one of the great influences in the development of Canadian art. As a young man, he went to Paris intending to study sculpture, but he was so struck by the work of the French Impressionists that he decided to study painting instead.

Returning home in 1895, Cullen settled in Montreal and proceeded to adapt the Impressionist style to Canadian scenes, and especially to snow scenes. He painted snow every colour except white, catching the reflections of sky and trees and water.

This was too new an approach to be very popular with the public, but it excited fellow artists. Cullen was a hero to younger painters like A. Y. Jackson* and the others who later formed the Group of Seven.

Burton Cummings
Born 1947, Winnipeg, Man.
Singer-pianist Burton Cummings was the leading songwriter and major on-stage personality of the Guess Who, the rock band from Winnipeg that conquered the world during the late 1960s and early 1970s. Cummings was 17 when he was asked to join the band, which immediately scored an international hit with "Shakin' All Over." Follow-up concert tours in England and the U.S. launched the group on their triumphant career, which saw a succession of million-selling records.

Guitarist and songwriter Randy Bachman (born 1946, Winnipeg) was also a key member of the band, though he left it in 1970 and formed another highly popular group, the Bachman-Turner Overdrive. In recent years, both Bachman and Cummings have had successful solo careers.

Samuel Cunard
Born 1787, Halifax, N.S.
Died 1865
The Cunard Line of steamships owes its origins to Samuel Cunard, the enterprising son of a Halifax carpenter. Even in his twenties, Cunard had an exceptionally good head for business, and his small sailing-ship company (which he had started in partnership with his father) soon grew into a large sailing fleet that traded as far away as China.

With the coming of steam, Cunard managed to outbid his rivals for the coveted contract to take mail by steamer across the Atlantic. He quickly had three steamships built and in 1840 launched the first regular trans-atlantic mail service. Constantly improving and enlarging his fleet, Cunard was one of the first Nova Scotians to build a successful business empire.

Cunard's shipping company later became one of the greatest passenger lines in the world, launching such mighty ships as the *Queen Mary*, as well as the original *Queen Elizabeth* and the *Queen Elizabeth II*.

Arthur Currie

Born 1875, Napperton, Ont.
Died 1933

Sir Arthur Currie was the first Canadian to be made a full general (in 1919). He began his career in British Columbia as a school teacher and then as a businessman. But he also joined the militia, and he was already a lieutenant colonel when World War I started. He quickly rose in rank during the war, succeeding Sir Julian Byng* in 1917 as commander of the Canadian Corps.

Shortly before Currie took over, the four Canadian divisions had fought together for the first time, achieving a fabled victory, despite appalling losses, at the battle of Vimy Ridge. Currie made sure the Canadian troops stayed together, instead of being mixed in with other units as the British generals wanted. This policy gave the troops a pride in being Canadian and winning as Canadians.

Currie was a popular commander, often called Barrage Currie because he favoured pounding the enemy with shellfire, rather than sacrificing men. Ironically, he was later accused of wasting lives needlessly, and he had to sue a newspaper to defend his reputation. Although millions of lives were lost needlessly in that War to End All Wars, Currie tried to protect his troops more than most generals. He spent his last years as principal of McGill University—a full circle to his early days as a school teacher.

Louis Cyr

Born 1863, St.Cyprien de Napierville, Que.
Died 1912

Louis Cyr was the strongest man in the world, a solid mound of muscle. His thighs were thicker than an average man's waist.

Taken up by a promoter in his twenties, Cyr took on every champion going and never lost a contest. He could lift a 250-kg weight with one finger. In Boston in 1895, he lifted a plank with 18 fat men on it. He may well have been the strongest man ever, though there were no official records in his day. It was left to Doug Hepburn,* in this century, to win the official world title for Canada.

When Cyr was not weightlifting, he liked to play the violin. And between tours, he ran a tavern in Montreal. Sadly, his magnificent strength was undermined from within, and he died of Bright's disease when only 49.

John Wesley Dafoe
Born 1866, Combermere, Ont.
Died 1944
A rumpled, fatherly figure with a thatch of red hair, J. W. Dafoe was one of Canada's greatest newspapermen. He started as a reporter in Ottawa, and after gaining experience on several newspapers, he was appointed editor of the *Manitoba Free Press* in 1901.

For 43 years Dafoe guided and nurtured the *Free Press*, building it into a national paper known for its firm viewpoints. Even cabinet ministers took note of what Dafoe wrote in his editorials. By the time he died, the *Winnipeg Free Press* (as it had by then become) was one of the most influential newspapers in all North America. And Dafoe himself had become a folk hero to many young journalists; for he stood firm to his beliefs, writing what he felt should be written, regardless of the attitudes of the newspaper's owner or any other powerful person.

Ken Danby
Born 1940, Sault Ste. Marie, Ont.
At the Crease, the famous picture of a hockey goalkeeper, was painted by Ken Danby, Canada's leading sports artist. He has produced hundreds of pictures of athletes in action: sprinters, divers, cyclists, gymnasts.

Danby had decided to be an artist by the time he was 10, and when he was 18 he enrolled at the Ontario College of Art. There he tried abstract painting, but he later turned to realistic pictures and finally found his true vocation when he chose sport as his subject. He lived in Toronto for several years and then moved to a century-old millhouse near Guelph, Ont.

Trump Davidson
Born 1908, Sudbury, Ont.
Died 1978
Jimmy "Trump" Davidson was a pioneer in making jazz a popular form of music in Canada. Principally a cornet player and singer, Davidson first performed publicly at the age of 12, playing the trumpet in Sudbury's Canadian Legion Band. A few years later, around 1925, he formed the Melody Five, which is thought to have been the first jazz-style group in Canada.

He went on to form several dixieland big bands, one of which toured England. For many years he and his band appeared at Toronto's Palace Pier, as well as being heard regularly on the radio. He had his own CBC shows, such as *Trump Davidson's Dixieland* and *Dixieland Downbeat*, and was still performing well into the 1970s.

Robertson Davies
Born 1913, Thamesville, Ont.
In 1960, William Robertson Davies was awarded the Lorne Pierce Medal for distinguished service to Canadian literature. The author of about 30 books, as well as countless articles, he has received many other honours and awards, including the Governor General's Award. One of his most celebrated works is the Deptford Trilogy—a three-volume saga that consists of *Fifth Business* and two connected novels, which tell the same story from different people's point of view.

Roberston Davies was an actor before he was known as an author, and he has written a number of plays. He also worked as a journalist and for many years was editor of the Peterborough *Examiner*. From 1962 to 1982 he was master of Massey College at the University of Toronto.

Nicholas Flood Davin
Born 1843, Ireland
Died 1901

In 1883, when Regina was little more than a collection of tents and shacks, Nicholas Flood Davin founded the city's first newspaper, the *Leader*. Davin was a journalist and lawyer from Toronto, a talented but unstable man who had great ambitions and great ingenuity. In 1885 he pulled off the scoop of the year by disguising himself as a priest so that he could get into Louis Riel's* cell and interview the condemned man. He published the interview after Riel was hanged.

Moving from journalism into politics, Davin was elected an MP, and he sold the *Leader* to Walter Scott (who later became first premier of Saskatchewan). But as time passed, Davin grew to dislike Scott, and his views, and the way he ran the *Leader*. Worse still, he lost his seat in Parliament to Scott in 1900. Drinking heavily, and overwhelmed by personal as well as career problems, he shot himself during a visit to Winnipeg.

John Davis
Born c.1550, England
Killed 1605

The navigator John Davis followed up on the voyages of Martin Frobisher* and sailed to the Arctic in the 1580s to search for the Northwest Passage. Though he didn't find the passage, he explored much of what is now called Davis Strait; and he made many charts which greatly helped later explorers, enabling Hudson* to find his strait and Baffin* to find his bay.

Davis also explored in the South Atlantic, where in 1592 he discovered the Falkland Islands. Later voyages took him east. He was killed by pirates off the coast of Malaysia.

William Davis
Born 1929, Brampton, Ont.

Premier of Ontario since 1971, William Davis is the member for Brampton, the town where he was raised and educated. He completed his education in Toronto and worked as a lawyer before going into politics. Running as a Conservative, he was first elected to the Ontario legislature in 1959 and three years later was made minister of education.

During his years as education minister, Davis expanded Ontario's educational facilities and created the community college system. As premier, he has worked to strengthen the province in many ways, and he played an important role in 1981 when the premiers were negotiating with Prime Minister Trudeau* on how to bring the constitution home to Canada.

George Mercer Dawson
Born 1849, Pictou, N.S.
Died 1901

Dawson City in the Yukon was named in honour of Dr. George Mercer Dawson, a geologist of small stature and great spirit. Working first for the Boundary Commission and then for the Geological Survey of Canada, he surveyed vast areas of territory, trekking across the prairies, then through northern British Columbia and the Yukon, round the Queen Charlotte Islands, and even to the Bering Sea. In 1883 he was appointed assistant director of the Geological Survey, and he was made director in 1895.

Simon James Dawson
Born 1820, Scotland
Died 1902
The Dawson Road was named after a civil engineer—Simon Dawson. During exploring expeditions to the prairies in 1857 and 1858, he mapped out a road-and-water route from Lake Superior to the Red River Settlement, and in 1868 was sent to build a wagon road along this route. The Dawson Road was no smooth highway; it involved 47 portages. But it provided access to the West. It was used by the Red River Expedition of 1870 (see Wolseley*), and it was the route taken by settlers until the railway was built.

Amor De Cosmos
Born 1825, Windsor, N.S.
Died 1897
The fiery journalist and politician was born William Smith, but in California (where he had gone to seek his fortune) he formally changed his name to Amor De Cosmos, which means "lover of the universe." It was an odd name for a man who was so hot-tempered that he would lash out with his fists when words failed.

De Cosmos settled in Victoria in 1858, and there he founded the *British Colonist* newspaper. It was an outspoken paper, frequently attacking the autocratic rule of Governor James Douglas*—who tried in vain to close down the paper.

Before long, De Cosmos was taking a more direct part in Vancouver Island politics as a member of the Legislative Assembly. Vigorously, he urged that B.C. should join Canada, and after this happened in 1871 he served as an MP in Ottawa. The following year he also became premier of B.C. But in 1874 a law was passed, saying one could not at the same time be a provincial and federal politician, so De Cosmos gave up the premiership and concentrated on federal politics.

In Ottawa, he was a strong spokesman for British Columbia, though not for all British Columbians. The "lover of the universe" had no love for the Chinese, and he did his best to keep them out of Canada. In 1882 he failed to get re-elected, and from then on he became more eccentric each year, until he was finally judged insane and shut in an asylum. By the time he died, this man who had done so much for British Columbia was almost forgotten. Only about 30 people attended his funeral.

Mazo de la Roche
Born 1879, Newmarket, Ont.
Died 1961
Mazo de la Roche was the author of a series of novels about Jalna, a rambling old farmhouse which was the home of the Whiteoak family. These popular books were based partly on an Ontario farmhouse she had known as a child, but mostly on her imagination.

From earliest childhood she had made up stories, often acting them out with her cousin, Caroline Clement. She first had a story published (in a magazine) when she was 23 and went on to write other magazine stories, and also novels. But she didn't have real success as a writer until, at the age of 48, she wrote the first novel about Jalna. It won a $10,000 prize and became an instant best seller. From then on, Mazo de la Roche had success after success. She wrote 17 Jalna novels in all, which were so popular that they were translated into 14 languages.

Cecil Denny
Born 1850, England
Died 1928
As NWMP officer and later as Indian agent, Cecil Denny was one of the best ambassadors to the Plains Indians during the 1870s and 1880s—though his superiors didn't always think so. Denny tended to go his own way and do what he thought best, regardless of orders. In 1879, when the Blackfoot were starving, he bought them meat with government money. Another time he dealt with a murder case by using Indian law rather than police law. Instead of arresting the murderer, he held a meeting of the chiefs, who arranged for the victim's family to be given some horses as payment.

Denny was Indian agent to the Treaty No. 7 tribes during the Northwest Rebellion, and this was one reason why they didn't join the rebellion. They knew that Denny would protect their interests, and indeed he did. But later, less caring Indian agents took over, and Denny spent his last years as provincial archivist of Alberta.

Joseph DesBarres
Born 1721, France(?)
Died 1824
Joseph DesBarres was remarkable for the length of his life as much as for what he did in it. He was 82 when he was made governor of Prince Edward Island, 90 when he retired, and 102 when he died. At the age of 100 he danced a jig on a tabletop.

DesBarres was as touchy as he was lively, constantly embroiled in quarrels and law suits, and consequently he was not a very good governor. An earlier stint as governor of Cape Breton Island had caused so much trouble that he was recalled. Yet he had many talents. Though impatient with people, he was painstaking in his work. For the first part of his life, he was a surveyor for the British army, and in this role he mapped much of the coastline of the Maritimes. This was an enormous job, taking more than ten years. The volume of charts and drawings he produced was so thorough that it was used by sailors for more than a century.

Yvon Deschamps
Born 1935, Montreal, Que.
Comedian Yvon Deschamps has been Quebec's top funnyman ever since the late 1960s, when he gave up straight acting roles and started his one-man comedy shows. With his dry, gloomy, witty comments on everyday life, he has spread gales of laughter across Quebec, playing to packed audiences night after night.

Deschamps grew up in the poor St.Henri district of Montreal and went to work aged 11 in the CBC record department. Later he took acting lessons, and this led him into an acting career. His first one-man show in English was in 1976, when he appeared on TV in *90 Minutes Live*. In recent years, Deschamps has also attracted an American audience, delighting them too with his comic characters, who deliver wry monologues about life and death and the way the world is.

Abraham de Sola
Born 1825, England
Died 1882
Abraham de Sola settled in Montreal at the age of 22 and spent the rest of his life working for the Jewish people of Canada. He helped form the Hebrew Philanthropic Society (to care for poor Jewish immigrants) and organized the Young Men's Hebrew Benevolent Society and several other benevolent societies. He also started a Jewish Sunday school in Montreal and a private school for Jewish children. And he served both as minister of the Shearith Israel congregation and as professor of Hebrew at McGill.

Meanwhile, de Sola played a very active role in the intellectual life of Montreal. He wrote books and scholarly papers, belonged to numerous science and arts clubs, and served as president of the Natural History Society. His activities gained him a great reputation, and not only in Canada. In 1872 he was invited to Washington to open the House of Representatives with a prayer. De Sola was the first person in all the British Empire ever honoured in this way.

Grant Devine
Born 1944, Regina, Sask.
In 1982, Grant Devine became premier of Saskatchewan, having led the Conservatives to a sweeping victory in the provincial elections. They won 55 of the 64 seats in the legislature.

The grandson of homesteaders, Devine grew up on the family farm at Lake Valley, Sask. He studied agriculture at university and then worked with Agriculture Canada in Ottawa. After gaining a doctorate from Ohio State University, he was appointed associate professor of agricultural economics at the University of Saskatchewan. In 1979 he ran for the leadership of Saskatchewan's Conservative party, winning the position on the first ballot.

Edgar Dewdney
Born 1835, England
Died 1916
The capital of Saskatchewan owes its location to Lieutenant Governor Dewdney, who bought up land on Pile of Bones Creek and then told the federal government that this was the perfect site for the new capital of the North-West Territories. In 1882, Pile of Bones was given the more noble name of Regina, and it became the capital city, firstly of the North-West Territories and later of Saskatchewan.

Dewdney had long associations with western Canada, having started his career as a civil engineer in British Columbia. He had then become a Conservative MP and was one of those who remained loyal to John A. Macdonald* during the Pacific Scandal. In 1879 Macdonald appointed him Indian commissioner and two years later also made him lieutenant governor of the North-West Territories.

In this dual role, Dewdney did what he could to help the Plains Indians, who came to trust him and view him as a friend. He was a strong influence in persuading Crowfoot* and other Blackfoot Confederacy chiefs to remain neutral during the Riel* rebellion of 1885. Dewdney was later made minister of the interior, holding the office until 1892, when he was appointed lieutenant governor of British Columbia.

Jacques Dextraze
Born 1919, Montreal, Que.
General Dextraze was chief of the defence staff of the Canadian Armed Forces in the 1970s. More than 30 years earlier, at the beginning of World War II, he had been turned down by the army because he had flat feet. He tried for almost two years before he was accepted.

Once in the army, Dextraze quickly made his mark, gaining promotions, medals, a reputation for daring, and the nickname Mad Jimmy Dextraze. Typical of his boldness was his 1944 assault on a contingent of Germans, who held a well-fortified position in a church in Normandy. Although the Germans had already mown down two Scottish companies, Mad Jimmy didn't hesitate. Leaping forward, he personally led the attack and took the German stronghold. He later served in the Korean War, and in 1963 he commanded the United Nations forces in the Congo. His post as head of Canada's combined armed forces lasted from 1972 to 1977.

Punch Dickins

Born 1899, Portage la Prairie, Man.

Punch Dickins first gained glory as a 19-year-old air ace in World War I. But he was at his most spectacular in the late 1920s when he flew for Western Canada Airways, the fledgling air service formed by bush pilot Doc Oaks (1896-1968). Doc Oaks took aircraft into remote regions of the West, and especially the North; and Dickins became a pioneer northern pilot. He was the first to fly over the Barren Lands of the Northwest Territories, the first to land in Aklavik. He flew some of the first air mail routes and took numerous parties of prospectors to search the North for minerals.

Unlike most bush pilots, Punch Dickins actually looked the part. He was known for his natty clothing—fur parka in winter, and in summer a deerskin jacket, matching breeches, and shiny boots. He was as meticulous about his aircraft, insisting that they be shiny bright and in perfect running order. This attention to detail may have kept him alive, for many pilots were killed during the dangerous pioneering days of bush flying.

Dickins survived, growing with aviation as the small airlines were taken over by larger companies. He was general manager of CP Air in the 1940s and then became a vice-president of de Havilland.

John G. Diefenbaker

Born 1895, Neustadt, Ont.
Died 1979

John G. Diefenbaker, the Conservative prime minister of Canada 1957-63, had many of the same qualities as his own great hero, John A. Macdonald.* Like John A., the gleaming-eyed John G. was a brilliant orator who could capture people's hearts with his impassioned, and often humorous, speeches. He knew when to pause dramatically, when to grunt with equal drama, and when to point the accusing finger.

Diefenbaker grew up in Saskatchewan and became a highly successful prairie lawyer, but he ran for office several times before he was first elected to Parliament in 1940. In 1958, the year after becoming prime minister, he called an election and campaigned across the country, speaking of his Vision of the North. He said he would open up the North and mine its resources. The voters were so inspired by this idea, and especially by Diefenbaker himself, that his Conservatives had a record-breaking election victory, winning 208 of the 265 House of Commons seats.

While Diefenbaker's Vision never got much beyond the visionary stages, he did much to promote multiculturalism during his years in office and in 1960 brought in the

Canadian Bill of Rights. On the international scene, he played a leading role in forcing South Africa out of the Commonwealth because of its apartheid policies. Known affectionately as Dief the Chief, he continued to serve in Parliament until his death at the age of 83.

Adrian Dingle

Born 1912, Wales
Died 1974

Adrian Dingle was creator of the comic strip *Nelvana of the Northern Lights* about a beautiful heroine who had magical powers and was a great protector of the Inuit. Dingle had come to Canada as a small child, and he began his career in an insurance office in Oakville, Ont. He brought out his first *Nelvana* strip in 1941, and it was so popular that he soon started other strips. One was *The Penguin* about a crime-fighter in a birdlike mask. Another was *Nils Grant, Private Investigator*.

But Dingle's success was fairly brief. By the late 1940s, so many American comic books were being sold in Canada that it was very difficult for Canadians to compete. Dingle gave up commercial art and spent his last years painting landscapes and semi-abstracts.

The Dionne Quintuplets
Born 1934, nr.Callander, Ont.
Yvonne, Annette, Cécile, Emilie, and Marie Dionne were the world's first quintuplets to survive—five identical baby girls, all born in a farmhouse in northern Ontario on May 28, 1934. Until they were nine years old, the Quints lived in a nursery complex which was built specially for them. During these years, about 3 million people came to have a peep at them as they played in their public observation garden. They were one of the world's biggest tourist attractions.

In 1943 they returned home to live with their brothers and sisters (there was a total of 11 children in the family). When the Quints grew up they moved to Montreal. Emilie became a nun and died during an epileptic fit when she was 20. Of the remaining four, Annette, Cécile, and Marie married, but in due course separated from their husbands. Marie has since died, but the three remaining Quints maintain close contact with one another.

Mary Dohey
Born 1933, St. Bride's, Nfld.
Canada's highest award for bravery, the Cross of Valour, has been won by very few people since it was introduced in 1972. The first person to be honoured with the award was Sergeant Lewis Stringer (1930-69), a supply technician on HMCS *Kootenay*, who gave his life to save his fellow crew members during a fire in the ship. The first living person to win the award was Mary Dohey, a stewardess on a hijacked plane.

During eight hours of terror (in which, at times, Mary Dohey had a gun held against her head) she not only remained calm but managed to calm the hijacker too. She persuaded him to release the passengers and some of the crew, but refused to escape to safety herself. The drama ended when, for a moment, the hijacker put down his gun—and one of the remaining crew pounced on him.

Dollard des Ormeaux
Born 1635, France
Killed 1660
In 1660, Adam Dollard des Ormeaux fought a legendary battle at the Long Sault (the rapids on the Ottawa River). This was during the Iroquois wars when the French, the Hurons and their allies were in bitter conflict with the Iroquois and their allies.

Dollard was a garrison commander at Montreal, and he had set out with a small band of men to ambush Iroquois hunters as they returned home with their furs. But instead of finding a few hunters, they ran into a large army which was mustering to attack Montreal and Quebec. Dollard's band consisted of only 17 French and 44 Hurons and Algonkins. They were no match for the Iroquois, who brought in 500 reinforcements. Nevertheless, they took shelter behind the stockades of an abandoned fort and held out for about a week. All the Frenchmen were killed and most of the Hurons and Algonkins. But as a result of the battle, the Iroquois dispersed and went home.

Donnacona
Birth unknown
Died c.1539

The Iroquois chief Donnacona was one of the first Indians to fall victim to the Europeans. He formed an alliance with Jacques Cartier* when the explorer arrived in 1534; and when Cartier returned to France, he took Donnacona's two sons with him. These young men came back with Cartier on his second voyage, and they showed him the way into the St. Lawrence River (which Cartier had missed on his first voyage).

But then the friendship turned sour. Cartier invited Donnacona to a feast, seized him and several other Iroquois, and again sailed for home. In France, though treated more as a guest than a captive, Donnacona sickened and died. So did most of the other Iroquois. Cartier's return without them on his third voyage set the scene for the future French-Iroquois wars.

The Donnellys
Murdered 1880

The Donnellys were Irish settlers who lived near Lucan, Ont. There was fist-fighting Jim Donnelly, who served a seven-year jail sentence for manslaughter, and his wife Johannah, who had a wispy beard and was tougher than most men. They had one daughter, Jennie, and seven muscular sons: James Jr., William, John, Patrick, Michael, Robert, and Thomas.

The Donnellys were the terror of the district. They stole their neighbours' cattle and burned their barns and houses. They ambushed travellers at night, beat them up and robbed them, and then galloped away into the darkness. They even scared off the police: few constables stayed long at Lucan.

This went on for more than twenty years before a man called James Carroll decided to silence the "Black Donnellys" once and for all. Gathering together the men of the district, he raided the Donnelly house and massacred most of the family. He was tried for murder, but the jury declared him not guilty.

All this happened more than a century ago, but it is said that on stormy nights when the wind is howling, the clatter of horses' hooves can still be heard near the old Donnelly homestead.

Antoine-Aimé Dorion
Born 1818, Ste. Anne de la Pérade, Que.
Died 1891

In the late 1840s, the young lawyer Antoine-Aimé Dorion helped form a new political party, the Parti Rouge. This party was the French Canadian wing of what later became the federal Liberal party.

Dorion was a disciple of Papineau* and a prominent political figure. In the years before Confederation, he was twice joint leader of the government of the Province of Canada. After Confederation, he was briefly minister of justice in Alexander Mackenzie's* Liberal government. He spent his last years as a judge.

Roger Doucet
Born 1919, Montreal, Que.
Died 1981

The tenor Roger Doucet was for many years a familiar sight at hockey games in the Montreal Forum—an erect, broad-chested figure, full-throatedly booming out a stirring bilingual version of "O Canada."

Doucet had been singing in public ever since he was a child, when he was a choir boy in Montreal. He first made his name as a cabaret artist and went on to perform in operas and musical comedies, and on TV and radio. In 1971 he began singing the national anthem at televised Forum hockey games, and he became so popular that he was asked to sing at other games, football and baseball as well as hockey. His voice can still be heard, for he made several LPs, including *Roger Doucet, Songs of Glory*.

David Douglas
Born 1799, Scotland
Killed 1834
The Douglas fir is named after the botanist David Douglas, who made several expeditions to the Pacific Northwest between 1825 and 1833, collecting seeds and specimens. He was the first European to climb a mountain in the Rockies (Mount Brown, which was named for another botanist). Douglas later went to Hawaii, and there on a mountainside, he fell into a bullock pit and was killed by a bull.

James Douglas
Born 1803, British Guiana
Died 1877

James Douglas was one of the great figures of British Columbia's early years. In 1843 he founded Fort Victoria (today's city of Victoria) and he was later governor of the two colonies which were started on the West Coast—Vancouver Island, and the mainland colony of British Columbia.

A long-time officer of the Hudson's Bay Company, Douglas tended to rule the colonies as if they were company posts. The settlers said he was a despot, and a pompous one at that. But he was the right man in the right place at the right time.

He acted very firmly when thousands of miners arrived to pan for gold on the Fraser River. Many of the miners were Americans, and Douglas feared that the United States might claim mainland B.C. So he went to the diggings and told the miners they were on British territory. He made them take out licences. And he sent Judge Begbie* to keep order among them. Thanks to Douglas, there was no American takeover; and today British Columbia is part of Canada, not part of the United States.

John Drainie
Born 1916, Vancouver, B.C.
Died 1966
John Drainie, the well-loved actor, spent most of his life with the CBC rather than going abroad to seek fame and fortune. But his fame spread abroad when he played the title role in the radio play *The Investigator*. This was a satire on Senator McCarthy's witch hunt against Communists in the United States. It was made into a record and gained worldwide popularity.

Drainie was also known for his delightful impersonations of Stephen Leacock.* Another of his roles was Professor Hunter in *The Incredible Journey*, a film based on Sheila Burnford's book about three family pets who trekked across northern Ontario.

Tommy Douglas,
Born 1904, Scotland
In 1944, Thomas C. Douglas formed North America's first socialist government when he led the Co-operative Commonwealth Federation (CCF) to victory in the Saskatchewan elections. He remained premier of Saskatchewan for 17 years, during which time he brought in many new measures, including a medical insurance plan (the first comprehensive government medicare in North America). Over the years, he became well known as a stirring orator as well as a committed social democrat, and when the New Democratic Party was formed in 1961, he was chosen its first national leader. Resigning from the premiership of Saskatchewan, he served as federal NDP leader in Ottawa until 1971, when he was succeeded by David Lewis.*

Although Tommy Douglas has spent most of his life in politics, he started his professional career as a Baptist minister in Weyburn, Sask. And it was as an MP for Weyburn that he first became a politician.

Jean Drapeau

Born 1916, Montreal, Que.

In 1982 Jean Drapeau was elected mayor of Montreal—for the eighth time. He had been mayor almost continually since 1954, when he first won office by promising to clean up the city and put down crime.

Over the years, Drapeau won the hearts of Montrealers, for he dared to think big, to dream up grandiose projects that seemed impossible, and then to carry them through with great style. Two of his largest projects were the world fair, Expo 67 (for which he built the Montreal subway system), and the 1976 Olympic Games (which involved construction of a multimillion-dollar Olympic Stadium). Although the stadium was a disaster financially, Drapeau's policies brought work to many of his citizens, and brought the world to his city, greatly increasing Montreal's international reputation.

Marie Dressler

Born 1869, Cobourg, Ont.
Died 1934

Marie Dressler, Hollywood's great character actress, was an Ontario girl called Leila Koerber. When she was 14, she ran away from home and from her Austrian father (whom she hated), joined a touring opera troupe, and gradually gained a reputation as a comedienne. She had her first big-time success in New York, in a musical comedy, when she was 25.

Like many other actors of the time, Marie Dressler made her way from live theatre to silent films to sound films. During the first years of sound films (and the last few years of her life) she became one of Hollywood's most popular stars, winning a best-actress Oscar in 1931. Her favourite parts were Min (in *Min and Bill*) and Tugboat Annie.

Marcel Dubé

Born 1930, Montreal, Que.

Canada's most prolific playwright, Marcel Dubé has written hundreds of dramas for radio, TV, and the theatre. He first became nationally known in 1953 when his play *Zone* won the top award at the Dominion Drama Festival in Victoria, B.C.

Zone is about a gang of teenage smugglers in the east end of Montreal, the district where Dubé was raised. Most of his plays have French Canadian settings and most are written in French. As very little of his work has been translated, many English-speaking Canadians have never seen a play by Marcel Dubé. Yet he is one of the most talented dramatists in all Canada.

Lord Dufferin
Born 1826, Italy
Died 1902

Canada's third Governor General was a British intellectual who read Latin and Greek, painted pictures, wrote poetry, and made flowery speeches. Some people thought Lord Dufferin delightfully cultured. Others thought him affected. Prime Minister Alexander Mackenzie* thought him a tiresome meddler who should keep his nose out of Canadian politics.

Dufferin was in Canada 1872-78, years of strife about the Canadian Pacific Railway: who would construct it, when, and if. Mackenzie was not keen on the project. Dufferin was; for British Columbia had threatened to leave Canada unless the railway was built.

So Dufferin paid a goodwill visit to B.C., and there he made a comment which became famous. Someone had put a notice on an arch, demanding Separation; and Dufferin refused to drive under it, saying he would only do so "if the S were turned into an R." As Lord Dufferin had a lisp, what he probably said was "if the Eth were turned into an R." Either way, his aim was Reparation—trying to patch up the quarrel between B.C. and the federal government. He succeeded. British Columbia remained part of Canada.

Sara Jeannette Duncan
Born 1862, Brantford, Ont.
Died 1922

Sara Jeannette Duncan was one of the first Canadian women to be really successful as a writer. She started out as a freelance journalist, calling herself Garth Grafton because pieces by a woman were likely to be rejected. Hers were not only accepted but appreciated, for she was a witty, observant writer. In 1888 she was made parliamentary correspondent for the *Montreal Star*, the first woman to hold such a position.

After making a trip round the world (which she wrote a book about) she married Everard Cotes, the curator of a museum in Calcutta. In India, she settled down to novel writing, producing a number of popular books, including her classic Canadian novel, *The Imperialist*.

Gabriel Dumont
Born 1838, Red River, Man.
Died 1906

Bold-hearted and cool-headed in the face of danger, Gabriel Dumont was one of the most celebrated Métis leaders. In his twenties he was elected captain of the buffalo hunt, a job that called for careful organization as well as boldness and panache. In his thirties he was chosen as ruler of the Métis on the Saskatchewan. And in his forties he became Louis Riel's* general in the Northwest Rebellion.

Dumont's plan during the rebellion was to harry the Canadian army, using guerrilla tactics. But Riel kept holding him back, and at Batoche the Métis had to fight a pitched battle against far superior forces—just what Dumont had hoped to avoid. Yet they held out for more than three days.

Fighting alongside Dumont was his 93-year-old father-in-law, José Ouellette. Only when Ouellette was hit did Dumont give up. But he didn't give in. He escaped to the United States, where for a time he toured with Buffalo Bill's Wild West Show. When a pardon was granted, he returned to Canada.

William Duncan
Born 1832, England
Died 1918

William Duncan was a lay missionary to the Coast Indians of British Columbia during the latter part of the nineteenth century. He built a special village for his converts (Metlakatla, near today's Prince Rupert) and there he did his best to turn them into English Christians.

Metlakatla was a self-supporting village with its own industries and police force, and of course its own church and schools. Because it was isolated from other communities, it escaped the terrible smallpox epidemic of 1862. This brought Duncan great prestige—and an increased number of converts. Most of his converts accompanied him when in the 1880s he set up another model village, New Metlakatla, on Annette Island in Alaska. Yet for all his good intentions, Duncan did great harm to Indian society. By banning traditional customs (which he viewed as sinfully pagan) and by altering the way of life of the people, he struck at the heart of the rich Coast Indian culture.

Tiger Dunlop
Born 1792, Scotland
Died 1848

William "Tiger" Dunlop was one of the larger-than-life characters of Upper Canada, the type of man who could turn his hand to anything, and did. Vigorous and outspoken, he was alternately soldier, doctor, colonizer, journalist, politician, author ... and always adventurer.

He first came to Canada as an army surgeon during the War of 1812 and then went to India, where he killed so many tigers that he earned his ferocious nickname. Back in Upper Canada in the 1820s, he worked for the Canada Company (the huge colonizing scheme that settled many parts of Upper Canada, including the land between Guelph and Lake Huron). But after ten years of helping settlers get established, Dunlop fell out with the company commissioners. Turning his energies to politics, he became a Reform member of the Legislative Assembly. He ended his days as superintendent of the Lachine Canal.

Maurice Duplessis
Born 1890, Trois Rivières, Que.
Died 1959

As leader of the provincial party called the Union Nationale, Maurice Duplessis was premier of Quebec for almost 20 years (1936-39 and 1944-59).

A tough, hard-headed lawyer, he first gained office, with a huge majority, by promising reforms and better conditions for Quebec workers. But once Duplessis was firmly ensconced as premier, he seemed to forget his promises. The "social reformer" turned out to be an arch-conservative—a dictator, in some people's view.

Duplessis allied himself with the bosses, not the workers. He supported the power of the Roman Catholic church. And he ruthlessly crushed those who opposed him, including such religious groups as Jehovah's Witnesses. In many ways he blocked progress in Quebec, though his policies did make the province stronger in its relations with the federal government.

Yvon Durelle

Born 1930, Baie Ste. Anne, N.B.

Canadian boxing champion Yvon Durelle came from a poor fishing family. When he was only seven years old, he was already a year-round fisherman helping his father and elder brothers. In his early teens, he worked in lumber camps around New Brunswick, and it was while he was in Chatham, N.B., at the age of 15, that he took part in his first boxing match. He knocked out his opponent in the first round. Three weeks later he was boxing professionally—for $8 a fight.

From this small beginning, Durelle fought his way to fame and fortune. He won the Canadian light-heavyweight title in 1953, and though he lost it that same year, he won it back in 1954 and held it until his retirement. In 1957 he won the Commonwealth title and held that until his retirement too. His last bout was in 1963.

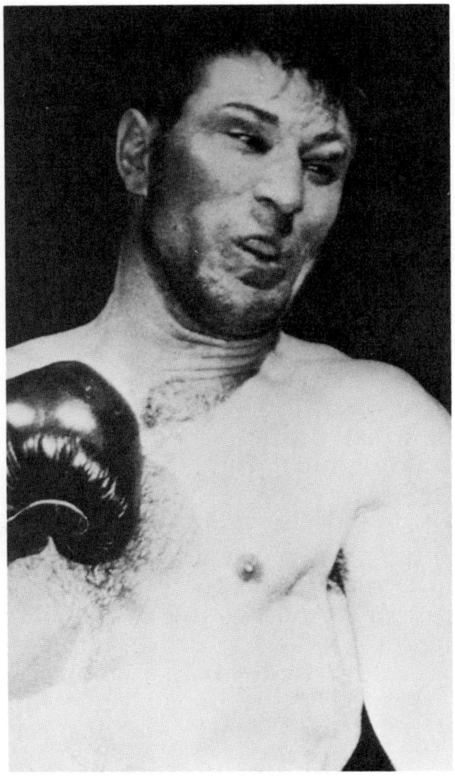

Lord Durham

Born 1792, England
Died 1840

Following the Rebellion of 1837, the British politician Lord Durham was sent to Canada to look into the causes of the trouble. The solution he recommended was to give the elected assemblies political power under the system known as responsible government. He also suggested that Upper and Lower Canada should become one single entity. As a result, the United Province of Canada was formed in 1841.

While the Durham Report paved the way for responsible government, it also aimed at making Canada completely British. Durham had little respect for French Canadians, whom he described as "a people with no history and no literature." He hoped that, with the two Canadas united, the French would gradually be assimilated into the British way of life. All this so infuriated French Canadians that they took vigorous steps to make sure that they did not lose either their language or their culture.

Timothy Eaton

Born 1834, Ireland
Died 1907

The founder of Eaton's chain of department stores started his career as an apprentice in Ireland and then ran general stores in Ontario with his brothers. The first store of his own, T. Eaton & Co., was established in Toronto in 1869.

Timothy Eaton's store did well from the outset, for he had a clever head for business. He set a fixed price for his goods (to prevent customers bargaining) and insisted on immediate cash payment (so that he wasn't plagued by unpaid bills). In addition, he offered to take back any articles that people weren't satisfied with. All these measures were novelties in the business world.

Then Eaton printed a catalogue and started a mail-order service, so that even the most remote homesteaders could buy his goods. Eaton's catalogue became so popular that it was called the Prairie Bible. Eaton also gained a name for treating his staff well and shortening their working hours. Although very strict, he acted as a father figure, head of a family of workers who were spread far across Canada as he opened branch stores in other cities.

His main competitor was Robert Simpson, a Scotsman who set up his first store a couple of years after Eaton and right nearby on Toronto's Yonge Street.

Bob Edwards
Born 1864, Scotland
Died 1922
"Some men spoil a good story by sticking to the facts," commented Bob Edwards, the roistering editor of the Calgary *Eye Opener*. He himself never let facts inhibit his stories. If something hadn't happened he invented it, and he invented people too, often placing them at real events. Readers of his paper were never sure what was fiction and what was factual reporting, but they were often laughing too hard to care.

Bob Edwards started the *Eye Opener* in 1902, a few years after settling in the West. It was extremely popular, attracting readers across Canada, for it was far more than a funny paper. Beneath his humour, Bob Edwards was a crusader. He ridiculed corruption, snobbery, just about every vice, while remaining undaunted by people in powerful positions. The paper was such a lively extension of himself that no one could carry it on after his death. A copy of the last issue was buried with him, along with a flask of whisky.

Ezra Eddy
Born 1827, U.S.A.
Died 1906
Ezra Butler Eddy was known as "the greatest matchmaker in the world." In the 1850s he settled in Hull, Que., where he started a small business, making wooden matches by hand. Several fires later (and after a lot of rebuilding and modernizing) he was president of one of the biggest and most successful companies in Canada, E. B. Eddy & Co.

Lord Elgin
Born 1811, England
Died 1863
As Governor General from 1847 to 1854, Lord Elgin firmly established the system of responsible government in the Province of Canada, a measure which the Reform party had long been demanding.

Elgin's first move was in 1848. In the 1847-48 elections, the Reform Party had won a majority of seats in the Legislative Assembly and then defeated the Tories during a vote in the assembly. Instead of asking the reigning Tory party to reshape its ministries (as had been the practice), Elgin turned to the party with the majority and asked the Reform leaders La Fontaine* and Baldwin* to form a government.

But the real test came the following year when La Fontaine's government passed the Rebellion Losses Bill (which would repay Patriotes for losses suffered during the Rebellion of 1837). Elgin signed the bill, even though he didn't like it. The Tories didn't like it either—they said the rebels were being rewarded—and they rioted in Montreal, burning the Parliament Building and hurling stones at Lord Elgin's carriage.

Nevertheless, Elgin held firm to the principle of responsible government: that the Governor General is duty bound to give his approval to laws which have been passed by the elected assembly.

(For the first responsible government in British North America, see J. B. Uniacke.*)

Marian Engel

Born 1933, Toronto, Ont.

Marian Engel won the Governor General's Award for fiction in 1976 for her novel *Bear*. Educated at McMaster and McGill universities, she went to France on a scholarship in 1960 to study French literature. Before returning to Toronto, she worked for several years in Europe, and her novels have been popular there as well as in North America. Her recent works include *Lunatic Villas* and *The Islands of Canada*.

Arthur Erickson

Born 1924, Vancouver, B.C.

Many of Canada's modern public buildings have been designed by Arthur Erickson, who grew up intending to be an artist rather than an architect. At 16 he was the youngest person ever to have his pictures exhibited in the annual British Columbia show at the Vancouver Art Gallery.

Erickson's interests turned to architecture after his service overseas in World War II. He studied the subject at McGill and then won a scholarship, which allowed him to travel for several years and see many of the world's great buildings. Settling back in Vancouver in the 1950s, he launched on his celebrated career as an architect. His works include such dramatic buildings as Simon Fraser University (designed with fellow architect Geoffrey Massey); the University of Lethbridge in Alberta; and the soaring glass-framed Bank of Canada building in Ottawa.

Leif Ericsson

Birth Unknown
Died c.1020

Leif the Lucky was possibly the first European to set foot in North America. He was a Norseman, the son of Eric the Red who had established settlements in Greenland. In 1000 A.D., Leif sailed west from Greenland and visited Baffin Island, Labrador, and Newfoundland.

Some stories say Leif the Lucky had already heard of these lands and went looking for them. Other stories say he found them by accident when his ship was blown off course. He lived so long ago that nobody is sure. But Norsemen were certainly in Canada very early. One of their settlements has been found at L'Anse-aux-Meadows on the northern tip of Newfoundland.

Sorel Etrog

Born 1933, Romania

The Genie—the stylized statuette of a human figure which is presented each year to Canada's award-winning film-makers and actors—was called the Etrog until 1980. It was named after the sculptor who designed it, Sorel Etrog. Etrog settled in Toronto in the 1960's, having emigrated from Romania to Israel, to the United States, to Canada. He has had numerous exhibitions of his sculptures, which vary from tiny figures to large pieces several metres high. One of his most celebrated works is *War Remembrances*, which is in the Montreal Museum of Fine Arts.

The other top media prize is the ACTRA award of the Association of Canadian Television and Radio Artists. It was designed by William McElcheran and was not named after its sculptor. It is called Nellie and is a little statue of a plump nude woman with flowing hair.

Ellen Fairclough
Born 1905, Hamilton, Ont.
Two women called Ellen were "firsts" as cabinet ministers. Ellen Fairclough, a former Hamilton alderman, was the first woman to hold a cabinet position in the federal government. This was in 1957 when Diefenbaker* made her secretary of state in his Conservative government. She held two more cabinet posts before the Conservatives were defeated in 1963.

About 40 years earlier, in 1921, Mary Ellen Smith of Nanaimo was appointed minister without portfolio in the B.C. legislature. A Liberal, she had been elected to take her husband's seat in the legislature after his death. She was the first woman to hold a cabinet post in a provincial government and also the first woman cabinet minister in the entire British Empire.

Pierre Falcon
Born 1793, Elbow Fort, Man.
Died 1876
The Métis poet Pierre Falcon was a popular songwriter and folksinger, though he earned his living by working for the fur trade. His most famous ballad celebrated the battle of Seven Oaks, in which a group of Métis under Cuthbert Grant* killed 20 Red River colonists and their governor, Robert Semple. This is often called the "massacre" of Seven Oaks, but Falcon described it from the Métis point of view—a strike for freedom against proud invaders.

His son Jean-Baptiste Falcon played a leading role in the greatest of all Métis victories, the battle of Grand Coteau. This was in 1851 when a small group of Métis, who were out on a buffalo hunt, were attacked by hundreds of Sioux. Despite the odds against them, the Métis successfully fought off the Sioux by using their well-tried tactics of placing their carts around them as a protective barrier.

Charles Fenerty
Born 1821, Upper Sackville, N.S.
Died 1892
A Nova Scotian farmer and lumberman, Charles Fenerty claimed he was the first person in the world to make paper from wood pulp. He got the idea by watching some wasps build a nest; the wasps were chewing wood fibres and producing a fine paper. Fenerty tried grinding wood fibre, rather than chewing it, and in 1838 he produced some usable paper. This was a very significant advance, for paper was commonly made from rags, which were often in short supply. By contrast, there was no shortage of trees in Canada.

Nevertheless, Fenerty's invention attracted little attention. Two other Canadians had a far greater impact on the birth of our pulp and paper industry. One was John Thompson of Napanee, Ont., who in the 1860s made paper from wood pulp on a commercial scale—the first person to do so in North America. He used a process that had been invented in Europe. The other pioneer was Alex Buntin, who in 1866 opened North America's first pulp mill near Montreal. From then on, Canada's pulp and paper business grew rapidly, and today it is our biggest industry.

Max Ferguson
Born 1924, England

For about 30 years, Max Ferguson had his own morning show on CBC radio, launching each day lightheartedly with his skits of whoever and whatever was in the news. He was nicknamed Rawhide after one of the characters he created, but was particularly famed for his take-offs of politicians, whose voices he captured with delicious accuracy.

Ferguson had been brought to Canada as a small child and grew up in London, Ont., where he attended the University of Western Ontario. He began his CBC career as an announcer in Halifax, and retired to the Maritimes when in 1976 *The Max Ferguson Show* finally left the air. His announcer and co-comedian on the show was Allan McFee, who now hosts the late-night music program *Eclectic Circus.*

Reginald Fessenden
Born 1866, East Bolton, Que.
Died 1932
Reginald Fessenden invented radio as we know it today. Although Marconi was the first to send a wireless message, he did so by Morse code using dots and dashes. Fessenden found a way of transmitting actual sounds so that people could talk to one another by radio. In December 1900 he first managed to transmit the sound of his voice between two radio towers on Cobb Island in the Potomac River, near Washington. Then, at Christmas 1906, he beamed the world's first radio broadcast to some United Fruit Company ships which were sailing in the Atlantic and Caribbean. The surprised crews found themselves listening to a Christmas concert, complete with Fessenden himself playing "Holy Night" on the violin.

Even as a boy, Fessenden had been fascinated by the possibilities of electricity. The son of a clergyman, he grew up in Ontario, at Fergus and Niagara Falls, completing his education at Bishop's College. In his early twenties, he went to New Jersey and pestered Thomas Edison until he was taken on at the famous Edison Laboratories. Over the years, Fessenden took a variety of jobs (including teaching at universities) as he struggled to raise money for his research. Only towards the end of his life did he become wealthy.

Peter Fidler
Born 1769, England
Died 1822
Appointed chief surveyor to the Hudson's Bay Company in 1796, Peter Fidler made numerous maps of the HBC territories. He helped lay out the Red River Settlement, surveyed the surrounding district of Assiniboia, and was the first person to find coal on the prairies. Like David Thompson,* he was trained by Philip Turnor.*

LeMoine FitzGerald
Born 1890, Winnipeg, Man.
Died 1956
LeMoine FitzGerald was the last artist to be a member of the Group of Seven. When J. E. H. MacDonald* died in 1932, the other members invited FitzGerald to join them. With them, the following year, he formed the new and larger association of artists, the Canadian Group of Painters.

FitzGerald was principal of the Winnipeg School of Art and he spent most of his life in Winnipeg, at times painting in the snow at temperatures well below zero. He painted in soft colours and often chose simple subjects for his pictures, such as a jug, or apples on a plate.

David Fife
Born 1805, Scotland
Died 1877
David Fife produced the wheat called Red Fife. He had a farm near Peterborough, and in 1842 he obtained some wheat from a cargo that had come from Gdansk, Poland. When he sowed the wheat, only a few heads developed, but he used them as seed the next spring and got a good crop.

Within 20 years, most of the farmers in eastern Canada were sowing their fields with wheat that had been bred from Fife's first handful of seed. Red Fife ripened earlier than other wheats, it produced an excellent flour, and was free of rust (a wheat disease). It was later used as the "male parent" of the famous Marquis wheat, which Sir Charles Saunders* developed.

Timothy Findley
Born 1930, Toronto, Ont.
Timothy Findley is the author of numerous short stories and several books, including *The Wars*, which won a Governor General's Award in 1977 and has been made into a film.

As a child, Findley intended to be an actor, and he did work as an actor early in his career. He also wrote scripts for radio and television. But even then he was working on his first novel. Now an established novelist who can spend his full time writing, he lives in a rambling old farmhouse near Cannington, Ont. He spent four years working on *Famous Last Words* (1981), his celebrated novel about the rise of fascism in Europe.

Robert Flaherty
Born 1884, U.S.A.
Died 1951

Raised in Canada, Robert Flaherty was an Arctic explorer and film-maker who in 1922 made the world's first full-length documentary film. Called *Nanook of the North*, it was about the Inuit and their day-to-day activities. Flaherty later made other films, including *Elephant Boy*, which he did not shoot in the Canadian Arctic.

Sandford Fleming
Born 1827, Scotland
Died 1915

Sandford Fleming made his mark in many different ways—as the inventor of Standard Time, the system of dividing the world into 24 different time zones; as a scientist and surveyor and railway builder; and as the designer of Canada's first postage stamp, the threepenny beaver (1851).

During the 1860s he was chief engineer in charge of building the Intercolonial Railway to the Maritimes, and in 1871 he was appointed chief engineer of the Canadian Pacific Railway. His main role with the CPR was to organize the surveys and choose a route for the railway. In 1872 he led an expedition right across Canada in order to find a good route, and he explored the Yellowhead Pass through the Rockies. Much of the journey was done on horseback, for there were no real roads in the West and of course no railways. Fleming went west again early in the 1880s when the CPR directors decided on a more southerly route for the railway. This time, he investigated the Kicking Horse Pass and found a way of building a railway line through it. (His route via the Yellowhead Pass was later used by Canadian National Railways.)

Meanwhile, in the late 1870s, Fleming had developed the system of Standard Time, which was adopted internationally at a conference in 1884. His next major project was to get a cable laid across the Pacific, and in 1902 he received the first message from New Zealand via the cable. He spent his last years as chancellor of Queen's University.

Maureen Forrester
Born 1930, Montreal, Que.

One of the world's leading contraltos, Maureen Forrester is famed not only for her deep, rich tone, but for the superb quality of her singing. Even on hectic concert tours, when moving from place to place, day after day, she offers a beautifully controlled and artistic performance.

As a child, Maureen Forrester sang in Montreal church choirs, and she studied music theory as well as singing. She first performed professionally in Montreal at the age of 21. Since then, she has sung in concerts and operas, with choirs and orchestras, all over the world, from Canada to China.

Eugene Forsey
Born 1904, Grand Bank, Nfld.

Eugene Forsey is the author of *Freedom and Order* and other classic works on politics. As a young man, he often stirred up a storm with his socialist views. In recent years, he has been a respected elder statesman, often interviewed by the media as the man who knows more about Parliament and constitutional law than anyone else in Canada.

Forsey virtually grew up in Parliament. His father died when he was a baby, so the family moved in with grandfather, who was a senior clerk in the House of Commons. Almost as soon as he could walk, Forsey was listening to parliamentary debates. He heard Sir Wilfrid Laurier* speak, as well as some of his predecessors and all the prime ministers since.

After sailing through his student years with honours, Forsey became a lecturer at McGill, where he taught British and Canadian government. Meanwhile, he was a leading spirit in the formation of the Co-operative Commonwealth Federation (CCF). In 1942 he took on the post of director of research for the Canadian Congress of Labour and spent the next 27 years serving the labour unions organization. In 1970 he was appointed to the Senate.

Robert Foulis
Born 1796, Scotland
Died 1866

Robert Foulis was the inventor of the steam fog-horn, which hooted automatically, serving instead of a lighthouse in foggy weather. In 1859 the first steam fog-horn in the world was installed on Partridge Island in the harbour of Saint John, N.B. For almost a century (until modern inventions, such as radar) steam fog-horns safely guided sailors into harbour, warning them of rocks and shoals.

Foulis had personal experience of the terrors of the sea. Emigrating as a young man from Scotland to the United States, his ship was blown off course and he found himself in Nova Scotia. He decided to stay in the Maritimes and at first earned his living as a portrait painter in Halifax. Then he moved to Saint John, where he worked as a civil engineer, started New Brunswick's first iron foundry, founded a School of Arts, taught, and invented the steam fog-horn. But Foulis did not take out a patent on his invention. In spite of his many talents, he had no head for business and died poor.

Edith Fowke
Born 1913, Lumsden, Sask.

Canadian folk songs have been a lifelong passion for Edith Fowke. For years she has been searching them out, recording them, and publicizing them. Educated in Saskatchewan, she moved to Toronto in 1938 and began to make collecting trips around Ontario, seeking out people who knew the old songs. Besides unearthing folk songs by the hundred, she also discovered numerous folksingers.

All Canada has been able to share these discoveries through Edith Fowke's radio programs, books, and records. Two of her publications (each with a companion record) are *The Penguin Book of Canadian Folk Songs* and *Sally Go Round the Sun*, which is a collection of children's songs and games.

Terry Fox
Born 1958, Winnipeg, Man.
Died 1981

In 1980 Terry Fox inspired the whole of Canada with his courage and determination. Although he had lost a leg to cancer, he set out to run across the country on his artificial leg—a Marathon of Hope to raise funds for cancer research.

Terry lived in Port Coquitlam, B.C., and there he had developed into a keen athlete. He was on the basketball team at Simon Fraser University and was thinking of a career in physical education. It was therefore a particularly bitter blow when in 1977 he learned that his leg would have to be amputated because of bone cancer. Yet, as he once said, "Nobody will ever call me a quitter." Soon after he was out of hospital, he was playing wheelchair basketball. And then he began to practise running. Already he was dreaming of his cross-Canada marathon, which eventually raised the incredible sum of more than $24 million. He ran east to west, starting in April 1980 in St. John's, Nfld.; and he got more than halfway to the Pacific before he had to call a halt near Thunder Bay. The cancer had spread to his lungs.

Before Terry died, he was made a Companion of the Order of Canada. He received many other honours, including the Lou Marsh Trophy as outstanding athlete of the year. His stubborn courage had kindled a flame which continues to inspire young and old, and especially those who have their own troubles to face.

Celia Franca
Born 1921, England

The National Ballet of Canada was shaped and nurtured by Celia Franca, the English ballerina who was invited to Toronto in 1951 to form the company. Besides being its chief organizer and inspiration, she was also the National Ballet's principal dancer for many years.

Celia Franca started the company with only 29 dancers, but even in those early days some of her troupe were superb performers: Winnipeg-born David Adams, who was hailed as one of the finest dancers in all North America; Lois Smith from Vancouver, who so often starred as his partner; and Earl Kraul from London, Ont., who later became a teacher at the National Ballet School.

The school was formed in 1959 so that talented young Canadians could have a thorough training in ballet, while also gaining a general education. Its principal from the outset was Betty Oliphant, the company's ballet mistress. Like Celia Franca, she aimed for perfection. It is largely due to these two dedicated enthusiasts that the National Ballet of Canada now ranks among the finest dance companies in the world.

John Franklin
Born 1786, England
Died 1847

In 1845 Sir John Franklin set out to search for the Northwest Passage with two well-equipped ships, the *Terror* and *Erebus*. Then . . . nothing. No word was heard of the expedition for year after year. What had happened to Franklin and his men?

The explorer John Rae* found the first evidence of their fate in the early 1850s, and gradually the story came to light. Franklin's ships had been trapped in the ice, and one by one the men had died of cold and hunger and scurvy. Some had tried to find a way south over the frozen wasteland, but they too had perished. In all, 129 men died on this tragic expedition.

Simon Fraser
Born 1776, U.S.A.
Died 1862

The Fraser River is named after Simon Fraser, a fur trader for the North West Company. In 1808 he followed the Fraser to its mouth, a hair-raising journey through thundering rapids and rock-lined canyons. Having braved all these dangers, Simon Fraser thought himself a failure. For the river was not (as he had hoped) the Columbia. And it was certainly not (as he had also hoped) an easy trade route to the Pacific.

In addition to this epic journey, Fraser established several trading posts in the region he named New Caledonia (today's central B.C.). He was the first to set up North West Company posts to the west of the Rockies.

In spite of all his good work, Fraser died poor, just as David Thompson* did. Both men were "doers" rather than self-advertisers. They didn't have the ruthless business drive of that other great B.C. explorer, Alexander Mackenzie,* who became both rich and famous in his lifetime.

Louis-Honoré Fréchette
Born 1839, Lévis, Que.
Died 1908

Louis-Honoré Fréchette was the first Canadian poet to gain international acclaim. This was in 1880, when a book of his poems was awarded a prize by the French Academy. Quebeckers took to calling him *le lauréat* (the poet laureate).

Fréchette's early life had been less laurel-strewn. At the age of 13 he had run away from his stepmother and to New York, where he got a job as a telegraph operator. He later returned home to study law, but could not make a living as a lawyer and before long was back in the States. There he published a book of poems that was bitterly critical of Canada. (He had this book burnt after he became *le lauréat*.)

Fréchette finally returned to Canada in 1871, and this time he did manage to make a living—as a lawyer, journalist, and politician. And after France had awarded him the celebrated literary prize, he was in great demand as a poet. His most famous work is *La Légende d'un Peuple*, a cycle of poems celebrating heroic events in Canadian history.

Martin Frobisher
Born c.1539, England
Died 1594

The swashbuckling Martin Frobisher was the first English seaman to search for the Northwest Passage, the fabled sea route to the Pacific Ocean. In the 1570s he made three voyages to the Arctic and discovered Frobisher Bay, which he thought was a strait. In passing, he claimed Greenland for Queen Elizabeth I (naming it West England).

Frobisher took rock samples wherever he went, for he was hoping to find gold. He was as much fortune-hunter as explorer, a pirate-adventurer who had once been held hostage in Africa. He was just the type of bold spirit Queen Elizabeth liked, and she later knighted him for his role in the defeat of the Spanish Armada.

Comte de Frontenac
Born 1622, France
Died 1698

Frontenac was governor of New France for 19 years all told (1672-82 and 1689-98). Haughty and autocratic, he ruled the colony as if it was his private kingdom—ignored Louis XIV's orders, quarrelled with his senior officials, and even imprisoned some because they didn't show him enough respect. There were so many complaints that Frontenac was dismissed, but he was reinstated as governor when war broke out with Britain.

Frontenac's hauteur stood him in good stead when in 1690 the British sailed up the St. Lawrence and demanded the surrender of Quebec. He told them sternly, "I have no reply to make except from the mouths of my cannons and muskets." The British departed with their tails between their legs. Frontenac fought the Iroquois with equal success, and he greatly increased the fur trade. Although this was against orders, it brought long-term benefits; for by sending out traders and explorers, Frontenac spread New France's empire far across the continent.

Barbara Frum
Born 1937, Niagara Falls, N.Y.

The well-known broadcaster was born Barbara Rosberg, daughter of a department store owner in Niagara Falls. She married young and settled down to life as a homemaker, but she wanted to do something more than being a wife and mother. She had her first opportunity in 1963, when she gave a talk on CBC radio, telling mothers how to amuse their children.

Within two years, Barbara Frum was working full-time as a journalist and broadcaster, and in 1971 she moved into high gear when she took over as host of the phone-out radio show *As It Happens*. Soon her tough, straight-ahead interviewing style brought her national acclaim, as well as many awards. She finally left the show in 1981 to take a similar job on *The Journal*, CBC TV's evening current affairs program. She was succeeded on *As It Happens* by Elizabeth Gray, another well-known journalist, broadcaster, and interviewer.

Northrop Frye

Born 1912, Sherbrooke, Que.

The distinguished literary scholar started out intending to be a minister. But as soon as he enrolled at the University of Toronto's Victoria College, he realized that this was the place for him, that he could best make a contribution in the academic world.

Northrop Frye did in fact complete his theological studies and was ordained a United Church minister. But a few years later he accepted a teaching post at Victoria College. He has been there ever since, rising from lecturer in English to chancellor of the college, while giving his celebrated courses on literature, criticism, and the Bible.

Over the years, Frye's reputation has spread far beyond Toronto. In 1947 he gained world acclaim as a literary critic when he published *Fearful Symmetry*, his tradition-breaking study of the English poet William Blake. Other books followed, among them Frye's masterworks, *Anatomy of Criticism* (1957) and *The Great Code: The Bible and Literature* (1982), which took him 10 years to write.

Frye's reputation is such that undergraduates across the world already study his works, writing theses on his thoughts and theories. Meanwhile, he continues to lecture to his own students, deeply committed to what has been his life's work—the passing on of knowledge.

Thomas Fuller

Born 1823, England
Died 1898

The Parliament Buildings in Ottawa were designed by the architect Thomas Fuller, who won a competition for their construction in 1859. The cornerstone was laid the following year by the Prince of Wales (the future Edward VII) and in 1865 the buildings were ready for occupation. They were first used as a seat of government when the Parliament of the Province of Canada met there in 1866. Fuller designed other public buildings in Ottawa and in 1881 was appointed chief architect for the Dominion.

In 1916, some years after his death, the Centre Block of the Parliament Buildings went up in flames. Architect John Pearson was in charge of the rebuilding. His new Centre Block was one storey higher than Fuller's—and it was made fireproof.

Robert Fulford

Born 1932, Ottawa, Ont.

Saturday Night magazine used to have a fine reputation but a small circulation. Since Robert Fulford took over as editor in 1968, the magazine has broken new ground, gaining a new look and a greatly increased readership.

Fulford has spent his life in journalism, working as both columnist and editor for newspapers as well as magazines. He has written on many subjects, but especially on the arts, and is known as a film critic under the name Marshall Delaney.

André Gagnon

Born 1942, St.Pacôme de Kamouraska, Que.

Since he first began writing music at the age of six, pianist and composer André Gagnon has covered an amazingly wide field, performing as everything from TV host to concert pianist, and writing everything from chamber music to pop songs. He won his first Juno Award in 1976 for his LP *Neiges*. That same year, he completed a concerto he had written for Jean Carignan.* He has composed music for ballet, films, TV, and has also had successful tours as a performer in many parts of the world.

Clarence Gagnon
Born 1881, Montreal, Que.
Died 1942
Clarence Gagnon painted scenes of habitant life, and he did the illustrations for Louis Hémon's* novel *Maria Chapdelaine*. In 1977, 18 of his sketches for the book sold for $58,000.

Gagnon's favourite sketching ground was the Baie St.Paul area, north of the St.Lawrence River. Some people in the villages there still remember him—a friendly man who took an interest in their work and painted cheerful pictures of their white-washed cottages and their daily activities.

John Kenneth Galbraith
Born 1908, Iona Station, Ont.
John Kenneth Galbraith is one of the world's leading economists, author of such international best sellers as *The Affluent Society*. Raised on his father's farm in Ontario, he attended agricultural college in Guelph, completing his education in the United States. He stayed on in the States, where he became a professor at Harvard University and an economic adviser to the U.S. government. He served as U.S. ambassador to India 1961-63.

One of Galbraith's most delightful books is *The Scotch*, about his Canadian upbringing. Although officially retired now, he continues to lecture and write. In 1981 he published his autobiography, *A Life in Our Times*.

Mavis Gallant
Born 1922, Montreal, Que.
Mavis Gallant's short stories have been read throughout the world, and especially in the United States, where for many years they have appeared in the *New Yorker* magazine. She started her writing career as a newspaper reporter in Montreal, but set off for Europe when she was 28, intent on being a fiction writer. Settling in Paris, she lived on a shoestring while gradually making her name. Her first collection of stories was called *The Other Paris*.

Most of Mavis Gallant's stories are set in Europe, but in 1981 she brought out a book of Canadian stories, *Home Truths*. It won a Governor General's Award. In 1983, after half a lifetime in France, Canada's famous expatriate author returned home to be writer-in-residence at the University of Toronto.

William Edward Gallie
Born 1882, Barrie, Ont.
Died 1959
The two outstanding figures in medical education in the early years of this century were Dr. William Gallie in Toronto and Dr. Edward Archibald in Montreal. Archibald (1872-1959) was professor of surgery at McGill and chief surgeon at the Royal Victoria Hospital. Gallie was professor of surgery in Toronto and successively chief surgeon at the Hospital for Sick Children and at Toronto General Hospital.

Both men were brilliant researchers who invented new techniques which enabled more problems to be corrected by surgery. But they are especially remembered for the changes they made in the way doctors and surgeons were trained. Most significant was the Gallie Course in Surgery, which was established in Toronto in 1932. A postgraduate course, the first of its kind in Canada, it was carefully structured to give young surgeons a wide experience, while encouraging them to pursue original research projects. Some of the "Gallie slaves" who took the course later led the world into new fields of surgery.

Alexander Tilloch Galt
Born 1817, England
Died 1893
Alexander Galt could be called *the* Father of Confederation. A leading politician in the Province of Canada, he formally suggested in 1858 that Britain's North American colonies should join together in a federal system of government. That same year, he was sent to England with two other ministers (George-Étienne Cartier* and John Ross) to discuss the scheme with the British.

There had in the past been some talk of a federal union, but Galt's proposal led directly to Confederation. George Brown* took up the cause in 1859. John A. Macdonald* played on-again off-again, and eventually became a Confederation enthusiast in 1864, a few months before the Charlottetown Conference.

Galt played an important role at all three Confederation conferences, often acting as financial adviser. A former railway promoter, he had twice served as finance minister of the Province of Canada, and after Confederation he was the first finance minister of the Dominion of Canada. He later served as Canadian high commissioner in England. Both at home and abroad, Galt was one of the men who built Canada.

Louis Gamache
Born c.1784, L'Islet, Que.
Died 1854
He was known in the Gulf of St.Lawrence as the Pirate of Anticosti and was said to be in league with the devil. Many hair-raising stories were told about Louis Gamache. He was a former Royal Navy seaman who set up house on the lonely island of Anticosti, remote from any settlement. Living there with his family, he supported himself with a little fishing, a little hunting, a little trapping . . . and, it was said, a lot of piracy.

Jean Garand
Born 1888, St.Rémi, Que.
Died 1974
During the 1930s, Jean Garand invented a semi-automatic rifle, known as the Garand rifle, which became standard issue for the U.S. army and marine corps during World War II. It was said to be the best rifle in the world.

Garand's family had moved to the United States when he was 11, and he patented his first invention (a new type of jack screw) while employed at a textile mill in Connecticut. He was 13 at the time. He invented his famous rifle while working at the U.S. Armory in Springfield, Mass.

François-Xavier Garneau
Born 1809, Quebec, Que.
Died 1866
During the last century, François-Xavier Garneau was hailed as Canada's "first national historian." Others had written histories before Garneau, but none had been so thorough or so all-embracing.

Garneau was a notary by training, not a historian. But after the Rebellion of 1837, when he realized that Upper and Lower Canada were going to be united, he set out to put French Canada's past on record. He feared that the union would mark the end of French Canada and wanted to disprove Lord Durham's* cruel statement that French Canadians had no history. Between 1845 and 1849,

Garneau brought out a mammoth three-volume *Histoire du Canada*, based on original documents; and he spent the rest of his life rooting out more documents, updating his work, and publishing revised editions.

Garneau also wrote poetry, and his great-grandson Hector de Saint-Denis Garneau (1912-43) was a famous poet, though a tragic one. Suffering from a heart disease, he shut himself off from the world, seeing very few people, and died at the age of 31.

Jean Gascon

Born 1921, Montreal, Que.

In 1975 Jean Gascon was named a Companion of the Order of Canada for his great contribution to Canadian theatre. He had trained as an actor in France, and after playing there in a number of roles he returned to Montreal, where in 1951 he was one of the founders of the Théâtre du Nouveau Monde. Gascon performed with this celebrated theatre company for the next 15 years. Meanwhile, he helped found the National Theatre School of Canada and was appointed its director general. He was artistic director of the Stratford Festival 1967-74 (being co-director with John Hirsch* for the first two years). Since 1977 he has been director of theatre at the National Arts Centre in Ottawa.

James Gay

Born 1810, England
Died 1891

One of our worst verse writers, James Gay was a kindly man with very little sense of humour and a firm belief in his own brilliance. He called himself Poet Laureate of Canada and Master of All Poets; and to prove it, he wrote odes to Queen Victoria, the Governor General, and other important figures.

Gay lived in Guelph, Ont., where he supported himself and his family by mending umbrellas, sharpening saws, and doing odd carpentry jobs. He owned a two-headed horse (which he had saved from being killed at birth) and he showed this strange creature at the Guelph Exhibition of 1875, charging 5 cents for a copy of his poems and 10 cents for a view of the horse. In his spare time, Gay played the flute. And he continually wrote poetry. He even spoke in rhyme. Citizens of Guelph who passed him in the street would be greeted with: "Nice day, fine day, so says Canada's poet, James Gay."

Another nineteenth-century poet of doubtful talents was James McIntyre, the coffin maker of Ingersoll, Ont. He is best known for his poems about cheese making, especially his "Ode on the Mammoth Cheese."

Gratien Gélinas

Born 1909, St.Tite, Que.

A little man with a big smile, Gratien Gélinas gave Canadian theatre such a shot in the arm that it has flourished with life and health during the past 40 years. He is one of our greatest all-round contributors: actor, playwright, producer, director, founder of his own theatre company, and, in the 1970s, chairman of the Canadian Film Development Corporation.

Gélinas began his career in the late 1930s, performing at first on radio and then in revues and plays. He was hailed as a Canadian Charlie Chaplin, because he so often played the funny-pathetic little man. His three most famous characters—Fridolin, Tit-Coq, and Bousille—have all been honest nice-guys who get hurt. It was largely because of Gélinas that Canadian theatre became a popular form of entertainment, especially in Quebec.

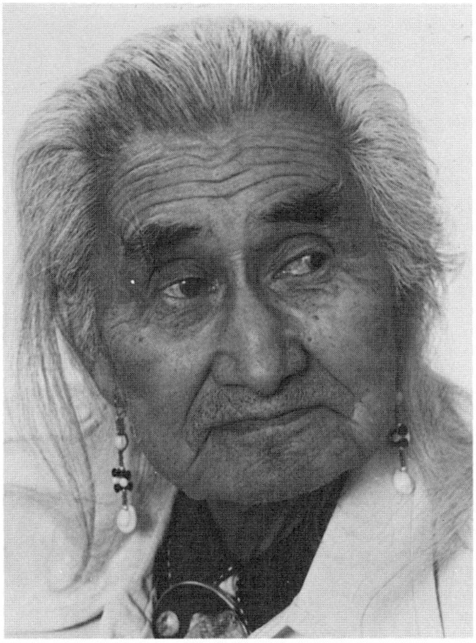

Chief Dan George

Born 1899, Burrard Reserve, B.C.
Died 1981

Stage, television, and film actor, Chief Dan George generally played the part of a wise, elderly Indian. He was 60 before he made his breakthrough as an actor.

He spent his youth working as a logger and longshoreman in British Columbia, and he might have remained in this work if some timber hadn't fallen on him, badly injuring him. Forced to retire, he saw this as a beginning, not an end, and took up entertaining. In 1960 he became known throughout Canada for his role as Antoine in the CBC TV series *Cariboo Country*. This led to work in films, including *Little Big Man*, for which he won the New York Film Critics Award as best supporting actor.

Dan George was made an honorary chief of the Shuswap and Squamish tribes, and he became a spokesman for the Indian people. In 1967, before a large audience, he delivered his "Lament for Confederation," a moving speech which recalled the sufferings of the Indians over the years.

Bruno Gerussi

Born 1928, Medicine Hat, Alta.

Star of *The Beachcombers*, the long-running TV serial, Bruno Gerussi spent his early childhood in Exshaw, Alta., moving to New Westminster, B.C., when he was nine. He was the son of poor Italian immigrants, and life was tough for the young Gerussi, getting even tougher during World War II when his classmates picked on him for being Italian. Meanwhile, there was a constant struggle to make ends meet, and at the age of 14 he went to work in a sawmill, earning 38 cents an hour. Later he attended technical school, and it was there he realized he wanted to be an actor. He won a scholarship to the Banff School of Fine Arts, and this launched him on his career.

Gerussi had early success, performing at the Stratford Festival and touring with the Canadian Players. Then, during an empty period, he turned to radio and made a success of that too, hosting his own morning show on the CBC. He was already well known throughout Canada when in 1972 he was offered a role in the new CBC TV series, *The Beachcombers*. It has been one of the most successful shows on Canadian television.

Abraham Gesner

Born 1797, Cornwallis Twp., N.S.
Died 1864

Abraham Gesner was the inventor of kerosene, a light oil that could be used instead of whale oil as a fuel for lamps. Gesner's importance rests not so much on the kerosene itself as on the way in which he produced it—by distilling hydrocarbons, such as asphalt and petroleum. His distillation process enabled James M. Williams* and other pioneers of the oil industry to refine the petroleum they discovered, converting it into a salable product. North America's giant oil-refining industry owes its origins to Abraham Gesner.

Gesner was a doctor by training, but he only practised medicine when no other work was available. His main interests were geology and scientific experiments. He made a geological survey of New Brunswick 1838-42, following this up with a survey of Prince Edward Island. And it was while Gesner was in Charlottetown in 1846 that he gave his first public demonstration of how to produce kerosene. At the end of his lecture, he lit a lamp containing the oil he had produced. Although none of his audience realized it, he had just lit the way to the future.

Humphrey Gilbert
Born c.1537, England
Drowned 1583

Sir Humphrey Gilbert landed on Newfoundland in 1583 and claimed it for Elizabeth I of England. He then laid down the law, telling the few fishermen who were already there (French and Portuguese, as well as English) that they would be executed for treason if they worshipped as Catholics and would have their ears cut off if they spoke against the queen. If they wanted to have fishing posts on shore, they must get a licence from him.

The bold Sir Humphrey then sailed away—but was caught in a violent storm, which sent him and his ship *Squirrel* to the bottom of the ocean.

Bobby Gimby
Born 1918, Cabri, Sask.

Trumpeter and songwriter Bobby Gimby has been nicknamed the Pied Piper of Canada—the magnetic music man who leads groups of children in cheerful songs.

Gimby started his career in the West, playing in boys' bands and dance orchestras, and in the 1940s moved to Toronto, where he formed his own orchestra. Over the years, he performed frequently on radio in such shows as *The Happy Gang* and *The Bobby Gimby Show*. Meanwhile, he was also writing music, and in 1967 he composed "CA-NA-DA," the catchy bilingual song which became so popular during the celebrations of Canada's 100th birthday. Gimby has also written centennial songs for Manitoba and British Columbia.

Gustave Gingras
Born 1918, Montreal, Que.

Dr. Gingras has spent most of his life helping the physically handicapped. Because of his determination and enthusiasm, even people with paralysing spinal damage have been able to get out of bed, out of hospital, into jobs, and sometimes into marriage. They live purposeful lives in the community.

A graduate of the University of Montreal, Gingras began his work by helping soldiers who had been paralysed in World War II. As time passed, he worked more and more with civilians, including children who were thalidomide victims. He founded the Rehabilitation Institute in Montreal, helped organize the first Wheelchair Olympics in Toronto, and in 1977 took charge of rehabilitation services in Prince Edward Island. A world authority on the disabled, Gingras served as president of the Canadian Medical Association 1972-73.

Frederick Gisborne
Born 1824, England
Died 1892

Frederick Gisborne laid the first underwater telegraph cable in all North America. This was in 1852 when he laid a cable between Prince Edward Island and New Brunswick.

Gisborne had long been a telegraph enthusiast. He had worked as an operator in Montreal and then helped to found the British North American Telegraph Company. He was also a rugged outdoorsman, prepared to face the dangers of laying a cable on the seabed. It was largely due to his efforts that in 1856 Newfoundland was linked to Cape Breton by cable. He was also involved in the laying of a cable across the Atlantic. This was completed in 1866, when the transatlantic cable was landed at Heart's Content, Nfld.

James Gladstone

Born 1887, nr. Pincher Creek, Alta. Died 1971

James Gladstone was the first Treaty Indian to be made a senator. Brought up on the Blood Reserve in southern Alberta, he developed into a successful farmer, setting an example to his neighbours by using chemical fertilizers and power machinery. He was the first farmer on the reserve to buy a tractor.

Gladstone became well known for his forward-looking attitudes, and in 1948 he was elected president of the Indian Association of Alberta. During the following years, he often negotiated with the federal government on Indian matters. He was appointed to the Senate in 1958, and there he continued to promote the interests of the Indian people. It was partly because of Gladstone's efforts that Treaty Indians gained the right to vote in federal elections.

Charles Gorman

Born 1897, Saint John, N.B. Died 1940

Known as "the man with the million-dollar legs," Charles Gorman set seven world speed-skating records. Although he had suffered a shrapnel wound in the leg during World War I, he practised steadily after the war and in 1924 had his first big success. That year he won both the U.S. national amateur outdoor championship and the international championship. His most amazing year was 1927 when he won four world championships.

More recently, Sylvia Burka has gained fame as a speed-skater. Born 1954 in Winnipeg, she won the women's world championship in 1976.

Oliver Goldsmith

Born 1794, St.Andrews, N.B. Died 1861

The first Canadian-born poet to write in English, Oliver Goldsmith is best known for his narrative poem *The Rising Village*. Published in 1825, it describes the various stages of settlement in "happy Acadia"—the first isolated cabin, the planting of crops, the bounteous harvest, and so on. But Goldsmith himself did not choose to till the soil. Joining the civilian supply branch of the British army, he travelled the world, ending his days in England.

Charles Goodeve

Born 1904, Neepawa, Man. Died 1980

During World War II, Charles Goodeve saved untold numbers of Allied ships from being sunk by enemy mines. A chemistry lecturer and a member of the Royal Naval Volunteer Reserve, he was taken into the navy as soon as war broke out and assigned to anti-mine research. By 1940 he had developed a method of demagnetizing the steel hulls of ships so that magnetic mines would not explode when ships passed near them. This system was called "degaussing" and it was used for the rest of the war.

Meanwhile, Goodeve worked on secret weapons for the Admiralty, promoting the Hedgehog anti-submarine depth bomb, the Oerlikon anti-aircraft gun, and other new weapons. After the war he became a director of the British Iron and Steel Research Association.

Glenn Gould

Born 1932, Toronto, Ont.
Died 1982

Canada's finest concert pianist, with a great reputation throughout the world, Glenn Gould presented a curious appearance on the concert stage. He liked a far lower seat than other pianists, so he brought his own chopped-down chair to performances and would sit hunched over the keyboard, humming as he played.

Gould had been a child prodigy, writing piano pieces when he was five and playing with the Toronto Symphony when he was 13. But despite successful tours throughout the world, he didn't really enjoy performing in public. In 1964 he abandoned the concert stage to concentrate on studio recordings. He was fascinated by the whole technology of recording, and by the way you could experiment to get just the effect you wanted.

In all, he made more than 80 discs, the most famous being Bach's *Goldberg Variations*. It was this record which launched Gould internationally when it first came out in 1955. Just before he died, he made a studio recording of the same work—a very different interpretation, thoughtful rather than impulsive. Through such digital recordings, Gould gave modern technology a central role in the age-old business of making beautiful music.

Igor Gouzenko

Born 1919, Russia
Died 1982

Igor Gouzenko launched a spy scandal that shook the world and helped bring on the Cold War between Russia and the West. He was a cypher clerk in the Soviet embassy in Ottawa, and in September 1945 he escaped from the embassy, taking with him a mass of documents which exposed a vast Russian spy ring. He said there were "moles" in the British secret service and that senior officials in Canada, Britain, and the U.S. were in fact Russian agents. He proved to be right.

Gouzenko spent the rest of his life in hiding. He was given an assumed name, and for many years his house was protected by the Mounties. On the rare occasions when he appeared on TV, he put a hood over his head so that he wouldn't be recognized. He lived in fear that the KGB would track him down and assassinate him (though it seems that the Russians did in fact know where he lived). So great was Gouzenko's fear of discovery that he refused to get hospital treatment for his diabetes. By the time he died at his Mississauga home, he had been blind for several years.

Robert Goulet

Born 1933, U.S.A.

Matinée idol Robert Goulet couldn't even get a job on radio at the start of his career. He was living in Edmonton at the time, the son of a French Canadian father and an American mother. English-language radio wouldn't take him as an announcer because he had a French accent. And the French-language station wouldn't take him because he had an English accent.

Goulet did eventually get work on radio, at CKUA in Edmonton, but a scholarship to the Royal Conservatory of Music changed the direction of his career. He performed in a number of musicals early in the 1950s and then starred in CBC TV's *Showtime* (1957-59). In 1960 he gained great acclaim in *Camelot*, playing Sir Lancelot opposite Julie Andrews and Richard Burton. Then came further successes—on Broadway, in films, in television—and a Grammy Award, a Tony Award, an Emmy. Now a resident of the United States, Goulet performs mostly in night clubs, especially in Las Vegas.

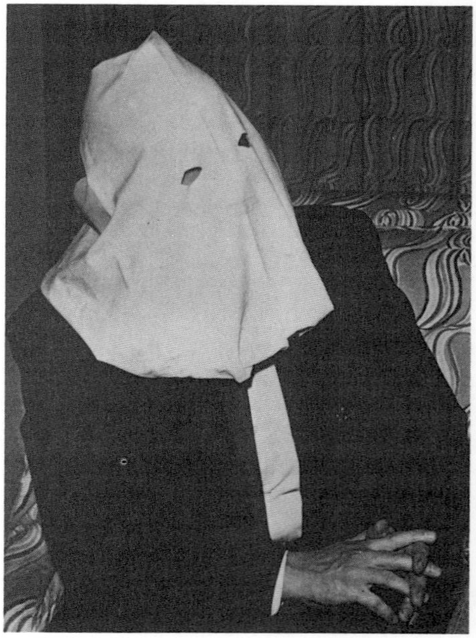

Alain Grandbois
Born 1900, St.Casimir de Portneuf, Que.
Died 1975

One of the leading poets of his time, Alain Grandbois was an adventurous spirit who roamed the world as a young man. He published his first book of poems in China in 1934. Two years later he was in Spain, fighting in the Spanish Civil War.

Grandbois returned to Quebec shortly before World War II and soon gained acclaim not only as a poet but as a writer of biographies and short stories. As a biographer, he wrote about other adventurers: Louis Jolliet* and Marco Polo. As a poet, he broke with tradition by writing unrhymed verse. His style greatly influenced younger poets. He received many awards, including the Lorne Pierce Medal for distinguished service to Canadian literature.

Cuthbert Grant
Born c.1793, Fort Tremblante, Sask.
Died 1854

The Métis leader Cuthbert Grant was the son of a North West Company trader, and he sided with the Northwesters in their feud against the Hudson's Bay Company and the Red River colonists. In 1816 he led the Métis horsemen who clashed with a group of colonists at Seven Oaks (now part of Winnipeg), killing 20 of them, along with their governor, Robert Semple. Grant was later arrested and taken to Montreal for trial, but he jumped bail, escaped back to the prairies —and lived to ride again.

In time, Grant made his peace with the Hudson's Bay Company officials, who appointed him warden of the plains, a type of magistrate. He spent his last years peacefully farming and dispensing the law.

George Monro Grant
Born 1835, Albion Mines, N.S.
Died 1902

George Monro Grant wrote *Ocean to Ocean*, an account of the cross-Canada journey he made in 1872 as a member of Sandford Fleming's* expedition to the Pacific. The book was tremendously popular, exciting people's imagination with its description of the West.

Grant wrote several other books, including one on world religions. He was a clergyman by profession, at first based in Halifax and then in Kingston, where for many years he was principal of Queen's University. A man of wide interests, he was one of the most distinguished Canadians of his time. In 1899 he was made moderator of the Presbyterian Church in Canada.

John Gray

Born 1946, Truro, N.S.

John Gray, the writer and composer of *Billy Bishop Goes to War*, began playing in rock bands when he was 13 and he continued to do so during his years as a student at the University of British Columbia.

After graduation, Gray became involved in theatre and in 1976 wrote *18 Wheels*, a musical about truckers. Three years later, he launched the two-man show about Billy Bishop,* which had highly successful runs in the United States and Britain, as well as in Canada. His co-star in the show was actor Eric Peterson, who played 17 human roles (and an airplane) while Gray accompanied him on the piano and joined in the choruses. Peterson was again the actor in Gray's 1982 musical for children, *Bongo in the Congo*. In 1983 Gray's *Billy Bishop* won him a Governor General's Award.

Lorne Greene

Born 1915, Ottawa, Ont.

Actor Lorne Greene started his career as an announcer and newscaster on CBC radio, gaining the nickname the Voice of Doom because of the ominous way he read the news in World War II. During the early 1940s, his deep sombre voice was one of the best known in Canada. This opened up an acting career on radio, which led him into theatre and television.

In 1959 he began his star role in NBC's popular television series *Bonanza*, which ran for 14 years. As Ben Cartwright, the dignified cowboy father of the series, he was known to millions of viewers across the world. In recent years, Lorne Greene has moved on to other television roles and has also performed in films, both as actor and narrator.

Nancy Greene

Born 1943, Ottawa, Ont.

Nancy Greene was the third woman champion to bring Canada fame on the ski slopes. First there was Lucile Wheeler (born 1935, Montreal) who in 1958 became the first skier from North America to win the world championship. Then there was Anne Heggtveit (born 1939, Ottawa) who in 1960 won the first gold medal ever gained by a Canadian in all the years of Olympic skiing. Nancy Greene's triumphs began in the mid-1960s, culminating with the gold medal in the giant slalom at the 1968 Olympics. In both 1967 and 1968 she was awarded the Lou Marsh Trophy as Canada's outstanding athlete of the year.

She had grown up in Rossland, B.C., and, like her predecessors, had been on skis ever since she could toddle. Like them too, she retired at the height of her success. She married a fellow Canadian-team skier, Al Raine, and together they settled down to develop the ski area at Whistler, B.C.

Meanwhile, another champion is following in her tracks. In 1982, Gerry Sorensen (born 1958, Kimberley, B.C.) won the women's World Cup downhill championship race at Haus, Austria.

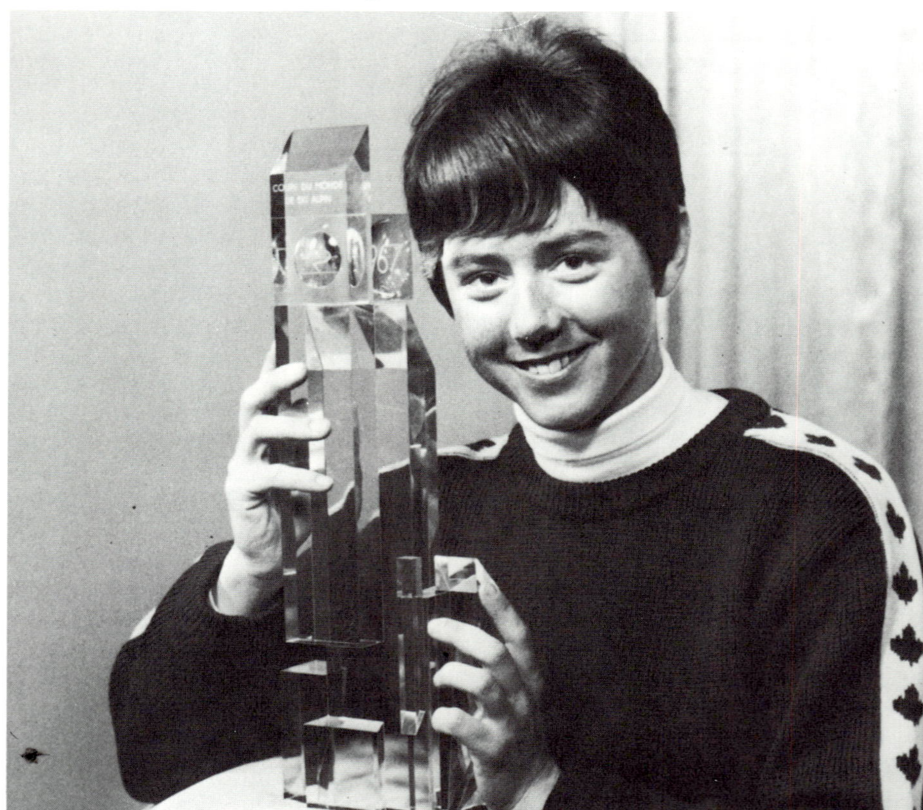

Wilfred Grenfell
Born 1865, England
Died 1940

The great missionary doctor of Labrador was a man of brimming enthusiasm—like an energetic youth leader, spurring people into action as he bounded cheerfully past difficulties and dangers. He was gut-and-pluck and onward-Christian-soldiers.

Grenfell started his life's work in 1892, when Britain's Mission to Deep Sea Fishermen sent him to serve on the northeast coast of Newfoundland and Labrador. He was horrified at what he found there. The people were unbelievably poor, underfed and living in hovels. They had no doctor and their nearest hospital was far away at St.John's.

During the next 40 years, Grenfell changed the whole scene. He established hospitals and orphanages, brought in doctors and nurses, and set the families to work making rugs, cloth, and other goods that could bring them an income. He even enlivened their social life, organizing everything from cricket matches to concerts.

Meantime, he publicized his cause so successfully, with books and lecture tours, that help poured in. Each summer, young volunteers came flocking to work unpaid for his mission. Others sent money to support the work. Today, the people of the outports still bless the name of Grenfell.

Earl Grey
Born 1851, England
Died 1917

Earl Grey was Governor General of Canada 1904-11 and he presided at the ceremonies when Alberta and Saskatchewan became provinces. A keen sportsman, he gave Canada its famous football trophy, the Grey Cup.

Wayne Gretzky
Born 1961, Brantford, Ont.

In the 1981-82 season, Wayne Gretzky made hockey history by scoring 50 goals in only 39 games. Later in the season, he stacked up another record with a total of 62 goals in 50 games. He then went on to break the record for the most goals in one season, the most assists in a season, and the most points in a season.

In 1982-83, he broke his own record for most assists in a season, as well as breaking or tying numerous other records. In 1982 he was awarded the Lou Marsh Trophy as outstanding Canadian athlete of the year. Early in 1982 he also won the Sporting News man-of-the-year award—one of the few Canadians who have ever won this prestigious American award.

These are just some of the amazing achievements of the Great Gretzky. The Edmonton Oilers star has been making news ever since he scored a goal shortly before his sixth birthday, when playing his first game in organized hockey. He has been hailed as the greatest, the youngest, the best . . . better even, in many people's view, than such superstars as Bobby Orr,* Bobby Hull,* and Gordie Howe.* Fan letters pour in. Wayne Gretzky T-shirts sell by the thousand. And President Reagan has joked that he would swap the entire state of Texas for one Wayne Gretzky.

Grey Owl
Born 1888, England
Died 1938

Grey Owl was one of Canada's most famous celebrities during the 1930s, author of *Pilgrims of the Wild* and other best-selling books. A former trapper who had taken to breeding beavers, he was a fervent spokesman for conservation, hoping to save the beaver from extinction. He went on lecture tours in Britain and the United States, and drew packed audiences, for he was the public's ideal of the noble Indian—a tall, gaunt figure with a great love of the Canadian wilderness.

The public received a big shock when Grey Owl died and it turned out that he was not Indian at all. He was Archibald Belaney, an Englishman who had been brought up in Sussex by two respectable English aunts.

But as a child he had loved to play at being Indian. And as an adult he had come to Canada and lived out his dream.

John Grierson
Born 1898, Scotland
Died 1972

In 1938, the British educator and film-maker John Grierson was asked by the Canadian government to set up a film policy for Canada. His report led to the establishment of the National Film Board in 1939. Grierson was appointed the NFB's first film commissioner.

Believing that film could be used to bring a better understanding among people, Grierson directed the NFB in a program of films which presented a broad view of Canadian life. His aim was "to interpret Canada to itself and to the world." The great reputation gained by Canadian documentary films is largely due to John Grierson. He is affectionately known as the father of documentary films.

Lionel-Adolphe Groulx
Born 1878, Chenaux, Que.
Died 1967

Historian, professor, and priest, Abbé Groulx was above all a French Canadian nationalist. The lectures he gave, the societies he formed, and the books he wrote all stressed the greatness of French Canada, its valuable folk traditions, its past glories. He gave French Canadians a new pride in their culture.

To keep the culture alive and strong, Groulx called for a French Canadian nation to be formed "within Confederation if possible, but outside if it is not possible." Over the years, Quebec separatists have drawn great inspiration from him.

Frederick Philip Grove
Born 1879, Germany
Died 1948
Frederick Philip Grove, the celebrated prairie novelist, was a curiously mysterious figure. While he wrote realistic stories of prairie life, he also wrote a very unrealistic account of his own life. He said he had been born in Russia of rich parents who owned a castle in Sweden. In fact, he was a German from a relatively poor family and his real name was Felix Paul Greve. Under this name, he had a successful literary career in Europe before being imprisoned for fraud.

In 1912 he turned up in Manitoba—as a school teacher calling himself F. P. Grove—and over the years he gathered a powerful reputation for his Canadian novels. He won a Governor General's Award for his misleading "autobiography" and also received the Lorne Pierce Medal for distinguished service to Canadian literature. *Fruits of the Earth* and *Over Prairie Trails* are two of his best-known books. Towards the end of his life he lived in Ontario.

Lydia Gruchy
Born 1895, France
The Rev. Lydia Gruchy, who was ordained at St. Andrew's Church, Moose Jaw, in 1936, was the first woman to be a minister of the United Church of Canada. She had graduated in theology from St. Andrew's College, Saskatoon, and at first worked as minister's assistant because the church rules forbade women to be ministers. These rules were changed mainly because of Lydia Gruchy's dedicated work. She later served in Ontario as well as Saskatchewan, retiring in 1962.

The highest position in the United Church has also been held by a woman, by Lois Wilson (born 1927). She served as moderator from 1980 to 1982.

Joseph Guibord
Born 1809, Varennes, Que.
Died 1869
Joseph Guibord was the most famous corpse in Canadian history. When alive, he had been a member of the Institut Canadien, a free-thinking society condemned by the Roman Catholic church. Consequently, when Guibord died, the church would not allow him to be buried in the Catholic cemetery of Côte-des-Neiges in Montreal, even though he had bought a plot there. The funeral procession was actually turned away at the cemetery gates.

Guibord was placed in a Protestant cemetery—temporarily—for his family fought a law suit over his burial rights. Their main adversary was the powerful Bishop Bourget of Montreal, who was determined the corpse would not be allowed in any Catholic graveyard. As most Catholics vigorously supported Bourget, there was a furious outcry when finally the Privy Council decided against the church. Armed police were called out to control the crowds on the day Guibord was dug up, taken in procession to Côte-des-Neiges, and dug in again.

But Bishop Bourget had the last word. He deconsecrated the patch of earth in which Guibord lay, making it unblessed ground.

Simon Gun-an-noot
Born 1874, Kispiox, B.C.
Died 1933
Simon Gun-an-noot made his name as a highly successful fugitive. A Gitskan Indian of the Skeena region he was a trapper and storekeeper, and a respectable family man. But one night in 1906 he had a row with a miner called Alex McIntosh, and next morning McIntosh was found dead, shot in the back. Max Leclair, a stranger to the district, was also found shot.

There was nothing to connect Gun-an-noot with either shooting, apart from the fact that he had threatened McIntosh. Nevertheless, he and his nephew Peter Hi-ma-dan were wanted for the murders and a reward was offered for their capture. For 13 years they lived as fugitives, evading all who came after them. Meanwhile, they carried on trapping, arranged for friends to sell their furs, and kept in close contact with their families (who spent long periods with them).

As time passed, prospectors as well as Indians came across the two men, yet nobody turned them in. Gun-an-noot voluntarily gave himself up in 1919, having arranged for a good lawyer to defend him.
At his trial, the jury took only 15 minutes to declare him not guilty. A few months later, Hi-ma-dan was also acquitted.

Casimir Stanislaus Gzowski
Born 1813, Russia
Died 1898
The International Bridge, which crosses the Niagara River at Fort Erie, was designed and built by Casimir Gzowski, the son of a Polish count. He arrived in Canada in his late twenties, a young man with a promising future and an adventurous past. (He had joined a national rebellion against the Russians who ruled his native Poland, and it had been ruthlessly put down.)

By training, Gzowski was a military engineer, and in Canada he set to work building some of our first railroads, including the Grand Trunk Railway from Toronto to Sarnia. Then in 1871-73 he built the bridge between Fort Erie and Buffalo. Some of the public parkways in Toronto were also designed by Casimir Gzowski. In many ways, he helped shape our nation. Peter Gzowski* is one of his descendants.

Peter Gzowski
Born 1934, Toronto, Ont.
Raised in Galt, Ont., broadcaster Peter Gzowski started his career as a journalist, working for smalltown newspapers and rapidly moving onward and upward. At 20 he was the youngest-ever city editor of the Moose Jaw *Times-Herald*. At 23 he was the youngest-ever managing editor of the Chatham *Daily News*. And at 28 he was the youngest-ever managing editor of *Maclean's* magazine.

After a stint as editor of the *Star Weekly*, Gzowski moved into broadcasting. From 1971 to 1974 he hosted the CBC radio show *This Country in the Morning*, bringing himself and the show immense popularity throughout Canada. He has since had his own late-night TV show, as well as a resumption of the morning radio show.

In addition, Gzowski has written books and articles, played just about everything from basketball to the banjo, and been an enthusiastic coach of little-league hockey teams.

Thomas Chandler Haliburton
Born 1796, Windsor, N.S.
Died 1865

T. C. Haliburton wrote a series of books about Sam Slick, a Yankee clockmaker, whose invented doings and sayings were chuckled over throughout the English-speaking world. Haliburton was the first Canadian to be a really popular international writer. He himself was neither a clockmaker nor a Yankee. He was a Nova Scotian judge and a red-blooded Tory who enjoyed good company, fine wine, fine women, and good conversation.

William Hall
Born 1827, Horton Bluff, N.S.
Died 1904

One of the very earliest Canadians to win the Victoria Cross was William Hall, the son of a slave who had been brought to Halifax during the War of 1812. Hall was the first Nova Scotian and the first Canadian sailor to win the medal.

He had gone to sea at an early age and was serving with the Royal Navy when in 1857 he took part in the relief of Lucknow in India, where the British garrison was besieged. Hall was ordered forward with the cannons to capture a heavily defended mosque which was the key to Lucknow. In the fierce fighting that followed, all but he and one officer were mown down. Both stayed at their post and Hall continued to man his gun, sending shell after shell into the walls. His gallantry saved the day, breaching the walls and allowing reinforcements to move forward and rescue the beleaguered garrison. He later retired from the navy and became a farmer near Avonport, N.S.

Hall's act of heroism was just three years after that of Lieutenant Alexander Dunn (born 1833, York, Upper Canada) who was the very first Canadian to win the VC. Dunn earned his medal in the Crimean War during the Charge of the Light Brigade, when he fought off the enemy with his sabre, having used up all the bullets in his revolver.

Théophile Hamel
Born 1817, Ste. Foy, Que.
Died 1870

Many of the portraits of nineteenth-century politicians that hang in the Parliament Buildings in Ottawa were painted by Théophile Hamel. He had his early training from Antoine Plamondon,* and after studying in Europe he opened a studio in Quebec. He soon became a most popular portrait painter, and his clients included leading citizens of both Upper and Lower Canada. His self-portrait, seen here, was painted when he was about 20.

Ned Hanlan

Born 1855, Toronto, Ont.
Died 1908

From far and wide, people flocked to watch Ned Hanlan, and not just because he was the world rowing champion. He streaked through the water so fast that he could take time off to amuse the crowds, and he often fooled around in the middle of a race, waving to friends or dropping his oars. Sometimes he skulled in a circle until his competitor caught up.

Hanlan was the son of a Toronto Island storekeeper, and he had grown up in boats, rowing himself to school as a child. He won the Canadian skulling championship in 1877 and was world champion 1880-84. He carried on skulling until well into his forties.

Lawren Harris

Born 1885, Brantford, Ont.
Died 1970

Lawren Harris and J. E. H. MacDonald* were the main founders of the Group of Seven. The two artists first met in 1911 and together they began to develop a new style of landscape painting. With bold brush strokes, they sought to capture the raw vigour of Canadian lakes and forests. Gradually, they gathered like-minded artists around them and in 1920 held their first Group of Seven exhibition.

Harris had studied art in Germany and he was the only member of the group who did not have to earn a living. His family had a share in the prosperous Massey-Harris farm-machinery company. He used his wealth to help his fellow artists, and with the art lover Dr. James MacCallum he built the Studio Building in Toronto, where some of the Group of Seven painters lived.

As Harris grew older, his style became increasingly abstract until he was doing only abstract paintings. This was a great contrast to his early work, some of which was very realistic (see his portrait of Salem Bland*).

Robert Harris

Born 1849, Wales
Died 1919

The original group picture of the Fathers of Confederation was painted by Robert Harris who, most appropriately, grew up in Charlottetown. He was one of the best-known portrait painters of his time and was president of the Royal Canadian Academy at the turn of the century.

Harris took more than a year to complete his huge canvas of the Fathers of Confederation, which was destroyed in a few minutes during the Parliament Buildings fire in 1916. Fortunately, a sketch for the portrait survived, and this served as a guide for Rex Woods, who was commissioned to repaint the picture in 1964. Rex Woods has specialized in historical paintings, and some of his works are reproduced in this book (see Credits, p.232).

There are also some of Robert Harris's paintings in this book. They include the self-portrait shown here and the sketch of John A. Macdonald,* which is on p.139.

Don Harron

Born 1924, Toronto, Ont.

In 1952, when performing in the annual revue *Spring Thaw*, actor Don Harron became Charlie Farquharson, and he has lived a double life ever since. As Charlie Farquharson, he is yer whiskery farmer from yer Parry Sound, a feller without much of that eddycashun, though heez written his own vershun of yer hist'ry of Canada, and other books too. Heez often on radio and TV, talking about everything from the guvermint to his harrowin' days on the farm.

As Don Harron, he's also often on radio and TV. He was host of CBC radio's *Morningside* 1977-82, and began his own daytime TV show in 1983. But Harron has fewer whiskers and far more education than Charlie Farquharson. A professional playwright, actor, and broadcaster, he has appeared in films and plays, including Shakespeare plays. He is married to singer-actress Catherine McKinnon (born 1944, Saint John, N.B.) who first became known through her performances on the TV shows *Singalong Jubilee* and *Don Messer's* Jubilee*.

Evelyn Hart

Born 1956, Toronto, Ont.

At the 1980 International Ballet Competition held in Varna, Bulgaria, the audience went wild when Evelyn Hart danced a modern duet called *Belong* with her Royal Winnipeg Ballet partner David Peregrine (born 1954, Wales). The couple's performance in the competition brought Peregrine the men's bronze medal and Hart the women's gold. She was the first Canadian to win this most coveted of all ballet awards. Even more remarkable, both dancers had been late starters in ballet—he at 15, she at 14.

Evelyn Hart had been turned down when at the age of 11 she first auditioned for the National Ballet School in Toronto (though she did later do a brief stint there). Her first serious training was at Dorothy Carter's school in London, Ont. Since the Varna success, Hart and Peregrine have continued to bring prestige to the Royal Winnipeg Ballet, delighting audiences both at home and abroad.

Ezekiel Hart

Born c.1770, Trois Rivières, Que.
Died 1843

Ezekiel Hart was the first Jew to be elected to a Canadian legislature. He was the son of Aaron Hart, who had come to Canada with Wolfe's* forces and was the first Jew to settle in Lower Canada. (During the French regime, Louis XIV had decreed that only Roman Catholics could settle in France's colonies.)

The Harts lived in Trois Rivières, where they soon became leading citizens, and in 1807 Ezekiel was elected to the Legislative Assembly of Lower Canada. At the opening session, when members had to swear an oath on the Bible, Ezekiel Hart would not do so, for it was against his religion. He said he would swear his oath on the Old Testament. This produced an uproar and he was expelled from the assembly. Re-elected the following year, he was again expelled. He stood for election a third time in 1809, but then withdrew, for he saw no chance of being allowed to sit in the assembly. People were saying that Jews should not make laws for Christians; after all, no Jews were allowed in Britain's parliament.

That was the end of Hart's political career, but not the end of his cause. In 1832, Lower Canada passed a law giving Jews the same rights as everyone else, including the right to sit in the legislature. This made Canada the first part of the British Empire to give equal rights to Jews.

Julia Beckwith Hart
Born 1796, Fredericton, N.B.
Died 1867

Julia Beckwith Hart wrote the first novel ever published in Canada. Called *St.Ursula's Convent, or the Nun of Canada*, it was a suspense-filled romance, full of throbbing hearts and daring escapades. Julia was 17 years old, and still Miss Beckwith, when she wrote the story. It was published 10 years later, in 1824, after her marriage to the bookbinder George Henry Hart. She later wrote two more novels, contributed numerous articles to the *New Brunswick Reporter*, and produced a family of six children.

Richard Hatfield
Born 1931, Woodstock, N.B.

In 1969 Richard Hatfield was chosen leader of New Brunswick's Conservative party, and in 1970 he became premier of the province.

Premier Hatfield holds a law degree from Dalhousie University and in 1957-58 served in Ottawa as executive assistant to the minister of trade and commerce. A director of the Canadian Council of Christians and Jews, he has received the Canada-Israel Friendship Award. He has also been made an honorary Micmac-Maliseet chief, with the name Chief Rolling Thunder.

Frederick Haultain
Born 1857, England
Died 1942

Saskatchewan and Alberta were created as provinces in 1905 largely through the efforts of Frederick Haultain, who had been raised in Ontario but moved west when he was 27. He opened a law office in Fort Macleod, was elected to the first Legislative Assembly of the North-West Territories and in due course became head of the executive. This was equivalent to being premier, except that Haultain did not have the power of a provincial premier. To a large extent, the Territories were controlled by Ottawa through a lieutenant governor.

Over the years, Haultain worked to get provincial status for the Territories, though he wanted one province to be formed, rather than two neighbouring ones. He also wanted the West to have control of its crown lands and natural resources, and Saskatchewan and Alberta did not get this when they were first formed. Haultain was later knighted and for many years was chancellor of the University of Saskatchewan, which he helped found. Though largely forgotten nowadays, he was one of the great men of western Canada.

Francis Bond Head
Born 1793, England
Died 1875

Sir Francis Bond Head was lieutenant governor of Upper Canada 1835-38 and was one of the causes of the Upper Canadian rebellion. For besides being brave and dashing, he was inexperienced and stubborn—an unfortunate combination.

First, he antagonized the Reform party by firing the leading Reformers from his Executive Council because they tried to reform it. Next, he made them even angrier by openly campaigning against them (and for the Tories) in the 1836 election. Then, despite rumours that some Reformers were planning armed revolt, he sent all his troops to fight the rebels in Lower Canada. This gave William Lyon Mackenzie* the chance to launch the revolt he had been planning in Upper Canada.

Bond Head returned to Britain in disfavour, and he was never again made governor of anywhere.

Sandy Hawley
Born 1949, Oshawa, Ont.
In 1969, just three years after Johnny Longden* retired, Sandy Hawley became Canada's leading jockey. The 20-year-old champion had begun professional racing the previous year, having worked at E. P. Taylor's* National Stud Farm since his mid-teens. In 1970 he won 452 races, gaining the North American riding title. Since then, he has ridden to victory in race after race, winning title after title, and breaking record after record. In 1973 he became the world's first jockey to win more than 500 races in one season. In 1976, at the age of 27, he was the youngest jockey to have won 3,000 races. In both 1973 and 1976 he was awarded the Lou Marsh Trophy as Canada's outstanding athlete of the year.

Samuel Hearne
Born 1745, England
Died 1792
Samuel Hearne was the first European to reach the Arctic Ocean by going overland. A Hudson's Bay Company man, stationed on the bay at Fort Prince of Wales (Churchill), he was sent into the Arctic wilderness to find some copper mines which were believed to exist there.

Hearne set out in December 1770, having already made two unsuccessful attempts. He was accompanied by his friend, the Indian chief Matonabbee, and by many of the chief's friends and relations. During the next year and a half, they walked all the way to the mouth of the Coppermine River and back, a distance of about 8,000 km. Much of the journey was across the tundra—barren windswept country which offered little in the way of food or firewood. Hearne survived by living the Indian way and eating whatever was available. He gained a great admiration for the resourcefulness of his Indian friends. The book he later wrote provided a wealth of information about the Indian people. And about the Arctic.

In 1774-75 Hearne built Cumberland House, the HBC's first inland trading post. He is seen here discussing the plans with the carpenter.

Anne Hébert

Born 1916, Ste. Catherine de Fossambault, Que.

In 1982 Anne Hébert won the Prix Femina, one of France's most coveted literary awards, for her novel *Les Fous de Bassan* (The Gannets). This is one of the many prizes she has won during her life. These include two Governor General's Awards (one of them for poetry) and, in 1970, France's Prix des Libraires for her celebrated novel *Kamouraska*, which was later made into a film by Claude Jutra.*

An invalid during childhood, Anne Hébert was educated at home by her parents and then briefly worked as a scriptwriter for the National Film Board. For many years now she has lived in France. She has written plays as well as film scripts and stories, and is especially admired for her beautiful symbolist poetry.

Louis-Philippe Hébert

Born 1850, Ste. Sophie d'Halifax, Que.

Died 1917

Many of the statues of great Canadians that stand in parks and squares throughout Canada are the work of the sculptor Louis-Philippe Hébert.

He started his career in Montreal, carving wooden images for churches, and later specialized in statues and monuments. His work includes the statues of Macdonald* and Cartier* on Parliament Hill, Ottawa; the Maisonneuve* monument in the Place d'Armes, Montreal; and the statue of Evangeline, the mythical Acadian heroine, at Grand Pré, N.S. This was designed by him and completed by his son Henri, who was one of the founders in 1928 of the Sculptors Society of Canada.

John Sebastian Helmcken

Born 1824, England

Died 1920

John Helmcken was one of the earliest European residents on Vancouver Island and one of the infant colony's leading citizens. A Hudson's Bay Company doctor, he arrived in Victoria in 1850, only a few years after the HBC post was established there. Two years later he married James Douglas's* daughter Cecilia, and throughout the early growth of B.C. politics he tended to support Douglas and to oppose De Cosmos,* Robson,* and others who wanted more power for the people and less power for the Hudson's Bay Company.

Helmcken played an active part in politics, served as speaker of Vancouver Island's first Legislative Assembly, and in 1870 was a member of the delegation that went to Ottawa to arrange B.C.'s entry into Confederation. After B.C. joined Canada, Helmcken retired from politics and concentrated on medicine.

Louis Hémon

Born 1880, France

Killed 1913

The classic French Canadian novel *Maria Chapdelaine* was written by Louis Hémon, who came to Canada in 1911 and worked for a while on a farm in the Saguenay district of Quebec. Having personally experienced the tough pioneer life, Hémon settled down to write his pioneer novel, which he finished in Montreal early in 1913. He was killed that summer in a railway accident, so didn't live to enjoy the success of his book. It fascinated readers, for it gave a realistic picture of habitant life, instead of making the hardships seem romantic, as had been the custom.

Anthony Henday
Born England
(Dates of birth and death unknown)

Anthony Henday was the first European to visit the territory that is now Alberta. This was in 1754, when he was sent by the Hudson's Bay Company to make contact with distant Indian tribes and try and persuade them to bring their furs to the HBC posts at Hudson Bay.

Henday had been outlawed in England for smuggling, but the HBC officers were unaware of this. They regarded him as a "good and brave servant." And so he was. Travelling with a band of Cree, he went far into Blackfoot territory and joined the Blackfoot in a buffalo hunt. But he could not persuade them to bring their furs to Hudson Bay. It was far easier for them to trade with the French, who had established posts inland (though not as far west as Alberta).

Josiah Henson
Born 1789, U.S.A.
Died 1883

Born a slave on a Maryland plantation, Josiah Henson escaped to Canada with his family in 1830 via the "underground railroad." Years later, he met the American author Harriet Beecher Stowe, who used some of his experiences in her book *Uncle Tom's Cabin*. Although this book was based on many people's lives, Henson has become identified with Uncle Tom.

He was a remarkable man, a Methodist minister and an author, though he worked as a farm labourer when he first arrived in Canada. He settled near Dresden, Ont., where he established a settlement for other former slaves and a school for their children.

Doug Hepburn
Born 1926, Vancouver, B.C.

The man who became the world weightlifting champion was born with a club foot, and though the condition was corrected by surgery, he was a weakling as a child—bullied by the boys and scorned by the girls. So . . . he went on a body-building program. And ate. And put on muscle.

Doug Hepburn was 22 when he had his first big success at a competition in Vancouver, where he pressed 136 kg. This was the greatest weight pressed by a Canadian since official records had been kept. The next year Hepburn beat the U.S. champion. Yet his success sparked little interest at home; it was a group of friends who raised the money to send him to the Stockholm championships in 1953. He came away with the title—strongest man in the world—with a lift of 468 kg. He was awarded the Lou Marsh Trophy as outstanding Canadian athlete of 1953, and the following year he won the gold medal at the British Empire Games.

Gerhard Herzberg

Born 1904, Germany

In 1971 Gerhard Herzberg won the Nobel Prize in Chemistry. This prestigious award was bestowed on him for his pioneering work on molecular spectroscopy—the science of studying molecules by measuring the light emitted or absorbed by them.

Herzberg had come to Canada when he was 30, having left Germany during Hitler's early years in power. At first he worked as a research professor at the University of Saskatchewan, then went to the United States for a few years, and finally moved to Ottawa in 1948, where he joined the National Research Council. He has spent most of his time there since, continuing a program of active research, even after his official retirement. From 1973 to 1980 he served as chancellor of Carleton University.

Foster Hewitt

Born 1902, Toronto, Ont.

Sportscaster Foster Hewitt will forever be identified with the words "He shoots! He scores!" which he first uttered on radio in 1923, when covering one of the first hockey games ever broadcast.

The son of the sports editor of the *Toronto Daily Star*, Hewitt had joined the *Star's* radio station the previous year—almost as soon as it was formed. When covering those early hockey games, he didn't have a microphone; he gave his commentary into a telephone (and the operator kept cutting in to ask what number he wanted). The technology became more sophisticated over the years, but Hewitt never lost his gutsy enthusiasm. For half a century he covered a wide range of sports, moving on to television when games were televised. He also found time to write several books on hockey as well as an autobiography called *Foster Hewitt, His Own Story*.

Dan Hill

Born 1954, Toronto, Ont.

Singer, songwriter, and guitar player, Dan Hill is the son of black civil rights leader Daniel Hill, who was chairman of the Ontario Human Rights Commission 1972-73. He was brought up to believe in making an effort to achieve his goals, and he taught himself to play the guitar. His first LP, *Dan Hill*, was released when he was 21, and during the next couple of years he soared to fame, gaining an international hit with his single *Sometimes When We Touch*, which sold more than a million copies.

James Hillier

Born 1915, Brantford, Ont.

In the 1930s, while a lecturer at the University of Toronto, Dr. James Hillier invented the electron microscope. His associate in this invention was Albert Prebus, a research student from Alberta, and both were continuing work that had been started by another Alberta research student, C. E. Hall. Directing the team was E. F. Burton, head of the Department of Physics at the University of Toronto.

All these men, except Burton, later took senior research posts in the United States. While this was a loss for Canada, their achievement was international. All over the world, researchers now use the electron microscope, for it has immense magnifying powers. It allows biologists and medical scientists to see structures thousands of times smaller than those that can be seen with an ordinary microscope.

Clarence Hincks

Born 1885, St.Marys, Ont.
Died 1964

Dr. Hincks, founder of the Canadian Mental Health Association, spent his life working to improve the lot of the mentally sick. By the time he began his work, there had already been some much-needed reforms, especially in Toronto, thanks to Joseph Workman* and other pioneers; and in London, Ont., Richard Bucke had made the asylum more like a hospital and less like a prison. But Hincks suspected that this was not the case in many parts of Canada.

Starting in 1918, he visited nearly all of Canada's mental hospitals to see what conditions were like. Conditions were terrible. In some asylums he found patients kept in cages. He saw dirt and neglect. And he came across several "patients" who should never have been hospitalized—a child who had been rebellious at school; an old man whose relatives wanted his money.

Shocked by his findings, Hincks raised a vast sum of money through his association and brought in sweeping reforms. Today's caring and highly professional mental hospitals owe a lot to Clarence Hincks.

Francis Hincks

Born 1807, Ireland
Died 1885

Francis Hincks was a key figure in the Reform party (the forerunner of the Liberals). He founded the party's Upper Canadian newspaper, the *Examiner*. And he made the first approaches to La Fontaine,* the Reform leader in Lower Canada. This led to a lifelong friendship between La Fontaine and the Upper Canadian leader Robert Baldwin,* who together built a strong French-English Reform party in the Province of Canada.

Like other Reformers, Hincks wanted responsible government, and when La Fontaine and Baldwin achieved this in 1848 he was made a cabinet minister in their government. On their resignation in 1851, Hincks became head of the government, along with Augustin-Norbert Morin. Later, after Confederation, he was a cabinet minister in John A. Macdonald's* government.

In between, Hincks did a most extraordinary thing. This champion of democracy served for 14 years as a colonial governor, a one-man ruler, in Barbados and then in British Guiana.

E. Cora Hind
Born 1861, Toronto, Ont.
Died 1942
Forthright and fearlessly individualistic, E. Cora Hind was agricultural editor of the *Winnipeg Free Press* and was known throughout the world for her crop forecasts. Each year she toured the prairie wheat fields and then predicted how much wheat would be harvested. Her predictions were so accurate that grain dealers staked their fortunes on them.

Success had not come easily. Moving to Winnipeg soon after she left school, Cora Hind could not get a newspaper job—because she was a woman. So she taught herself to type and became the first typist in the West. Meanwhile, she wrote freelance articles and gradually gained a reputation as an expert on farming. When Dafoe* was made editor of the *Free Press* in 1901, he immediately took her on staff. Cora Hind was 40 at the time, but only halfway through her life. She spent the next 40 years championing the cause of Canadian farmers and writing articles for and about them.

Henry Youle Hind
Born 1823, England
Died 1908
The Toronto geology professor Henry Youle Hind made two expeditions to the West, in 1857 and 1858, and reported that there was a broad strip of fertile country along the North Saskatchewan River and its tributaries. His glowing reports of the Saskatchewan valley attracted great interest, especially when plans were set in motion to build the Canadian Pacific Railway. Sandford Fleming's* original survey for the railway routed the line through Hind's "fertile belt."

Hind also made geological surveys in Labrador, New Brunswick, and Nova Scotia, and he spent the last part of his life in the Maritimes. His expeditions inspired his brother, William Hind, to journey throughout Canada too. William Hind was an artist, and he painted the scenes he saw and the adventures he had on his travels. On one of his journeys, he accompanied the Overlanders to the Cariboo gold fields.

John Hirsch
Born 1930, Hungary
For more than 20 years John Hirsch has been a driving force in the development of Canadian theatre. He spent his early childhood in Hungary, where several of his relatives were connected with the theatre. But Hirsch is of Jewish origin, and many of his relations died during the Holocaust of the early 1940s when the Nazis killed 6 million Jews. His mother died in a concentration camp, his father was shot during a forced march, and his eight-year-old brother was suffocated in a gas chamber. Hirsch survived because a family maid took him to Budapest.

After the war, the Canadian Jewish Congress brought him to Canada and settled him with adopted parents in Winnipeg. At the time, there was no professional theatre company in Winnipeg, so Hirsch proceeded to create one, starting with a puppet theatre. By 1958 he had helped found the Manitoba Theatre Centre, a true community theatre. The first of its kind in Canada, the Manitoba Theatre Centre has since served as a model for other regional theatres. Meanwhile, Hirsch was busy directing and producing plays. Among his many activities, he was co-director (with Jean Gascon*) of the Stratford Festival 1967-69, and for four years was head of CBC TV drama. Since 1981, he has been artistic director of the Stratford Festival.

Abby Hoffman

Born 1947, Toronto, Ont.

Track star Abby Hoffman first made the headlines at the age of nine, when she played goalie with a Toronto boys' hockey team. There was a great uproar when it came to light that there was a girl on the team.

By the time she was 15 she was again in the news—as a middle-distance runner, and such a fast one that she was picked for the Canadian team in the 1962 Commonwealth Games. Over the years, she represented Canada at two Commonwealth Games, four Pan American Games, four Olympics, three World University Games, and the Maccabiah Games. In the course of all this, she won four international gold medals and was an eight-time winner of the Canadian 800-metre title. In 1981 Abby Hoffman was appointed director of Sport Canada.

Adelaide Hoodless

Born 1857, South Dumfries, Ont.
Died 1910

Adelaide Hoodless was the founder of the Women's Institute. She organized the first meeting in 1897 at Stoney Creek, Ont., and before long other branches were formed. Today, the organization has thousands of branches throughout the world.

Mrs. Hoodless started the WI so that women could be taught to care for children and run the home in a hygienic and efficient manner. In those days, many children died because their mothers didn't know the basic rules of hygiene. Mrs. Hoodless's own son had died from drinking infected milk, and it was his death which started her on her life's work. This work spread far beyond the Women's Institute.

Adelaide Hoodless helped promote the YWCA, started domestic science schools, and sponsored every cause that could help train women to be knowledgeable and careful homemakers.

Camillien Houde

Born 1889, Montreal, Que.
Died 1958

Camillien Houde, the controversial mayor of Montreal, was a larger-than-life figure—gigantically fat, spectacularly outspoken, and hugely popular, especially among the Montreal poor.

Born poor himself, Houde had started work as a butcher's boy, gradually making his way up through various jobs and businesses. He was first elected mayor in 1928 and held the position until 1954, with only a few periods out of office. One of these periods was during World War II, when he was interned for advising Montrealers not to register for military service as the federal government had demanded. On his release from prison in 1944, he was mobbed by cheering crowds. Although some Canadians were strongly anti-Houde, he was a folk hero among his own people. When he died, thousands turned out to mourn at his funeral.

James Houston

Born 1921, Toronto, Ont.

He is known by the Inuit as Saumik, the man who showed them how to adapt their carving skills to printmaking. And he is known by children everywhere as James Houston, author and illustrator of *The White Dawn* and other popular adventure books.

An artist by training, Houston first visited the Arctic on a holiday in 1948, and he couldn't believe what he saw—beautiful carving, ancient skills, a tradition of art that had barely been noticed in the rest of Canada. He returned to the Arctic as a government administrator, and during his years there he taught the Inuit the techniques of printmaking, which he had seen during a year he spent in Japan.

This had a double benefit. It gave some of the people of the North a new way of earning a living in the modern Canadian world that had overtaken their traditional world. And it gave people throughout the world the chance of enjoying Inuit art. Kenojuak,* Pitseolak,* and many other famous Inuit artists had their first inspiration from James Houston. Although he has now left the North, he continues to work for the Inuit in many different ways.

C. D. Howe

Born 1886, U.S.A.
Died 1960

He was nicknamed the Minister of Everything, and Clarence D. Howe did seem to be in charge of everything. Between his first election to Parliament in 1935 and his defeat in the 1957 elections, he held a succession of cabinet posts in the Liberal government—acting like a dictator, some people said.

C. D. Howe was at heart a businessman, not a parliamentarian. Trained as an engineer (and briefly an engineering lecturer at Dalhousie) he had moved west to the Lakehead in 1913 and made a fortune out of building grain elevators. As a cabinet minister, he continued his hard-nosed business methods, his aim being to get things done. He certainly succeeded. It was C. D. Howe who set up the airline that became Air Canada *and* the Trans-Canada pipeline. During World War II, he stirred the whole country into activity to help the war effort, organizing hundreds of private firms into making arms and supplies. And after the war, he reorganized this great industrial machine to fit it for peacetime purposes.

Gordie Howe

Born 1928, Floral, Sask.

Gordie Howe was still playing professional hockey when he was a grandfather. He was a superb player, one of the all-time greats. Howe had joined the Detroit Red Wings at the age of 18 in 1946, and between then and his first retirement in 1971 he played in 1,687 regular season games, scored 786 goals, won the Hart Trophy six times as most valuable player, and won the Art Ross Trophy six times as leading scorer.

Howe's 1971 retirement didn't last long. In 1973 he joined the Houston Aeros and after three years moved to the New England Whalers. The reason? He wanted to play with his sons. For several seasons, Gordon, Marty, and Mark Howe were all playing on the same team. Gordie Howe was over fifty before he hung up his skates.

Joseph Howe
Born 1804, Halifax, N.S.
Died 1873

Joseph Howe, the spirited journalist and politician, was the great champion of the people of Nova Scotia. He was their loyal family watchdog, snapping and growling (and sometimes getting kicked) as he protected their freedom and fought for their rights.

Howe was the editor of the *Novascotian*, and in 1835 he was sued for libel for writing an article criticizing the Halifax magistrates and police. Conducting his own defence in court, he won the case—a great victory for the freedom of the press. In 1848 he won another victory when Nova Scotia was given responsible government, which he had long been calling for. But James Uniacke,* not Howe, was made premier of the new government. Howe had made himself too unpopular with the authorities, though he served as second-in-command in the government.

Later, he vigorously opposed Confederation, for he thought it would be bad for Nova Scotia. He even went to Britain in 1868 to try and get the British North America Act repealed. However, he came to accept Confederation and served as a cabinet minister in the federal government. Just a few weeks before his death, he was appointed lieutenant governor of Nova Scotia.

David Hubel
Born 1926, Windsor, Ont.

In 1981 Dr. Hubel won the Nobel Prize in Medicine for his work in brain and eye research. Sharing the prize were Torsten Wiesel of Sweden and Roger Sperry of the United States.

A McGill graduate, David Hubel worked at the Montreal Neurological Institute early in the 1950s and then moved to the States. In 1959 he joined Harvard University Medical School, where he is a senior professor.

Monica Hughes
Born 1925, England

Monica Hughes has gained a large and enthusiastic audience among young people with such science-fiction best sellers as *Crisis on Conshelf Ten* and *Earthdark*. Before becoming a writer, she had a variety of jobs, from bank clerk in Rhodesia to lab technician at the National Research Council in Ottawa.

Having settled in Edmonton with her husband Glen and four children, Monica Hughes first began to work seriously as a writer in 1971. Since then, she has brought out well over a dozen books, including her recent works, *My Name Is Paula Popowich!* and *Space Trap*. Her books have been translated into several languages and are popular throughout the world.

Henry Hudson
Birth unknown
Died 1611

Hudson Bay and Hudson Strait are named after the navigator Henry Hudson, who in 1610 sailed through the strait and into the bay—the first explorer to do so. He was seeking the Northwest Passage to the Pacific, and he thought he had found it as he sailed south down the bay. This was surely a great ocean! Too late, Hudson realized his mistake. By then the ice had closed in to the north and he had to winter in the bay.

It was a long, hard winter. Food was scarce, many of the men fell sick and most fell out with Hudson. Though a great seaman, he was a poor leader with no understanding of how to keep a crew loyal. On the way home next year, the crew mutinied and cast Hudson and his son adrift in an open boat, together with the sick. The castaways were never seen again.

Sam Hughes

Born 1853, Darlington, Ont.
Died 1921

Sam Hughes first made his mark as an athlete, as a runner and lacrosse player. Later in life he served as an MP and was also an officer in the militia, taking part in the Boer War in Africa. Partly because of his war service, Hughes came to be regarded as an authority on military matters, and in 1911 Robert Borden* appointed him to the cabinet as minister of militia and defence.

This was unfortunate, since Hughes was a stubborn, disorganized man with his feet firmly planted in the nineteenth century; and he was still in office when World War I broke out. He did not gain the affection of the troops as he sent them hither and yon, often without arranging accommodation or notifying the British command that they were coming. Nor did he gain the affection of the officers, who found themselves being outranked by Hughes's protégés.

There was a sigh of relief all round when in 1916 Borden asked Hughes to resign from the cabinet. But Hughes stayed on in the militia, and when he died he was Lieutenant General Sir Samuel Hughes.

Bobby Hull

Born 1939, Pointe Anne, Ont.

One of modern hockey's greatest stars, Bobby Hull joined the Chicago Black Hawks in 1957, and during the next 15 years he won just about every available award, including the Lady Byng Trophy for good sportsmanship combined with ability. A fast skater and a superb stick-handler, he was especially famed for his booming slap-shot.

Having starred so long with the Hawks, Hull caused a sensation when he left them and the National Hockey League in 1972, and signed a $1-million contract with the Winnipeg Jets of the newly formed World Hockey Association. But this new league disbanded after a few years and the Jets became part of an enlarged and reorganized NHL. So Hull ended his playing career in the league he had first joined. During his career, Hull scored more than 900 goals.

Tommy Hunter

Born 1937, London, Ont.

Known as "Canada's country gentleman," Tommy Hunter has won several Juno Awards as best male country singer, and his television show has won the Big Country Award.

He first became keen on country music as a small boy, when the Grand Ole Opry show visited London. During his early teens he played the guitar every possible moment . . . and dreamed of country and western. By the time he was 16 he was performing on Hamilton radio, and a few years later he joined the CBC as a rhythm guitarist. For many years now he has hosted *The Tommy Hunter Show*, one of the most popular variety shows on Canadian television. "Mary in the Morning" and "Family Tree" are two of his big hits.

Walter Huston

Born 1884, Toronto, Ont.
Died 1950

Walter Huston, one of the greatest movie stars of his day, was a graduate in engineering, and at the beginning of his career he worked as an engineer whenever he couldn't get acting jobs. But by the 1920s he was starring on Broadway in New York, and this led to stardom in Hollywood. In 1948 he won an Oscar for his performance in *The Treasure of the Sierra Madre*.

Another of the many Canadians who made it in Hollywood was Walter Pidgeon (born 1897, Saint John, N.B.). He made his name as the handsome, honest hero in such classics as *Mrs. Miniver*. More recently, he starred with Barbra Streisand, playing an elderly senator in *Funny Girl*.

Pierre Le Moyne d'Iberville

Born 1661, Montreal, Que.
Died 1706

Iberville was one of New France's greatest heroes. Part soldier, part sailor, part explorer, and part pirate, he raided British ships, burned British settlements, and in 1696 he sacked St.John's, Nfld. Wherever Iberville sailed, France ruled the waves. Striking swiftly and suddenly, he spread terror all along the coast.

Iberville's most celebrated victory was in Hudson Strait. There, in his lone ship *Pélican*, he outfought three British warships and went on to capture the British forts on Hudson Bay. His most renowned discovery was the Mississippi delta. La Salle* had not been able to find the river when approaching it by sea. Iberville did find it.

Typically, Iberville died on campaign. He was struck down with fever in the West Indies, having just captured the British island of Nevis.

Harold Adams Innis

Born 1894, Otterville, Ont.
Died 1952

The economic historian Harold Adams Innis was one of Canada's intellectual giants. He produced nine volumes of history, covering a phenomenally wide scope, and is known especially for his "staple theory" of Canadian history. This theory emphasized the great importance of the trade in staples —fish, fur, lumber—in shaping the way Canada developed.

An academic to the core, Innis spent most of his life at the University of Toronto, rising from lecturer to dean of the School of Graduate Studies. He was a powerful influence on younger historians, especially those who knew him and worked with him. Donald Creighton* in Toronto and A. R. M. Lower (who taught in Winnipeg and then at Queen's in Kingston) both became leading historians and men of great influence themselves. Innis was also an influence on Marshall McLuhan,* for in his later years he turned to the study of mass communications, a subject popularized by McLuhan in the 1960s.

May Irwin
Born 1862, Whitby, Ont.
Died 1938

In 1896, in the very earliest days of film, May Irwin shocked North America with her one-minute movie *The Kiss*. It was the first film to show a couple kissing—and in close-up too. May Irwin didn't care. The daughter of an Ontario logger, she was a plump and cheery variety artist who had been performing since she was a child.

Her mother had taken her to the United States at the age of 11, seeking fame and fortune for her in the theatre. May Irwin achieved both in her teens, drawing an enormous salary as New York's favourite ragtime singer-comedienne. She was the toast of Broadway during the Gay Nineties. She bought a summer cottage in the Thousand Islands and filled it with gaiety and laughter, with six grand pianos, and with a crowd of theatrical friends. Still cheerful in old age, she insisted on being buried in a red satin dress when she died.

A. Y. Jackson
Born 1882, Montreal, Que.
Died 1974

Group of Seven artist A. Y. Jackson lived to the age of 92. He was the grand old man of Canadian painting. He had been a grand young man too. When he was 23, he and his brother worked their way to Europe on a cattle boat—just for a brief visit so that they could see something of the world. Two years later, Jackson returned to Europe to study painting in Paris. Living on a shoestring, he mingled with other painters, sketched to his heart's content, and visited every gallery he could get to.

Life seemed a bit dull when Jackson settled back in Montreal a few years later. But his work soon attracted attention, and in 1913 he was invited to join the group of Toronto artists who were trying a new style of landscape painting. Jackson shared a studio in Toronto with Tom Thomson* for a couple of months, and both men had a stimulating effect on each other's work. Jackson's paintings had a prominent place when, in 1920, he and his fellow artists formally called themselves the Group of Seven and held their first exhibition. For the rest of his life, Jackson continued to paint, producing many pictures.

Russ Jackson

Born 1936, Hamilton, Ont.

Hailed as the greatest Canadian-born quarterback in the history of the CFL, Russ Jackson was an outstanding athlete from his early years. At high school in Hamilton he won all-star honours in football, baseball, and basketball. And at McMaster University he not only played with the Varsity Marauders but won the scoring title one year. He also graduated with honours, receiving the Governor General's Medal for Excellence.

Jackson then joined the Ottawa Rough Riders, and by the end of his first season he was recognized as the team's number-one quarterback. In the course of 12 years, he helped Ottawa win three Grey Cup victories. In 1969 he was awarded the Lou Marsh Trophy as Canada's athlete of the year.

Ferguson Jenkins

Born 1943, Chatham,Ont.

In the 1982 season, Fergie Jenkins became the seventh pitcher in the history of major league baseball to strike out 3,000 batters.

Ferguson Jenkins grew up in Chatham, and it was while playing there that he was noticed by a big-league scout, who liked the young pitcher but told him he wasn't muscular enough to succeed in the majors. So Jenkins spent that winter chopping wood to increase his upper-body size and to strengthen his pitching power. His dedication paid off and he was signed on by Philadelphia. He spent three years in the Phillies' farm system before playing in the big leagues. Since then, he has proved to be the greatest Canadian ever to play professional baseball and has gained particular success as a member of the Chicago Cubs. In 1974 he was awarded the Lou Marsh Trophy as Canada's outstanding athlete of the year.

C. W. Jefferys

Born 1869, England
Died 1951

The historical artist C. W. Jefferys is known particularly for his three-volume *Picture Gallery of Canadian History*, which contains hundreds of carefully researched pictures: battles and explorations, military uniforms and household implements, and even a drawing of Montcalm's* skull.

Jefferys was brought to Canada as a child, and he first earned money for his drawings during his schooldays in Toronto. He used to illustrate his classmates' schoolbooks, charging one cent for illustrating Canadian history, two cents for English history, and five cents for Algebra (which he hated). As an adult, Jefferys worked as a newspaper illustrator and for many years taught art at the University of Toronto. Some of his pictures have been reproduced in this book.

Pauline Jewett

Born 1922, St.Catharines, Ont.

As president of Simon Fraser University 1974-78, Pauline Jewett was the first woman in Canada to head a completely co-educational university. She had previously taught at Carleton and had also served as a Liberal MP. After leaving Simon Fraser, she again ran for Parliament, though not as a Liberal. She was elected as the NDP member for New Westminster-Coquitlam. In 1983 she campaigned vigorously to prevent the U.S. cruise missile from being tested in Canada. She is one of the most highly regarded women MPs in the history of our Parliament.

Norman Jewison

Born 1926, Toronto, Ont.

Jesus Christ Superstar and *Fiddler on the Roof* are two of the films made by Norman Jewison, who started his career in broadcasting. He worked as a scriptwriter and actor with the BBC in England and from 1952 to 1958 was a director for CBC TV. He then moved to the United States, where his television shows attracted the attention of Universal Studios and other big movie companies, who offered him contracts to direct films. His 1967 film *In the Heat of the Night* won several Academy Awards. Other awards followed, establishing him as Jewison Superstar, one of the many Canadians who have made it internationally.

Albert Johnson

Origins unknown

Killed 1932

He was known as the Mad Trapper of Rat River, though he probably wasn't mad. His name may not even have been Albert Johnson. Nobody knows who he was or where he came from. What is known is that he went trapping in the far North during the winter of 1931-32. And that he shot and wounded a Mountie who came to his lonely cabin to inquire about his activities.

So began one of the biggest man hunts in Canadian history. Mounties, Indians, trappers, all were after the dangerous "maniac," searching with dog teams and bush planes in temperatures of 40° below zero. For 48 days the Mad Trapper eluded his pursuers, killing one Mountie and wounding yet another before he was finally gunned down on the frozen ice of Eagle River in the Yukon. That was the end of the Mad Trapper, but it wasn't the end of the mystery. Who was this man? And was he a villain or a victim? People are still wondering to this day.

Raoul Jobin

Born 1906, Quebec, Que.

Died 1974

Raoul Jobin was hailed as the greatest French tenor of his time. The son of a Quebec tavern keeper, he completed his musical education in France, where he became the star of the Paris Opera. Although spending much of his life in France, Jobin sang with New York's Metropolitan Opera during the 1940s, and in the 1960s he was director of Quebec's Conservatory of Music.

Edward Johnson

Born 1878, Guelph, Ont.

Died 1959

One of opera's all-time greats, the tenor Edward Johnson called himself Edoardo Di Giovanni when he launched his career in Italy. This was partly because he had met and married the daughter of a Portuguese viscount. She thought Giovanni sounded more operatic than Johnson.

After his wife's death in 1919, Johnson left Europe and his exotic name behind and eventually settled in New York, where he sang with the Metropolitan Opera. As one of the Met's most admired artists, he was appointed general manager in 1935, a position he held for 15 years. Meanwhile, he served as chairman of the board of the Royal Conservatory of Music in Toronto. He died in Guelph, the city where he had first sung in public as a choir boy.

Pauline Johnson
Born 1862, Six Nations Reserve, Ont.
Died 1913

The poet Pauline Johnson was one of the great attractions of the 1890s and early 1900s as she toured North America and Great Britain, giving dramatic recitals of her poems. She was often described as an Indian princess, for although her mother was English, her father was a Mohawk chief. His house near Brantford, Ont., was called Chiefswood, and there Pauline Johnson grew up, gaining a pride in her Indian heritage from her father and a love of literature from her mother.

She started writing poetry young, but could not make a living from it. Her best-known poem, "The Song My Paddle Sings," brought in only a few dollars. But once she began to recite her poems on stage she was a sell-out success, for she was as much actress as poet, playing brilliantly on the emotions of her audience.

Bill Johnston
Born 1782, Trois Rivières, Que.
Died 1870

The Pirate of the St.Lawrence—that's what people called William Johnston. During the War of 1812 he declared himself pro-American, and from then on he burned Canadian farms, hijacked Canadian ships, looted and robbed . . . all in the name of loyalty to the United States. In the process, he amassed a rich pile of booty.

Johnston had a hideout in the Thousand Islands, and there he held sway with his ruffianly band of followers. For about 30 years he spread terror along the St.Lawrence. He was particularly active during the Rebellion of 1837, when he looted and burned the steamboat *Sir Robert Peel*. Nowadays, Johnston is considered rather glamorous. But Canadians who encountered him viewed him more clearly—as a greedy and cruel opportunist.

Lynn Johnston
Born 1947, Collingwood, Ont.

Lynn Johnston's comic strip *For Better or for Worse* is printed regularly in more than 250 newspapers, not only in Canada and the United States, but also in Europe, Australia, and South Africa. The strip is based mainly on her own family: her dentist husband and two children. But the setting is different. Unlike Elly Patterson in the cartoons, Lynn Johnston lives in a small mining community—Lynn Lake in northern Manitoba.

She grew up in Vancouver and attended art school there, later moving to Ontario where she had a job as a commercial artist. Shortly before her son Aaron was born, she drew a series of cartoons, which she published in 1973 as a book. It sold so well that she brought out more books and was then offered a 10-year contract by Universal Press to draw a family comic strip for the newspapers. The first of these strips appeared in 1979, and Lynn Johnston hasn't looked back since.

Louis Jolliet
Born 1645, Quebec, Que.
Died 1700

Louis Jolliet was a trader-explorer who was sent by Intendant Jean Talon* to look for "the great river they call the Mississippi" and travel down it until he found the China Sea. French missionaries had heard of the river from the Indians, and Talon hoped it would provide a water route to the West Coast, and thus a trade route to Asia.

Jolliet reached the Mississippi in 1673, accompanied by the missionary Jacques Marquette and five others. They followed the river far into present-day Arkansas, but turned back when they realized it was leading them to the Gulf of Mexico.

Pauline Julien

Born 1928, Trois Rivières, Que.

Singer and songwriter Pauline Julien began her career as an actress in France, where she had gone to study dramatic arts. But she gained fame as a Quebec singer, one of French Canada's most celebrated performers. At one time, she sang only Quebec songs, for she believed passionately in Quebec nationalism. She was so well known as a separatist that she was arrested during the October Crisis of 1970 (see Laporte*). In recent years, she has been a strong supporter of the women's movement.

Juliette

Born 1927, St.Vital, Man.

The popular singer was born Juliette Sysak, the daughter of Polish-Ukrainian Canadians. On her marriage, she became Juliette Cavazzi. But to many Canadians she was simply Juliette, the familiarly friendly figure who for many years performed regularly on radio and TV.

Juliette began her career when she was 13, singing with the orchestra at the Vancouver Hotel in British Columbia, and she first sang on CBC radio in Vancouver when she was 15. Moving to Toronto, she embarked on her successful career, often hosting her own shows on the CBC.

Conrad Kain

Born 1883, Austria
Died 1934

Conrad Kain was one of the most renowned mountaineers who ever risked his life among Canada's snow-capped ranges. Born of a poor Austrian family, he trained himself as a mountain guide in the Alps, moving to Canada in 1909 to become the Alpine Club of Canada's first official guide.

Over the next 25 years, Kain's skill and ice-cold courage became famed throughout the world as he conquered peak after peak. In 1913 he was the first to lead a party to the top of Mount Robson, the highest peak in the Rockies, and the following year he was the first up Mount Farnham, the highest peak in the Purcells. He achieved more Canadian first ascents than any climber before him. Kain made first ascents in other countries too and continued his climbing until one year before his death.

Claude Jutra

Born 1930, Montreal, Que.

Film director Claude Jutra started his career in the sciences rather than the arts, graduating in medicine from the University of Montreal. But instead of becoming a doctor, he became a student actor at the Théâtre du Nouveau Monde. In 1949 he made the film *Mouvement Perpetuel*. It won a Canadian Film Award in the amateur category and then carried off a prize at the Cannes Film Festival in France.

In 1955 Jutra joined the National Film Board, where he gained increasing acclaim for his films. One of his most celebrated productions, *Mon Oncle Antoine*, won eight Etrogs at the 1971 Canadian Film Awards, as well as being judged best picture at the Chicago Film Festival. Jutra has worked in television as well as film, and in English as well as French.

Karen Kain

Born 1951, Hamilton, Ont.

Karen Kain enrolled with the National Ballet School when she was 11 and in due course joined the National Ballet of Canada. By her second season with the ballet she had been promoted to a principal dancer and was performing the role of the Swan Queen in *Swan Lake*. A few years later, in 1973, the prima ballerina had a phenomenal success at the International Ballet Competition in Moscow, winning a silver medal as soloist, as well as gaining first prize in the *pas de deux* in partnership with Frank Augustyn (born 1953, Hamilton, Ont.). Both Kain and Augustyn continue to rank among the world's very finest dancers.

Paul Kane

Born 1810, Ireland

Died 1871

Many of the early pictures of the Indian people and their culture are the work of the artist Paul Kane. Brought to Canada as a child, he grew up in Toronto, where he had his first training as a painter.

In the 1840s he set out for the West with sketchbooks and notebooks and pencils and paints, intent on recording the Indian culture while it could still be seen in its pure state. He visited the Great Lakes area, the prairies, and the West Coast, and in 1859 published the illustrated story of his travels, *Wanderings of an Artist Among the Indians of North America*. Thanks to Paul Kane, we have a vivid record of North American civilization before it was deeply affected by the Europeans.

Yousuf Karsh

Born 1908, Armenia

Portrait photographer Yousuf Karsh came to Canada with his uncle at the age of 15. After schooling in Sherbrooke, Que., and a photographic apprenticeship in Boston, Mass., he opened his own studio in Ottawa in 1932. There he gradually built up a reputation for his expressive photographic portraits, and in 1941 he made a portrait of Winston Churchill which brought him wide fame.

Since then, Karsh has photographed many of the world's leading men and women, including many Canadians. His photographs are on display in major galleries and art museums, and they may also be seen in such books as *Karsh Canadians*.

Thomas Keefer

Born 1821, Thorold, Ont.
Died 1915

During the 94 years of Thomas Keefer's life, Canada moved into the industrial age, not only with factories but with a great surge of engineering projects: canals, railways, bridges, waterworks. Thomas Keefer was a central figure in this activity.

His father had been a partner in William Merritt's* Welland Canal Company, and one of Keefer's first engineering jobs was to work on the enlargement of the canal. He moved on to be chief engineer of the Ottawa River Works, the Montreal Harbour Commission, and several railway projects. He constructed a public water system for Montreal, complete with reservoirs, pumping stations, and underground pipes, and then planned similar systems for other cities. He was considered one of the leading hydraulic engineers in all North America. Not least of his achievements were two books, one on the importance of railways and one on canals. Both had great influence on the way Canada was developed.

His half-brother Samuel Keefer was also a noted engineer, and he built some of Canada's earliest suspension bridges.

Frances Oldham Kelsey

Born 1914, Cobble Hill, B.C.

Dr. Frances Kelsey is the thalidomide heroine, the woman who would not allow the drug to be used in the United States. Thalidomide was thought to be a safe sleeping pill; and in many parts of the world, including Canada, pregnant women took it during the late 1950s, unaware of the harm they were causing their unborn babies.

Unfortunately, Dr. Kelsey was not working in Canada at the time. Having graduated from McGill, she had continued her studies in Chicago, where she met and married a university professor. When he took a job in Washington, so did she—with the Food and Drug Administration. And one of her first tasks was to test thalidomide and clear it for general use in the United States. But she refused to clear it. She had doubts about it.

She was accused of being absurdly fussy, but she stuck to her guns. She was still doing so when a German scientist proved a connection between thalidomide and the alarming number of handicapped children being born.

Henry Kelsey
Born c.1667, England
Died 1724

Henry Kelsey, a young HBC employee, was sent inland from York Factory, Hudson Bay, in 1690 to make contact with the "remoter Indians" and get them to come to the bay to trade. He returned in the summer of 1692, having walked all the way to the Saskatchewan River and back. He was the first European to set foot on the prairies and the first to see buffalo and grizzly bears.

Kelsey spent almost 40 years working for the Hudson's Bay Company and ended up as overseas governor. Even in his last years he was still exploring, this time by sea in search of the long-sought Northwest Passage.

John J. Kelso
Born 1864, Ireland
Died 1935

The Toronto Children's Aid Society was formed in 1891 mainly through the efforts of J. J. Kelso, the son of Irish immigrants. Kelso was a reporter for the *Globe*, well known for the stories he wrote about the Toronto poor. The state of the children especially upset him. There were so many of them on the streets—ragged, barefoot waifs (some no more than three years old) who sold newspapers to make a few cents, or begged or pilfered. If they were caught stealing, they were sent to an adult prison, along with hardened criminals.

Kelso helped get the laws changed so that juvenile offenders were given suitable treatment. And he set up a shelter for neglected children and then found them foster homes or arranged for their adoption. In many ways, he laid the basis of the child welfare programs we have today.

Betty Kennedy
Born 1926, Ottawa, Ont.

As host of *The Betty Kennedy Show*, the popular radio program of views and interviews, and as a regular panelist on the TV show *Front Page Challenge*, Betty Kennedy has long been one of Canada's best-known broadcasters and interviewers. She has also been very active in community affairs as a company director and busy committee woman. And she is a best-selling author, known especially for her book *Gerhard* about her first husband and his long fight against cancer.

The mother of four children, she herself grew up with working parents. Her mother was employed at Bell Telephone, while her father ran the narcotics squad as an RCMP sergeant. Encouraged by them, she applied for her first job when she was 16. She began her long-standing association with CFRB radio, Toronto, in 1959.

Kenojuak

Born 1927, Ikirisaq, N.W.T.

One of Canada's most famous prints is *Enchanted Owl*, which Inuit artist Kenojuak Ashevak made from a stonecut in 1960. This print has been reproduced countless times and was used on a commemorative stamp in 1970.

Kenojuak spent her early years in the traditional manner, moving from camp to camp with her family and living off the land. She first began to make drawings and soapstone carvings in the late 1950s, when she and her husband Johnniebo were encouraged by James Houston* to take up art. Since then, her work has brought her a great international reputation. She is the first of Canada's Native people to be awarded the country's highest honour—Companion of the Order of Canada.

David Kirke

Born c.1597, France
Died 1654

The adventurer David Kirke was born in Dieppe (when that part of France belonged to England). So the French thought him a traitor as well as an enemy when he sailed up the St. Lawrence and tried to capture Canada for Britain. In 1629 he did, in effect, capture Canada. He blockaded Quebec, forced its surrender, and took Champlain* and most of the inhabitants prisoner. As this happened two months after France and England had made peace, Quebec was returned to the French. But the British were pleased with Kirke. They gave him a knighthood and also gave him Newfoundland, making him governor of the island.

Sharif Khan

Born 1945, Pakistan

Sharif Khan, king of squash, settled in Great Britain with his family as a teenager and later moved to Toronto. He was trained by his father, Hashim Khan, who stunned the squash world in the 1950s by winning six British Opens. Both father and son use "the Khan style," a brilliant combination of volleys and delayed wrist shots. Sharif has been world squash champion 12 times and has won every major title and tournament in North America

George Knudson

Born 1937, Winnipeg, Man.

George Knudson, the champion golfer, started his career when he was 10 by offering to pick up balls on the range at Winnipeg's St.Charles Country Club. Before long he was a caddy, and when he was 12 he decided to play the game himself. Over the years he has won a long string of championships, including the World Cup in 1968 (in partnership with Al Balding of Toronto) and the Peter Jackson Cup in 1976.

In recent years, another Manitoban has hit the headlines in professional golf, Dan Halldorson. In 1982 Halldorson became the first Canadian to win the World Cup since the Knudson-Balding victory. He was named Canada's outstanding professional golfer in both 1981 and 1982.

The year 1983 saw the emergence of Jim Nelford of Burnaby, B.C., as Canada's leading golfer on the world scene.

Moe Koffman
Born 1928, Toronto, Ont.
One of Canada's leading jazz musicians, Moe Koffman plays the flute, the clarinet, the saxophone, and also the violin, which he started to learn when he was nine. He composes music as well as playing it, performs as a soloist as well as with his own band, and plays every type of piece, from bebop to popular arrangements of Bach and Mozart.

Koffman began his career when he was a teenager, playing with dance bands in Ontario, and then spent some time in the U.S., performing in big bands under such greats as Jimmy Dorsey. He first gained wide recognition in 1958 with his "Swinging Shepherd Blues," which was an international hit.

Another leading jazz musician is Phil Nimmons (born 1923, Kamloops, B.C.), a clarinetist, composer, and bandleader.

Diane Jones Konihowski
Born 1951, Vancouver, B.C.
At the 1978 Commonwealth Games in Edmonton, the athlete chosen to carry the ceremonial baton into the stadium—and present it to the Queen—was Diane Jones Konihowski. She had won the gold medal in the pentathlon at the 1975 Pan American Games. She proceeded to win another gold at the games in Edmonton, and another at the next Pan American Games the following year.

Diane Jones had first competed internationally in track-and-field at junior meets more than ten years earlier. She won her first big medal, a bronze, at the World University Games in Moscow in 1973. In 1977 she married a fellow athlete, John Konihowski.

Gordon Korman
Born 1963, Montreal, Que.

Gordon Korman was 13 when he published his first book, *This Can't Be Happening at Macdonald Hall!* He wrote the story as a school assignment for his Grade 7 English teacher. Since then, he has written several more best sellers about the irrepressible Bruno and Boots and their fellow students at Macdonald Hall. Korman himself went to German Mills Public School in Thornhill, Ont., and then to Thornlea Secondary School in North York. After leaving school, he enrolled at New York University to study film and dramatic writing.

Cornelius Krieghoff
Born 1815, Holland
Died 1872
Today, a painting by Krieghoff can be worth $500,000 or more. When he lived in Montreal in the 1840s, he was lucky to get $5. He sold his pictures from door to door, and with so little success that he sometimes had to support himself by working as a house painter.

Krieghoff had come to Canada via the United States, where he met and married a French Canadian girl; and French Canadian scenes became his speciality. He liked to paint the daily life of Quebec: habitants at work and at play, village scenes and snow scenes. Early in the 1850s his pictures attracted the attention of an auctioneer, who took him to Quebec City and publicized his work. From then on Krieghoff did very well, painting portraits as well as Quebec scenes, and gaining wide recognition for his work.

William Kurelek
Born 1927, Whitford, Alta.
Died 1977

The son of Ukrainian homesteaders, the artist William Kurelek grew up on the prairies during the harsh years of the Great Depression. Many of his paintings are of prairie scenes: huge skies, huge fields, and small figures at work or play. There is also a religious element in much of his work. A convert to Roman Catholicism, Kurelek had a missionary zeal, which he expressed in paint, often portraying scenes from the Bible in Canadian settings.

Kurelek passed his childhood on small farms in Alberta and Manitoba, and later studied art in Toronto, Mexico, and England. He swept to fame almost overnight in 1961, when a celebrated art collector singled out one of his pictures at a Toronto exhibition. Kurelek's work is the subject of several books, among them *A Prairie Boy's Winter* and *Kurelek's Vision of Canada.*

François-Xavier-Antoine Labelle
Born 1833, Ste. Rose de Laval, Que.
Died 1891

Abbé Labelle was known in Quebec as "the king of the north" and "the apostle of colonization." A priest at St. Jerome in the Laurentians, Labelle was very concerned at the number of French Canadians who were emigrating to the United States because they could not make a living at home. His answer to the problem was to open up new areas for farming. So he set to work to get this done, enlisting the support of a wide range of people.

Largely through Labelle's efforts, the Canadian Pacific Railway company built the Quebec Colonization Road in 1883, which opened up the Gatineau area. A few years later, an extension was built to Lake Timiskaming. Then, in 1888, Labelle was appointed Quebec's deputy minister of colonization. In all, he founded about sixty settlements, giving many Quebeckers the chance to have their own farms and make an honourable living, just as settlers were doing at that time on the western prairies.

Gilbert LaBine
Born 1890, Westmeath, Ont.
Died 1977

Canada's nuclear industry owes its origins to Gilbert LaBine, the determined prospector who spent years searching the North for minerals. In 1929, when flying along the shores of Great Bear Lake with bush pilot Punch Dickins,* LaBine saw below him the type of rock that he knew contained cobalt deposits. Returning to the area the following year, he found rich veins of copper and silver. He also found pitchblende, one of the world's scarcest ores and the source of radium and uranium. At the time, the only big source of supply was in Africa.

Gilbert LaBine and his brother Charles decided to mine the pitchblende and take it out of the North, though it seemed an impossible project. But by 1936 they had moved quantities of ore to their refinery at Port Hope, Ont., and had produced their first few grams of radium. One of the results of their work was to spur on medical research. Because radium was readily available, Canadian scientists were able to develop the cobalt "bomb" for treating cancer.

Albert Lacombe

Born 1827, St.Sulpice, Que.
Died 1916

The missionary priest Father Lacombe spent most of his life in the West, first in the Red River region and later on the western prairies, where he founded the mission of St. Albert. Greatly admired by the Métis and Indians, he was one of the strongest influences on the prairies during the years when treaties were signed and the CPR was built and the life of the Plains Indians changed forever.

Although preaching peace, Lacombe was at times caught up in war. One night in 1865, the Blackfoot camp he was visiting was ambushed by a band of Cree. When Lacombe tried to stop the fighting, he was very nearly killed by the attackers, who didn't recognize him in the dark. He was saved by Crowfoot,* the young Blackfoot chief, who came charging to the rescue, scattering the Crees.

This was the beginning of a long-standing friendship between Lacombe and Crowfoot. In the years that followed, the two men often consulted together in their efforts to bring peace to the prairies.

Rodolphe Laflamme

Born 1827, Montreal, Que.
Died 1893

Rodolphe Laflamme was a lawyer and journalist who was passionately for Quebec and passionately against the Roman Catholic church. In 1844 he and other free-thinkers formed the Institut Canadien, a society for the liberal-minded. (The young Wilfrid Laurier* was a member.)

The institute had a library containing books banned by the church, and soon it too was banned. Bishop Bourget of Montreal told priests to deny the Sacrament to anyone who remained a member. As a result, a certain Joseph Guibord* was not only refused the last rites when he was dying, but his body was refused burial in a Catholic cemetery. Laflamme acted as lawyer to Guibord's corpse, fought the church, and won his case. Later in life, he won a seat in Parliament and served as a Liberal cabinet minister.

Guy Lafleur

Born 1951, Thurso, Que.

Hockey star Guy Lafleur grew up on skates. From the age of seven he often went to bed wearing his equipment, so that he would be ready to play in the morning. He practised every moment he could: before school, at noon, after school. By the age of 10 he was already a star, having won the scoring championship at the peewee tournament in Quebec City.

Lafleur moved up to Junior A when he was 14 and a few years later was the first draft choice of the Montreal Canadiens. He has played for the Canadiens since 1971, their colourful right-winger and one of their leading scorers. In 1977 he was awarded the Lou Marsh Trophy as Canada's outstanding athlete of the year.

Louis-Hippolyte La Fontaine
Born 1807, Boucherville, Que.
Died 1864

The great Reform leader La Fontaine was the first person to be premier of the Province of Canada under a system of responsible government. This was in 1848-51, when with Robert Baldwin* he led the government which was called the Great Ministry.

The two Reformers had made their first steps towards responsible government in 1842, when Sir Charles Bagot was Governor General. But Bagot was followed by Sir Charles Metcalfe, who felt that the Governor General should be the chief ruler. Only when he left and Lord Elgin* took over did La Fontaine and Baldwin establish that the governing should be done by the leaders of the largest party elected to the assembly.

A very determined man, La Fontaine looked like Napoleon; he combed his hair the same way and often stood the same way, with his hand tucked into his jacket. (He caused a flurry when he visited France some years after Napoleon's death.) But, unlike Napoleon, La Fontaine worked ardently for political justice: to get Canadians a fair system of government and to get French Canadians a fair share in the government.

(For the first responsible government in British North America, see J. B. Uniacke.*)

Newsy Lalonde
Born 1888, Cornwall, Ont.
Died 1970

Newsy Lalonde was the star player on the original Montreal Canadiens hockey team. He was a superstar long before the term was invented—very rough, very tough, and a very good player. In one season alone, he scored 38 goals in 11 games.

Lalonde played for the Canadiens from 1910 to 1922, and during this time he also made a name as a lacrosse player. He was elected to the Lacrosse Hall of Fame as well as the Hockey Hall of Fame, and in the Canadian Press poll of 1950 was voted outstanding field lacrosse player of the half-century. His real name was Edouard Lalonde, but he was nicknamed Newsy because he once had a job in a newsprint plant.

Lord Lansdowne
Born 1845, England
Died 1927

The British politician Lord Lansdowne was Governor General of Canada in the 1880s. He was one of the most capable men to hold this position. On leaving Canada, Lord Lansdowne was sent to India to be Queen Victoria's representative there. This much-coveted appointment was awarded to a few other Governors General too. Lords Dufferin,* Minto,* and Willingdon* all later served as Viceroy of India.

Pierre Laporte
Born 1921, Montreal, Que.
Murdered 1970

On October 10, 1970, the Quebec minister of labour, Pierre Laporte, was kidnapped by the FLQ, a group of extremists who used terrorist tactics in their efforts to gain independence for Quebec. This was the second FLQ kidnapping in what is called the October Crisis. A few days earlier James Cross, the British trade commissioner, had been kidnapped. Cross was eventually released unharmed, but Laporte did not survive. He was strangled, and his body was dumped in the trunk of a car. His murderers were later captured and sentenced to prison terms.

Only a handful of Quebeckers had anything to do with Laporte's murder, but hundreds were rounded up and imprisoned during the crisis. All sorts of people who had no thought of violence found themselves behind bars, just because they were known to be separatists. There have been other occasions in recent times when innocent people have suffered as the result of a crisis situation (see Takashima*).

Laporte's murder caused great shock, for in all Canada's history, political assassinations have been very rare.

Henry Larsen
Born 1899, Norway
Died 1964

Henry Larsen was the first person to sail through the Northwest Passage both ways and the first to attempt the passage since Roald Amundsen had successfully "conquered" it in his epic voyage of 1903-06. Like Amundsen, Larsen was a Norwegian seaman with a passion for Arctic exploration; but unlike Amundsen, he became a Canadian. Joining the RCMP in 1928, he was put in charge of the patrol ship *St.Roch*, and for 12 years he patrolled the Arctic waters.

During World War II he was ordered to take the *St.Roch* through the Northwest Passage. Here at last was the challenge he had been hoping for. Larsen did the journey from the Pacific to the Atlantic during 1940-42 and made the return journey in one single season in 1944.

Robert Cavelier de La Salle
Born 1643, France
Murdered 1687

In 1682, nine years after Jolliet* discovered the Mississippi, La Salle followed the river to its mouth and explored its delta. There he dressed up in scarlet and gold, and formally claimed the whole region for France, naming it Louisiana.

La Salle was an ambitious fur-trading explorer who had a large estate near Montreal and owned several trading posts, including Fort Frontenac (Kingston) on Lake Ontario. But he wanted more. After his journey down the Mississippi, he drew a false map of the river and told the French authorities that it led to the rich mines of New Mexico. As a result, he was provided with several ships and a large force of men, and sent to colonize the territory.

But La Salle was quarrelsome as well as ambitious, too high-handed to be a good leader. And he couldn't find the river when he approached it by sea. The "discoverer" of the Mississippi delta had now lost it again! The whole expedition was a failure, and after a series of muddles and disasters La Salle was gunned down by his own men.

Bora Laskin

Born 1912, Fort William, Ont.

As chief justice of the Supreme Court of Canada, Bora Laskin had to make a ruling in 1981 on how Canada's constitution, the British North America Act, could be brought home. The BNA Act was an act of the British parliament which could only be changed with the consent of that parliament. Prime Minister Trudeau* had decided that this situation had to end, and he had tackled the difficult task of working out a satisfactory procedure by which the Canadian parliament, the provinces, and the Canadian people could amend the constitution. The Supreme Court studied his proposals for six months and then brought down a judgement which allowed the constitution to be "patriated."

Bora Laskin is an expert on constitutional law and was professor of law at the University of Toronto. First appointed to the Supreme Court in 1970, he became chief justice in 1973.

Margaret Laurence

Born 1926, Neepawa, Man.

Margaret Laurence is one of the great figures of Canadian literature, author of such classics as *The Stone Angel* and *The Diviners*. She has also written books for children, including *The Olden Days Coat*.

She was raised in Neepawa, the small Manitoba town that figures as Manawaka in several of her novels. Then came university and marriage and seven years in Africa, where her husband worked as an engineer. Margaret Laurence's experiences in Africa gave her material for her first novel, which was published in 1960. Six years and several books later, she won the Governor General's Award for *A Jest of God*, which was made into the film *Rachel, Rachel*. In 1974 she won another Governor General's Award for *The Diviners*.

André Laurendeau

Born 1912, Montreal, Que.
Died 1968

As editor-in-chief of *Le Devoir* in the 1950s, André Laurendeau helped bring in Quebec's Quiet Revolution. A former member of the Quebec legislature, he was strongly against the repressive provincial government of Maurice Duplessis,* which he denounced boldly in his editorials. He pressed for social reforms, and when these were brought in under Jean Lesage* he became the Quiet Revolution's main spokesman.

Laurendeau also pressed for a royal commission on bilingualism and biculturalism, and was appointed co-chairman, with Davidson Dunton, of the commission when it was set up early in the 1960s. In many ways he was the voice of Quebec, a fearless campaigner and a strong Quebec nationalist.

Sir Wilfrid Laurier

Born 1841, St.Lin, Que.
Died 1919

Our first French Canadian prime minister and one of our greatest politicians, Wilfrid Laurier was a Liberal in belief as well as name. He believed in tolerance and in respect for the rights of people, especially those who were in a minority.

As a young man, Laurier campaigned to get Roman Catholics the freedom to vote as they chose (the priests had been telling them who to vote for in elections). Later, he bravely spoke up for Louis Riel* and the Métis. As prime minister, he arranged for French-speaking children in Manitoba to be able to attend their own schools, and he made it possible for immigrants to keep their language and religion.

Laurier was prime minister 1896-1911, prosperous years which he made even better by his policies. New railways were built, thousands of immigrants were brought from Europe, and the prairies were settled. In 1905 the provinces of Alberta and Saskatchewan were formed.

Besides helping Canada to grow, Laurier tried to make it more united. One of his chief aims was to get English and French Canadians to be more friendly, accepting one another's differences. With great skill, he tackled the tricky problem of pleasing both French Canadian nationalists and pro-British imperialists—two diametrically opposed groups. He was most successful in English Canada, where he gained a large following by his silver-voiced oratory and silver-haired charm. Some French Canadians were less impressed, thinking Laurier too pro-British.

Yet one of Laurier's aims was to make the dominion less dependent on Britain and more self-reliant. He gave Canada its first navy (instead of relying on the British navy). And in 1911 he signed a reciprocity agreement with the United States, which enabled many Canadian goods to be sold duty-free in the U.S. This opened up American markets and made Canada less dependent on trade with Britain.

Laurier was keenly aware of the facts—the geographical connection with the United States and the historical connection with Britain. He was also well aware of the divisions within Canada. Yet he had a strong belief in the spirit of the Canadian people, if only everyone would pull together. "The twentieth century belongs to Canada," he once said.

François de Laval
Born 1623, France
Died 1708
François de Laval was the first bishop of Quebec and founder of its first seminary (which later became Laval University). He started the seminary so that New France could train its own priests. There were only 24 priests when Laval arrived in Canada in 1659. By the time he retired almost 30 years later, he had increased their number to 102 and had organized the basis of a national church.

As leader of the church in New France, Laval had political as well as religious power. This led to clashes with various governors and other officials, who thought Laval far too imperious. But the settlers adored him, for he was courageous and truly dedicated, a pious man who helped the needy in many ways.

Pierre Gaultier de La Vérendrye
Born 1685, Trois Rivières, Que.
Died 1749
The fur-trading explorer La Vérendrye was constantly in debt and short of supplies, yet this didn't prevent him pursuing his dream—to search for a route to the great Western Sea (the Pacific).

By sticking firm to this purpose, La Vérendrye and his sons penetrated farther west than any previous explorers, setting up trading forts as they went and forming firm friendships with the Indians they encountered. Although none of them reached the Pacific, they were the first to explore the region west of the Lake of the Woods (where they built their main post). And in 1742-43 two of La Vérendrye's sons, François and Louis-Joseph, made a great journey southwest to the Missouri and beyond, possibly almost to the Rockies.

La Vérendrye opened up the interior to French trade and claimed vast areas for France, yet he received few rewards. When he died, his sons had to sell the family lands to pay off his debts.

Calixa Lavallée
Born 1842, Verchères, Que.
Died 1891
Calixa Lavallée wrote the music of "O Canada," which was first sung in public in 1880 at a banquet in Quebec City. The words had been written earlier that year by Adolphe-Basile Routhier, a well-known judge and author; they were later translated into English by Robert Stanley Weir, who was also a judge and author.

Lavallée himself was a prominent Quebec musician, a composer and conductor who had first drawn attention at the age of 11 when he played the organ at a choir concert in Montreal. He had an adventurous life: went to the United States as a teenager and fought in the Civil War; then spent some time in Boston, where the performance of an opera he had written was cancelled because the owner of the opera house was murdered. Because of such setbacks, Lavallée was often short of money, yet he had a great reputation in both Canada and the U.S.

Charles Lawrence
Born 1709, England
Died 1760

As lieutenant governor of Nova Scotia, Charles Lawrence was responsible for the deportation of the Acadians in 1755. In that year about 6,000 Acadians were forcibly taken from their homes and shipped to other colonies, and more were evicted in the years that followed.

There had been threats of expulsion ever since Acadia had been ceded to Britain in 1713. This was partly because Britain wanted to settle the region with British settlers—and the Acadians occupied most of the best land. But it was also because the French-speaking Acadians refused to swear an oath of loyalty to Britain. Lawrence saw them as a danger, a hostile people. Yet most Acadians were not dangerously hostile. They didn't want to take part in the French-British conflict; they simply wanted to be left in peace to farm their lands.

Lawrence's name has been darkened by shame for uprooting these hardy pioneer farmers. But he was basically just a military man of action and no more unprincipled than the French secret agent Jean-Louis Le Loutre.* Like Le Loutre, he was doing what he clearly saw to be his patriotic duty. He was promoted to governor in 1756.

Irving Layton
Born 1912, Romania

Irving Layton's poetry is like the man himself—vigorous, outspoken, straight from the chest. It has caused some people to hail him as a genius. It has caused others to turn purple with rage.

Layton was brought to Canada as a baby and grew up in Montreal, where he graduated from McGill. For much of his life he has taught English at universities, and ever since he was a teenager he has been writing poetry. The result is more than 30 books of very strong verse, which have inspired praise and outrage, won Layton the Governor General's Award, and gained him a reputation as one of Canada's very finest poets.

Stephen Leacock
Born 1869, England
Died 1944

"I owe a lot to my teachers," wrote Stephen Leacock, "and I mean to pay them back some day." Leacock was himself a teacher, a master at Upper Canada College in the 1890s and then for many years professor of political science at McGill University. But he is best known as a humorist, the writer of gently chaffing books which expose unfairness and other human failings, but without bitterness.

Leacock wrote more than 30 humorous books, as well as a number of scholarly works. One of his most famous books is *Sunshine Sketches of a Little Town*, a send-up of Mariposa, a fictional town based on Orillia, Ont., where he had his summer home. Even now, years after his death, Leacock's works are still best sellers throughout the world.

Eric Leaver

Born 1915, England

E. W. Leaver was the inventor of the hand-arm machine, which enabled machine tools to be operated automatically (instead of by skilled workmen) to do complex repetitive jobs like making parts. He developed the machine in Toronto, shortly after the end of World War II, in co-operation with his Nova Scotian colleague G. R. Mounce. Both young men had worked at the government radar plant in Toronto during the war, and both had highly inventive minds. Leaver had already patented several inventions.

Their hand-arm system was called AMCRO, and it led to the development of today's automated machine-tool industry. Thousands of assembly-line factories throughout the world now use hand-arm machines.

Ozias Leduc

Born 1864, St.Hilaire, Que.
Died 1955

The artist Ozias Leduc is far better known today than he was during his lifetime. Except for one brief trip to Europe, he lived all his 91 years in St.Hilaire, southeast of Montreal. He had little contact with the fashionable art world, though some fellow artists appreciated his work.

Leduc earned his living by decorating churches. Meanwhile, in his spare time, he painted pictures of his friends and neighbours at their everyday occupations. These paintings have a marvellous warmth and understanding. One of the best known is *L'Enfant au Pain*, a picture of a village boy seated at a table. But Leduc had more than one style of painting. He produced a wide variety of pictures during his long life, experimenting with new techniques and changing with the times.

Dennis Lee

Born 1939, Toronto, Ont.

Alligator Pie and *Garbage Delight* are two of the popular books by Dennis Lee, who was a lecturer and editor before he became a full-time writer. He started by composing rhymes for his own children and published the first collection of them in 1970 in *Wiggle to the Laundromat*. In addition to his books for young readers, Dennis Lee has written works for adults, and in 1972 he won the Governor General's Award in poetry for *Civil Elegies*.

James Lee

Born 1937, Charlottetown, P.E.I.

In 1981 James Lee became premier of Prince Edward Island, heading a Conservative government. Educated at Queens Square School and St.Dunstans University in Charlottetown, Lee trained as an architectural draftsman and then started his own real estate company. He was first elected to the Prince Edward Island legislature in 1975 and was made a cabinet minister in 1979.

Jules Léger

Born 1913, St. Anicet, Que.
Died 1980

Our fourth Canadian-born Governor General grew up in rural Quebec, where his father ran a small country store. His career as an adult was to take him all over the world.

Léger began his working life as a journalist, but joined the Department of External Affairs in 1940. As a career diplomat, he served in Chile, Italy, and other countries, and during the 1960s was ambassador to France. This was a difficult posting, since President de Gaulle was at the time encouraging Quebec separatism. Léger's quiet diplomacy carried him skilfully through his years in France and then through a delicate role as undersecretary of state in Ottawa.

As Governor General 1974-79, Léger exhibited yet another impressive quality—courage. Although partially paralysed by a stroke a few months after taking office, he put his country above his illness, carrying out his duties with determination and with great dignity.

Paul-Émile Léger

Born 1904, Valleyfield, Que.

Cardinal Léger, the elder brother of Jules Léger,* has for many years been one of Canada's most respected and most beloved churchmen.

Except for his childhood in the small town of St. Anicet, Que., Paul-Émile Léger spent most of his early life in colleges: training to be a priest, founding and running a seminary in Japan, running a college in Rome. When in 1950 he was ordained archbishop of Montreal, he had very little experience of non-church life and was therefore expected to be rigid in his views. But Léger proved to be a liberal-minded reformer, a man of tolerance and understanding. Created a cardinal in 1953, he played a key role in Vatican congresses, pressing for modernizations within the church.

Cardinal Léger was above all a Christian, more interested in a life of service than in high office, and in 1967 he resigned as archbishop so that he could help some of the world's most needy people—Africans who were suffering from leprosy. For more than ten years he served as a missionary in the steamy heat of Cameroon. Not until he was in his mid-seventies did Cardinal Léger leave the mission and retire to Montreal.

Jean-Louis Le Loutre
Born 1709, France
Died 1772

Jean Le Loutre worked as a special agent in Acadia during the 1740s and 1750s. Sent there as priest to the Micmac Indians and Acadian farmers, he did undercover work for the French, while carefully staying out of reach of the British authorities. Governor Cornwallis* denounced him as "a good for nothing Scoundrel as ever lived" and offered a reward for his capture, dead or alive. The later governor, Charles Lawrence,* also saw him as a number-one enemy. Besides keeping the French informed of British movements, Le Loutre encouraged the Indians to attack British settlers (paying them for British scalps). And he stirred up discontent among the Acadians, whom he pressed to move to French territory.

Yet, like Lawrence, Le Loutre was principally a patriot. He was sincerely working for his country and for his religion, the Roman Catholic faith. He thought it a disaster for the Acadians to be ruled by foreign Protestants. Finally captured in 1755, he was imprisoned for eight years and then sent home to France, where he ministered to Acadian exiles.

Jean-Paul Lemieux
Born 1904, Quebec, Que.

In 1965 Jean-Paul Lemieux held an exhibition of his paintings in Montreal, and people lined up to get into the gallery and buy his work. All the pictures found buyers within 15 minutes of opening time.

Lemieux's reputation had been building ever since he had won a prize, more than 30 years earlier, from the Art Association of Montreal. Many of his paintings are of lone figures against a smooth landscape—a nun, for instance, standing in the snow; and they are often Quebec subjects. Lemieux has spent most of his life in Quebec City, where he taught at the École des Beaux Arts from 1937 to 1965.

Roger Lemelin
Born 1919, Quebec, Que.

Roger Lemelin gave Canada the Plouffe family, the working-class family who first appeared in his novels and later became the subject of popular radio and TV sagas. Lemelin drew from his own background in creating his characters. His family was so poor that when at the age of 17 he shattered his ankle skiing, there was no money for an operation. So for the next six years he was laid up in a wheelchair. This was when he started writing.

His first book, *Au Pied de la Pente Douce*, was published in 1944. It was an immediate success for it was about ordinary Quebeckers, the type of people that readers could relate to. The book won Lemelin several prizes and was later translated into English as *The Town Below*. Besides working as a novelist, Lemelin has been publisher of *La Presse*, where he set up an annual literary prize to help other authors.

Jean Lesage
Born 1912, Montreal, Que.
Died 1980

As Liberal premier of Quebec from 1960 to 1966, Jean Lesage brought in what was called the Quiet Revolution—a series of reforms which greatly improved conditions for Quebeckers.

During the long reign of Premier Duplessis,* virtually all reform had been blocked. The Roman Catholic church maintained great power, with a firm hold over education among other things. As a result, Quebeckers were lagging behind other Canadians. In many ways, they were still living in the nineteenth century. They did not have the chance to explore new ideas or get a thorough scientific training. And in the business world, they had the junior jobs. The bosses were often English Canadians. One of the slogans of the Quiet Revolution was "We must be masters in our own house."

Lesage's reforms touched almost every aspect of Quebec life. Schools were placed under provincial control. New education programs were started, emphasizing scientific and business training. Some of the big businesses were taken over by the province. New highways were built. All round, there was a great sweep of modernization.

Although Lesage later retired from politics and returned to his original career as a lawyer, the results of his policies are still being felt. One of the results was that Quebeckers gained a new sense of nationalism, a new pride in being Quebeckers.

Marc Lescarbot
Born c.1570, France
Died 1642

Marc Lescarbot, a French poet and lawyer, wrote and staged the first play that was ever performed in North America. This was during 1606-07 when Lescarbot was visiting Port Royal, the tiny trading settlement which had recently been built in Acadia.

The play was called *Théâtre de Neptune*, and it was a lively show in which the Roman god Neptune sailed in from the sea—to the accompaniment of French songs, Micmac poems, sounding trumpets, and booming cannons. When Lescarbot returned to France, he wrote an enormously long history about French exploits and exploration in North America.

René Lévesque
Born 1922, New Carlisle, Que.
Quebec separatist leader René Lévesque was a well-known broadcaster before he took up politics. During the Korean War he served as a war correspondent and commentator for the CBC, and he later had his own current affairs show, *Point de Mire*, which was extremely popular.

In 1960 he was elected as a Liberal to the Quebec legislature and was appointed a cabinet minister in Jean Lesage's* government. For seven years Lévesque served as a Liberal, but his views became more and more separatist—and more and more at odds with those of his Liberal colleagues. So he left the party and in 1968 helped found the Parti Québécois, which was dedicated to making Quebec independent.

In 1976 the Parti Québécois was voted into office and Lévesque became premier of the province. But when he held a referendum on whether or not Quebec should leave Canada, the majority of Quebeckers voted against separation. Lévesque could not therefore go ahead with his plans for independence. But he could take steps to preserve Quebec's culture and individuality. His government has passed a number of laws, such as the controversial Bill 101, which were aimed at strengthening the use of the French language within the province and keeping Quebec vigorously Québécois.

David Lewis
Born 1909, Poland
Died 1981
David Lewis was leader of the New Democratic Party 1971-75. But long before that he was a dedicated social reformer. He spent his whole life working for Canada's working people and against what he called "corporate welfare bums"—the highly paid executives.

Brought to Canada when he was 12, Lewis grew up in Montreal and then worked as a lawyer in Ottawa. He could have grown rich out of his law practice, but instead he devoted himself to the CCF (forerunner of the NDP). He was national secretary of the party 1937-50 and became national vice-president of the NDP when it was formed in 1961. The following year he was first elected to Parliament.

Under Lewis's leadership in the 1972 elections, 31 NDP members were elected, a large enough group to be able to hold the balance of power between the Liberals and Conservatives. But Lewis lost his seat in the 1974 elections, as did many other NDP members. His son Stephen Lewis was leader of the Ontario NDP 1970-78.

Monique Leyrac
Born 1928, Montreal, Que.
In 1965 Monique Leyrac won a first prize at the International Song Festival in Poland for her heartfelt singing of Gilles Vigneault's* "Mon Pays." That same year she also won first prize at a song festival in Belgium. She sings in both English and French, as well as in other languages, and has more than once been proclaimed Canada's best singer of the year and woman of the year.

Monique Leyrac started her career as an actress, performing at first on radio and then in cabaret, plays, and musicals. As well as singing and acting, she has hosted CBC TV programs and given poetry recitals. One of her many records is *Monique Leyrac Chante Nelligan*, a song recital of Émile Nelligan's* poems.

Alex Lifeson

Born 1953, Fernie, B.C.

The rock trio Rush was formed in 1968 by guitarist Alex Lifeson and singer and bass guitarist Geddy Lee (born 1953, Toronto). The third founding member was drummer John Rutsey, who was replaced in 1974 by Neil Peart (born 1952, Hamilton, Ont.).

During the 1970s, Rush thundered its way to success as Canada's most popular power trio, a high-volume, high-energy band, backed by an arsenal of special effects. Smoke bombs, search-lights, booming drum rolls—all became part of the scene at a Rush concert.

The band has won gold-record sales awards for several of its LPs, achieving international hits with such albums as *Fly by Night* and *Moving Pictures*.

Gordon Lightfoot

Born 1939, Orillia, Ont.

Folksinger Gordon Lightfoot has composed well over 200 songs and has recorded more than 160 of them. He began his career young, singing as a boy soprano on local radio in Orillia and in Kiwanis concerts. After studying jazz at Westlake College in Los Angeles, he performed with small groups in Toronto as a singer and guitar player. He also sang in Europe and the United States.

Although Lightfoot first made his way as a performer, it was as a songwriter that he first became widely known. This was during the 1960s, after Ian and Sylvia Tyson* began to sing and record his "Early Morning Rain" and other songs. Before long, his ballads were also being sung by Peter, Paul, and Mary, and by other top American artists. This gave Lightfoot's own performances new impetus and he embarked on a series of tours. He has crossed Canada time and again, and gone as far afield as Australia. He has won numerous Juno Awards, both as a singer and composer. One of his most popular compositions is "Canadian Railroad Trilogy."

Beatrice Lillie

Born 1898, Toronto, Ont.

Beatrice Lillie made people laugh. She has been called "the mistress of sophisticated slapstick"—a clever, witty actress, known especially for her one-woman shows.

She first performed in public in Ontario, singing with her mother and sister in the Lillie Trio; but the family moved to England in 1914, and there Beatrice Lillie made her stage debut. Ten years later she took New York by storm. She has appeared in revues and plays, on radio and TV, on stage and film. She has also written an autobiography, *Every Other Inch a Lady*. In private life, she is a Lady—she married Sir Robert Peel, an English aristocrat.

Lord Lisgar
Born 1807, India
Died 1876
Canada's second Governor General was an elderly statesman who had been a British MP and civil servant. Lord Lisgar was thought very capable, but he was not particularly popular. He couldn't chat easily, and the "entertainments" he gave tended to be dull rather than entertaining. He was in office 1869-72, during John A. Macdonald's* first period as prime minister.

Arthur Lismer
Born 1885, England
Died 1969
Arthur Lismer was one of the original members of the Group of Seven. He had come to Toronto in 1911 to work as a commercial artist but soon turned to teaching, for which he had exceptional talent.

Lismer was principal of the art school in Halifax 1916-19, vice-principal of the Ontario College of Art 1919-27, and then educational supervisor at a variety of art galleries.

Lismer is especially remembered for his work with children. In 1932 he founded the Children's Art Centre in Toronto, where his progressive and exciting approach inspired many young people with a great enthusiasm for painting.

Rich Little
Born 1938, Ottawa, Ont.
Rich Little, the man with a thousand voices, grew up in Ottawa, and it was there that he first practised as a mimic: in the classroom at school, to the delight of his classmates and the undelight of his teachers. One teacher told him that he was so good at making people laugh that he ought to take up a stage career.

This, in effect, is what Little did. By the early 1960s he had his own television show and was convulsing audiences across Canada with his impressions of politicians and other public figures. His first record album, *My Fellow Canadians*, was a sell-out success. Moving to the United States, he again drew packed audiences, while continuing to make records—and to make fun of politicians. Each year he performs at Las Vegas, but he also goes on tour, maintaining strong ties with Canada, and especially with his home town of Ottawa.

Dorothy Livesay
Born 1909, Winnipeg, Man.
Dorothy Livesay published her first book of poems when she was 19. She won her first Governor General's Award in 1944. Three years later she was awarded the Lorne Pierce Medal for distinguished service to Canadian literature.

Long recognized as one of Canada's leading modern poets, Dorothy Livesay has brought out more than a dozen books. Much of her writing reflects her deep concern for people, especially the poor and disadvantaged. She has worked as a social worker and as a UNESCO teacher in Africa, and in recent years has lectured in creative writing at Simon Fraser University.

Of Canada's many women poets, several came to prominence in the 1940s, around the same time as Dorothy Livesay. These include Margaret Avison, Anne Marriott, P. K. Page, and Miriam Waddington.

Guy Lombardo
Born 1902, London, Ont.
Died 1977
The dance band called Guy Lombardo and His Royal Canadians was said to make "the sweetest music this side of heaven." For 60 years Lombardo was leader of this famous band, which he started aged 15 under the name Lombardo Brothers' Orchestra. It was very much a family group, composed of Guy himself (who was violinist as well as leader), his three brothers, and at times his sister and father.

Over the years the band increased in size, took in non-family players, adopted the name Royal Canadians —and moved to the United States. But Canadians could still hear the "sweetest music," especially on New Year's Eve. Televised live from New York, Lombardo was annually seen by millions as he brought in each New Year with a zestful "Auld Lang Syne."

Tom Longboat
Born 1887, Brantford, Ont.
Died 1949

Tom Longboat was Canada's first national sports hero since Ned Hanlan.* An Onondaga from the Six Nations Reserve, he won the Boston marathon in record time in 1907 and went on to win several other major races. The crowds flocked to see him, and on his marriage he was given a wedding reception in Massey Hall.

But Longboat was taken up by promoters who exploited his talent, made money out of his races, and then dropped him. He was only in the limelight for a few years—his most vigorous years of youthful strength. For most of his life he had to scratch a living, and at one time he was a helper on a garbage truck. By the time he died on the Six Nations Reserve, he had long been forgotten by the crowds who once cheered him.

Johnny Longden
Born 1910, England

Johnny Longden was the first jockey in the history of horse racing to ride more than 6,000 winners.

Brought to Canada as a small child, he grew up in Taber, southern Alberta, where his father worked as a coal miner. Longden himself went into the mines when he was 14, but he also rode at local fairs on the weekends. His family were devout Mormons, and in 1927 he visited Salt Lake City, where besides seeing the home of Mormonism he was given the chance to ride in a thoroughbred race. He won the race. This was the end of Johnny Longden's career as a coal miner and the beginning of his career as a jockey. Over the next 39

years, he and his horses won most of the highest honours in the racing world, including the Triple Crown.

Frances Loring
Born 1887, U.S.A.
Died 1968

The sculptor Frances Loring came to Canada in 1912, and the following year she was joined by fellow sculptor Florence Wyle (1881-1968) with whom she had shared a studio in New York.

The two women settled in Toronto, producing between them a great body of work. Frances Loring's sculptures include the statue of Sir Robert Borden* on Parliament Hill and the lions at the eastern entrance to the Queen Elizabeth Highway. Florence Wyle's work includes the Edith Cavell Memorial in Toronto.

Marquis of Lorne
Born 1845, England
Died 1914

The Province of Alberta owes its name to the Marquis of Lorne, who was Governor General 1878-83. After journeying through the prairies, he asked that one of the districts there be named in honour of his wife, Princess Louise Caroline Alberta.

Princess Louise was Queen Victoria's daughter and very like the queen in character. She didn't enjoy her time in Canada. She thought Canadians unpleasantly forward—she was once patted on the shoulder and told she had a nice plump figure. But both she and her husband greatly admired the Canadian scenery, and they drew some beautiful sketches of it.

Peter Lougheed
Born 1928, Calgary, Alta.

Premier Lougheed of Alberta first gained celebrity as a young football player, starring with the Edmonton Eskimos. In 1965 he was chosen leader of Alberta's Conservative party. At the time, there were no Conservatives in the legislature; but in 1967 he and five others were elected, and in 1971 he swept his party into power, ending the long reign of Social Credit (see Aberhart*).

As premier, Lougheed has stood up for provincial rights, insisting that the provinces should control the profits from their mineral resources. This is of particular importance to Alberta because of its oil and gas industry. To preserve some of the oil revenues for future Albertans, Lougheed established the Alberta Heritage Fund, which has amassed billions of dollars. This fund also supports present-day projects, such as medical research.

Angus McAskill
Born 1825, Scotland
Died 1863

Angus McAskill was known as the Cape Breton Giant. Brought to Nova Scotia by his parents as a child, he grew so tall that his father had to raise the ceilings in the kitchen and living room.

McAskill is said to have been 236 cm tall. He was very muscular and was credited with the most amazing feats of strength. For several years he toured with circuses. Then, having made a small fortune, he settled back in Nova Scotia, where he farmed in the region of St. Ann's Harbour. He died at the age of 38 of an illness which was probably meningitis. He is seen below with Tom Thumb.

Samuel Lount
Born 1791, U.S.A
Hanged 1838

Samuel Lount was executed publicly, along with Peter Matthews, for taking part in the Rebellion of 1837. A blacksmith by profession, he was for a while a Reform member of Upper Canada's legislature and was a colleague and admirer of William Lyon Mackenzie.* Like Matthews, he supported Mackenzie during the rebellion, leading a group of armed Patriots. Both men were present at Montgomery's Tavern and both were later caught while trying to escape to the United States. Although they were not such "wanted" men as Mackenzie and John Rolph* (both of whom did escape to the States), Lount and Matthews were condemned to death. In a way, they served as scapegoats for the absent leaders.

In Lower Canada, 12 men were hanged for their part in the rebellion. More than 100 others from both Upper and Lower Canada were sent as convicts to the penal colonies in Australia.

Brother Luc
Born 1614, France
Died 1685

The first trained artist to work in Canada was Brother Luc (born Claude François). He had been the king's painter in France, and when his mother died he became a Recollet friar, calling himself Luc (after St.Luke, the patron saint of artists). In 1670 he was sent to the settlement at Quebec to paint religious pictures and to help restore the Recollet monastery, which had been abandoned when Kirke* captured Quebec in 1629. Brother Luc designed the monastery's chapel, which still stands today. It is part of the Hôpital Général and is the oldest existing chapel in Canada.

Brother Luc stayed in New France less than two years, unlike the other outstanding artist of the French era, François Beaucourt (1740-94). Beaucourt was born in the colony, near Montreal. Although he studied and then worked in Europe, he eventually returned to New France, where he painted everything from portraits to stage sets.

Richard McBride
Born 1870, New Westminster, B.C.
Died 1917

The premier of British Columbia from 1903 to 1915 was Richard McBride—Glad-Hand Dick—the genial Conservative politician who not only charmed the voters with his affable manners but led B.C. into an era of prosperity.

Glad-Hand Dick had the type of optimism that inspired confidence, abroad as well as at home. New settlers poured into the province during his years in office; investors invested, and there was a great activity in lumbering, fishing, fruit growing, and railway building. Meanwhile, McBride charmed the British as well as the British Columbians, and in 1912 he was knighted. When the boomtime began to turn into a bust-time, he retired from the premiership and went off to England, where he was appointed B.C.'s agent general at the newly built British Columbia House. He died there, of Bright's disease, a couple of years later.

D'Alton McCarthy
Born 1836, Ireland
Died 1898

A hero to many Ontario Protestants (and a villain to most French Canadians) D'Alton McCarthy was above all an Orangeman, the son of Irish immigrants who had brought him to Canada as a child. Having started his career as a lawyer, he was elected to Parliament in 1876, and he remained an MP for the rest of his life.

In Parliament and outside it, McCarthy was the spokesman for the most extreme Protestants—a loud, angry voice, railing against the Roman Catholic religion and the use of the French language. He raised a storm of protest when Honoré Mercier* paid the Jesuits compensation for land they had earlier lost in Quebec. In Manitoban affairs, McCarthy supported the move to close the separate schools where French-speaking children were taught. He even tried to get French abolished as an official language throughout the North-West Territories.

Time and again, McCarthy stirred up the simmering resentments of French and English Canadians, causing them to boil up into bitterness and hatred.

John McClelland
Born 1877, Scotland
Died 1968

John McClelland was the founder of McClelland and Stewart, which was built into a large and successful publishing company by his son Jack McClelland.

Brought to Canada as a child, John McClelland left school when he was 13 and went to work at the Methodist Book House in Toronto. In 1906 he started his own bookstore, in partnership with Frederick Goodchild, who had also worked at the Methodist Book House. They published their first book a few years later.

At first the company was called McClelland and Goodchild, but the name was changed when a new partner, George Stewart, entered the business and when Goodchild retired. The policy of the company did not change, though. One of its main aims has always been to publish the works of Canadian authors and to bring promising writers to the attention of the Canadian public.

Nellie McClung
Born 1873, Chatsworth, Ont.
Died 1951

Nellie McClung was one of the West's most fiery and eloquent speakers in the struggle to get women the vote. Raised on a Manitoba homestead, she at first concentrated her campaign in Winnipeg, continuing it in Alberta when her husband was relocated there in 1914.

Even after the vote was won, Nellie McClung went on campaigning, trying to get reforms that would improve the lives of women and children. She was a member of the Alberta legislature 1921-26 and was one of the Famous Five, who with Emily Murphy* got women legally recognized as "persons." Nellie McClung herself received full recognition. In 1936 she was the first woman appointed to the newly formed CBC's board of governors, and two years later was one of the Canadian delegates at the League of Nations.

She also made her name as an author. Her first novel, *Sowing Seeds in Danny*, was the best seller of the year when it was published in 1908. She wrote 16 books altogether, including a two-volume autobiography: *Clearing in the West* and *The Stream Runs Fast*.

Robert McClure
Born 1807, Ireland
Died 1873

The naval officer Robert McClure was sent to the Arctic in 1850 to search for Sir John Franklin.* He didn't find any trace of Franklin, but he did find a route through the Northwest Passage.

McClure entered the passage from the Pacific and sailed as far as Banks Island. There his ship was trapped in the ice, but he explored further by sled and found a way into Viscount Melville Sound, which he was convinced would lead through towards the Atlantic. After four years in the Arctic, he and his men went by sled to Beechey Island, where they boarded a transport ship. They had thus been right across the Arctic Archipelago, though they had not sailed the route. The first person to sail through the passage was the Norwegian explorer Roald Amundsen on his expedition of 1903-06.

Robert B. McClure

Born 1900, U.S.A.

Robert McClure was moderator of the United Church of Canada 1968-71, the first layman to hold the position. He was a doctor and surgeon rather than a minister, a long-time medical missionary and the son of missionaries. His parents were en route to China when he was born.

Of the Canadian missionaries who served in China early in this century, two of the leading families were the McClures and the Kilborns. The Kilborns, who were Methodists, ran the West China Mission, while the McClures worked in northern China running the Presbyterian mission. In time, both families became connected by marriage, just as their churches became one when the United Church of Canada was formed.

Having spent his early years in China, Robert McClure returned home to complete his education and study medicine. He then went back to China as a doctor and worked there for more than 20 years. He has since served in the Middle East, India, Malaysia, and South America. His whole life has been dedicated to reducing suffering in countries where help is needed most.

John McCrae

Born 1872, Guelph, Ont.
Died 1918

John McCrae wrote "In Flanders Fields," the poem that is recited on Armistice Day each year. He wrote it in 20 minutes, early one morning in 1915.

McCrae was a doctor by profession. He trained in Toronto, then practised in Montreal, and when World War I broke out he volunteered for the army and served with No. 3 General Hospital in France. Unfortunately, he did not survive the war. He died of pneumonia early in 1918.

Grant McConachie

Born 1909, Hamilton, Ont.
Died 1965

Grant McConachie was known for his cheerful grin, his overpowering optimism, and his passion for airplanes. Whether working as a bush pilot or top airline executive, he was constantly pioneering new ideas, new routes, new types of planes. He grew up in Alberta when bush pilots were first venturing north from Edmonton, and at the age of 22 he launched his own airline. It had one plane, bought with money borrowed from his Uncle Harry, who ran a fairground concession. This was the beginning of a shoestring air service which was often close to financial ruin but which struggled through, buoyed up by McConachie's enthusiasm and resourcefulness.

His airline flew fresh fish out of the North, carried mail and passengers to the Yukon, and gradually increased in size and scope. With other bush airlines, it was bought by the Canadian Pacific Railway during World War II; and with other bush pilots, McConachie was taken on staff of the new Canadian Pacific Airlines.

In 1947 he was appointed president of the airline, and he spent the rest of his life expanding it. He started passenger services to Australia and the Orient, pioneered transpolar flights to Europe, and bought the newly invented jet planes. Because of McConachie's dynamic policies, CP Air became one of the world's leading airlines.

Thomas McCulloch
Born 1776, Scotland
Died 1843

Thomas McCulloch, the great Nova Scotian educator, was a Presbyterian clergyman who immigrated to Pictou, N.S., in 1803. There in 1816 he founded the Pictou Academy, but the academy was not allowed to grant degrees to its students. Only Anglican colleges were allowed to do that. Over the years, McCulloch headed a vigorous reform movement to get education out of the hands of the Anglicans, giving equal status to other denominations. He was successful, and when Dalhousie was opened in Halifax in 1838, McCulloch was made president of the college.

Besides teaching and preaching, McCulloch was also an author. His works include *The Stepsure Letters*, a witty satire in which he picked on gossip, flashy clothes, and other things which were not approved of by the strict Presbyterians of his day.

J. A. D. McCurdy
Born 1886, Baddeck, N.S.
Died 1961

John McCurdy made the first airplane flight in Canada—and in all the British Empire. This was in 1909 (one year after Casey Baldwin's* flight in the United States) when McCurdy flew the *Silver Dart* about a kilometre over the ice of the Bras d'Or Lakes at Baddeck Bay, Cape Breton Island.

McCurdy was the designer of the *Silver Dart* as well as its pilot. He was one of the aircraft pioneers in Alexander Graham Bell's* Aerial Experiment Association—a small group of enthusiasts whose aim was to build successful flying machines. McCurdy spent most of his life flying, often risking his neck as he demonstrated the wonders of the air age to admiring crowds. He formed an aircraft company, started a school for pilots, worked with the government on aircraft production; and from 1947 to 1952, with his feet firmly on the ground, he served as lieutenant governor of Nova Scotia.

Flora MacDonald
Born 1926, North Sydney, N.S.

Flora MacDonald is the first Canadian woman to be minister of external affairs (in Joe Clark's* Conservative government of 1979-80). One of her main concerns during her time in office was to arrange for many of the homeless Boat People from Indochina to be resettled in Canada. She was first elected to Parliament in 1972 as the member for Kingston and the Islands. A leading figure in the Conservative party, she is also one of the party's most vigorous MPs, speaking out strongly on a wide range of issues.

John A. Macdonald
Born 1815, Scotland
Died 1891

Our first prime minister was called everything from a lovable rogue to a scoundrel and a drunk. He was also hailed as Canada's great nation builder—the man who brought about Confederation and who then made the young dominion into a functioning country by getting a railway built across it. Though John A. Macdonald did have a roguish side to his character, he was an exceptionally able man, clever, witty, sophisticated, and highly skilled at the art of politics.

John A. had been brought to Canada as a child and raised in Kingston, where he started his career as a lawyer before going into politics. By the 1860s he was the dominant Conservative in the Province of Canada. He played a leading role at the three Confederation conferences, skilfully guiding his fellow politicians as they planned Confederation and drafted the BNA Act. After Confederation, when John A. first became prime minister, he was the public's darling.

He had two periods in office (1867-73 and 1878-91). The gap between them was due to the Pacific Scandal. This came about because John A.'s efforts to build the Canadian Pacific Railway were tied in with his efforts to ensure that he was re-elected in 1872: he gave the contract for the railway to Sir Hugh Allan;* and Allan gave the Conservatives $350,000 for their election campaign. When news of all this came to light in 1873 (see J. J. C. Abbott*), there was such a furore that John A. had to resign. Although there was nothing illegal about accepting campaign funds, people said that John A. had acted incorrectly, that he had given Allan the railway contract in return for the campaign funds. Some of his Liberal enemies went so far as to say that he had been bribed into giving Allan the contract.

It looked as if John A.'s political career was over, but five years later he got back into power with a National Policy that promised to develop Canadian manufacturing and to settle the West. Once again he tried to get the railway built, and this time he gave the contract to George Stephen's* company, which successfully completed the job.

While John A. has been praised for getting the CPR built, he has often been blamed for the two Riel* rebellions. Both took place while he was in office, and both might have been avoided if he had paid more attention to the problems of the West. But he was mostly interested in personal politics—winning the hearts of the voters with his humorous remarks, or outwitting the Liberals in the House of Commons. It was there that he shone most brilliantly, overshadowing all his contemporaries.

J. E. H. MacDonald
Born 1873, England
Died 1932

J. E. H. MacDonald and Lawren Harris* were the two main founders of the Group of Seven, the group of artists who brought a new, dramatic style to Canadian landscape painting. MacDonald had come to Canada as a child, and he started his career as a commercial artist, painting in his spare time. He was a senior designer at Grip Ltd. (the Toronto engraving and graphic design firm) during the years when the group was gradually assembling and when Tom Thomson* was still alive and painting with them.

MacDonald's new style was not popular with the public at first. In 1916 an art critic said that his picture called *Rock and Maple* might just as well have been called *Drunkard's Stomach*. But MacDonald went on painting, and in 1920 he and his fellow artists formally named themselves the Group of Seven and held their first exhibition.

The original members of the group were MacDonald, Harris, A. Y. Jackson,* and four artists who had worked at Grip Ltd.: Franklin Carmichael, Frank Johnston, Arthur Lismer,* and Frederick Varley.* Soon after their first show, MacDonald was appointed to the staff of the Ontario College of Art and he was made principal in 1929.

Miles Macdonell
Born 1769, Scotland
Died 1828

Miles Macdonell was in charge of the handful of Selkirk* colonists who established the Red River Settlement in 1812. He was given the imposing title Governor of Assiniboia.

Macdonell was not a skilful governor. His overbearing manner did little to put heart into the colonists as they tried to protect themselves from the North West Company men and their Métis allies. Neither of these groups wanted settlers on the prairies, so they made life as tough as possible for the colonists—and for Macdonell. When Macdonell passed "laws" against the Northwesters and tried to enforce them, the Northwesters took him prisoner. Before long he gave up being governor, and he spent his later years farming in Upper Canada.

Grant MacEwan
Born 1902, nr. Brandon, Man.

From 1966 to 1974 Grant MacEwan was lieutenant governor of Alberta. This was but one of many achievements in a life devoted to the people of western Canada, their land and their history.

MacEwan grew up as a farm boy in Manitoba and Saskatchewan, then studied agriculture, and in due course became dean of agriculture at the University of Manitoba. After moving to Alberta early in the 1950s, he served as leader of the provincial Liberal party, mayor of Calgary, and then lieutenant governor. Meanwhile, he had also become known as a writer. For years he wrote a newspaper column, and he is also the author of many popular books on western history. One of his best-known books is *Fifty Mighty Men*.

Kate and Anna McGarrigle
Born 1946 (Kate), 1944 (Anna), Montreal, Que.
The singing McGarrigles grew up in a musical family with an Irish father, a French Canadian mother, an assortment of musical instruments, and family singsongs round the piano. All this is reflected in their performances. They sing with equal ease in English and French—everything from traditional folk songs to modern rock. They both play a wide range of instruments. And their concerts have the informality of family singsongs, with plenty of fun and laughter. Adding to the family atmosphere is Anna's husband Dane Lanken, who plays the trumpet in the band which generally accompanies them. Their older sister Jane often sings and performs with them too.

Kate and Anna began by performing in Montreal coffee houses during the 1960s, and then they tried writing songs as well as singing them. This brought them international fame during the early 1970s and they have since had successful tours in Europe as well as North America. Their records include *Love Over and Over*, which came out in 1982.

Thomas D'Arcy McGee
Born 1825, Ireland
Assassinated 1868

D'Arcy McGee was one of the "big seven" of the Fathers of Confederation, a gifted orator who helped persuade Canadians that Confederation would be good for them. Joseph Howe,* though not agreeing with his policies, described McGee as "a man of genius—an elegant writer, an eloquent speaker, and a pleasant fellow over a bottle of wine."

McGee was an Irish Catholic who had emigrated to the United States in his youth. He moved to Canada in 1857 because the Irish Catholics of Montreal asked him to. They felt he would look after their interests. As a journalist and writer of books and poems, he had gained a powerful reputation in the United States, speaking up for the Irish against the British.

In Montreal, McGee was elected to the legislature of the Province of Canada. He served as a cabinet minister and did look after Irish interests. But he gradually became less of a rebel and more of a Canadian patriot, a great enthusiast for Confederation. This caused the most extreme Irish, especially the Fenians, to label him a traitor to Ireland; and less than a year after Confederation, one of them shot him on the steps of his Ottawa boarding house.

James McGill
Born 1744, Scotland
Died 1813
The founder of McGill University was an independent fur trader and a very successful one. From his headquarters in Montreal he sent out traders, formed partnerships with fellow merchants, and in due course made a large fortune. James McGill was also a politician, a member of the Executive Council of Lower Canada. When he died, he left a large part of his estate to endow a university, on condition that it be named after him.

Frances McGill
Born 1882, Minnedosa, Man.
Died 1959

Dr. Frances McGill worked with the RCMP long before women were officially allowed to join the Force. From the 1920s on, she was provincial pathologist for Saskatchewan, which meant that when people died in mysterious circumstances, she had to do medical tests and dissections, and find what had caused their death. She never accepted the obvious answer. With the patience of a born detective, she investigated every angle until she found the truth; and the truth was sometimes very different from what people had thought. Her painstaking work solved several murder cases.

Gruff and matter-of-fact, Frances McGill was greatly respected by the Mounties, who admired her unsqueamishness as much as her ability. If anyone fainted at the sight of blood, it certainly wasn't Dr. McGill. ("Pull yourself together, you sissy!" she once told a pallid young constable.) She became so much part of the team in Regina that in 1946 she was appointed honorary surgeon of the RCMP.

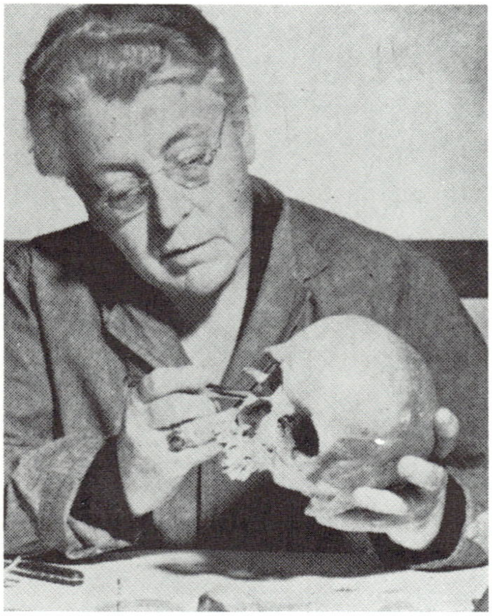

William McGillivray
Born c.1764, Scotland
Died 1825

William McGillivray was one of the most powerful men in the fur trade. A nephew of Simon McTavish,* he had joined the North West Company as a young man, and he became its head when McTavish died in 1804. Under his aggressive leadership, the company did so well that it rivalled the Hudson's Bay Company.

But then the Hudson's Bay Company let Lord Selkirk* set up a colony on the Red River. This was a great blow to McGillivray, for a settlement on the prairies would block the North West Company trade routes between Montreal and Athabasca. He and his brother Simon McGillivray did all they could to prevent the Red River Settlement from getting started. And when settlers arrived regardless, McGillivray made sure they were harassed by his traders and their Métis allies. In the strife that followed, some settlers were killed (see Cuthbert Grant*). Many had their homes destroyed. Yet for all McGillivray's ruthlessness, he couldn't dislodge the colony. He realized he would have to join forces with the Hudson's Bay Company if trade was to prosper, and in 1821 the two great fur-trading companies became one.

John McIntosh
Born 1777, U.S.A.
Died (?)
The McIntosh apple is named after John McIntosh, who in 1811 settled on a farm in Matilda Township, Upper Canada (at today's Dundela, Ont.). When clearing his land, McIntosh found several apple trees, which he transplanted and tended. The luscious red apples from one of these trees became so popular in the neighbourhood that McIntosh's son started a nursery to grow the trees. All the McIntosh apples found today throughout North America are descendants of the tree McIntosh found on his land.

Ada Mackenzie
Born 1891, Toronto, Ont.
Died 1973
One of Canada's most celebrated women golfers, Ada Mackenzie started to play the game when she was 10, and she was still competing in tournaments at the age of 80. Besides winning a great many championships, she helped to promote golf as a women's game. In 1924 she founded the Toronto Ladies' Golf and Tennis Club, and in 1928 she established the Ontario junior ladies' championships. She received the Canadian Press Award in 1933 as Canada's female athlete of the year.

The McKenzie Brothers
Created 1980
In real life, the comics Bob and Doug McKenzie are Rick Moranis (b.1953, Toronto) and Dave Thomas (b.1948, St. Catharines, Ont.), and neither of them are the dumb guys they play on camera. Dave (Doug) graduated in literature and then worked in advertising. Rick (Bob) was a Toronto disc jockey before he was 20.

They first performed together on the show *SCTV Network* when it was on Global TV. In 1980, when the show was moved to the CBC, there were 2½ minutes of empty air time that had to be filled with Canadian content. So they dreamed up Bob and Doug McKenzie and their mini talkshow "The Great White North." They reckoned that Bob and Doug were solid Canadian content, eh?

The two hosers left *SCTV* in 1982 to make their first movie, *Strange Brew*. To their surprise, they had become wildly popular pop heroes, not only in Canada but throughout North America.

Alexander Mackenzie
Born 1764, Scotland
Died 1820

Several famous Canadians were named Mackenzie, and quite a few were named Alexander Mackenzie. The most celebrated of these was the determined young fur trader who found his way overland to the Pacific.

Alexander Mackenzie ran the North West Company post on Lake Athabasca, and he had two great ambitions: to be rich and to be famous. He believed he could achieve both if he could find a water route to the Pacific Ocean so that furs could be shipped out easily. On his first attempt in 1789, he followed the river now named after him, but this took him to the Arctic Ocean. Undeterred, he tried again in 1793 and triumphantly reached the Pacific, though not by a navigable waterway. Only Mackenzie's willpower and leadership kept his voyageurs struggling on across portages and through rain forests.

Mackenzie was the first explorer to get through to the Pacific by land, and the book he wrote about the journey, a best seller, brought him the fame and fortune he had hoped for. He became a popular celebrity, especially in Britain. Society women lionized him, a famous artist painted his portrait, and George III gave him a knighthood.

Alexander Mackenzie
Born 1822, Scotland
Died 1892

Prime Minister Alexander Mackenzie was very different from his fur-trading namesake—dour, stiff, and flinty. He had been a stonemason before taking up politics and everything about him was rather stony, as if he had been carved out of granite. Most appropriately, he was a Grit (a Liberal).

Mackenzie took office in 1873, following John A. Macdonald's* disgrace over the Pacific Scandal. What Canada needed right then was a prime minister who was unquestionably honest, and Mackenzie fitted the part perfectly. He even looked upright. But he was not a successful leader. He was overshadowed (and overawed) by his powerful second-in-command, Edward Blake.* And he got himself into such a muddle over whether or not to build the CPR that British Columbia threatened to leave Canada. By the 1878 elections, Canadians had had enough of Mackenzie and they voted the Conservatives back into power.

William Lyon Mackenzie
Born 1795, Scotland
Died 1861

The leader of the 1837 rebellion in Upper Canada was a tiny firecracker of a man. Fiercely outspoken, he was a storm-centre of trouble long before he launched the rebellion.

Mackenzie was a newspaperman by profession, editor of the *Colonial Advocate*, in which he constantly attacked the power of the Family Compact and called for a fairer system of government. Elected to the Legislative Assembly as a Reform member, he carried on his campaign there, and did so with such vigour that he was expelled from the assembly several times. But he was re-elected each time by an admiring public and in 1834 was made Toronto's first mayor.

Mackenzie took to armed revolt in 1837 partly out of impatience, for he was making no progress in his attempts to reform the system of government. His rebellion was a failure. His forces were routed by the Loyalists at Montgomery's Tavern, north of Toronto, and he had to flee to the United States. He lived there for 11 years before a pardon allowed him to return to Canada.

Vehement to the last, Mackenzie died of an apoplectic fit.

William Mackenzie
Born 1849, Kirkfield, Ont.
Died 1923

Two railway contractors, William Mackenzie and Donald Mann (1853-1934), planned and built the Canadian Northern Railway system, starting with a line which ran from Gladstone to Winnipegosis in Manitoba. This stretch of track was opened to trains early in 1897.

Over the following years, the two contractors built up a network of railways—buying some, building others—and by 1915 they had completed a line which ran from coast to coast to the north of the CPR. But Mackenzie and Mann had tried to do too much, and their company was in financial difficulties. A few years later it was taken over by the government, becoming part of Canadian National Railways.

William Lyon Mackenzie King
Born 1874, Kitchener, Ont.
Died 1950

As Liberal prime minister for almost all the 1920s, and again 1935-48, William Lyon Mackenzie King was in office longer than any other prime minister in the entire British Commonwealth. He was the grandson of William Lyon Mackenzie* but a totally different character. Whereas rebel Mackenzie had been a passionate figure, sparking intense admiration or intense hatred, Mackenzie King was cautious, conventional, calculating. He appealed to people's minds rather than their emotions.

He was a very skilful politician, always weighing decisions carefully. At the beginning of World War II he made a point of declaring war on Germany several days after Britain had done so, thereby establishing Canada's right to act as an independent nation. And during the war, when some Canadians were calling for compulsory military service and others were campaigning against it, he came out with a classic piece of double-talk; he said there would be "conscription if necessary, but not necessarily conscription."

In the meantime, Mackenzie King was living a curious secret life. Unknown to the public, he used to hold seances in which he talked (or believed he talked) with his dead mother, dead grandfather, and such eminent former politicians as Sir Wilfrid Laurier.* He even sent messages to his dead dogs.

James McLachlan
Born 1870, Scotland
Died 1936

Jimmy McLachlan, one of Canada's greatest labour leaders, was 11 years old when he first worked in a coal mine in his native Scotland. Immigrating to Canada in 1900, he got a job in the mines at Sydney, N.S., where he was a strong union man.

McLachlan was leader of the Cape Breton miners during the bitter strikes of 1909 and the 1920s. The strikes were viciously put down, and when McLachlan complained of police violence, he was imprisoned for libel. He ran for Parliament several times but was never elected. A lifelong crusader for the workers, he died in great poverty, honoured but unrewarded.

Jimmy McLarnin
Born 1907, Ireland

In the Canadian Press poll of 1950, Jimmy McLarnin was named Canadian boxer of the half-century. Born in Belfast, he came to Canada with his family when he was three, living first on a farm near Moose Jaw and then in Vancouver. He began boxing when he was 12 and turned professional at 16.

In the years that followed, the baby-faced Irishman became Canada's most successful boxer, defeating a host of champions, ex-champions, and future champions. Twice he won the world welterweight title, though he twice lost it again in his very next fight: won it 1933, lost and rewon it in 1934, lost it again in 1935. In all, McLarnin won 63 professional fights out of a total of 77. On retiring from the ring in 1936, he went into business.

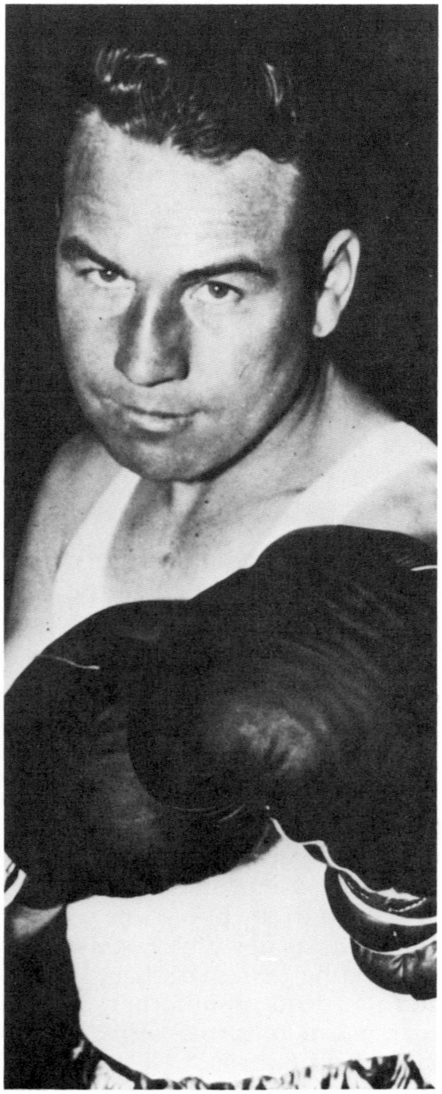

Murray McLauchlan
Born 1948, Scotland

Singer and songwriter Murray McLauchlan was brought to Canada when he was five and began his singing career in Ontario and Quebec coffee houses. Early in the 1970s he brought out his first albums, scoring a hit with his "Farmer's Song," which won a gold-record sales award in 1973. That same year, McLauchlan won his first Juno Awards.

Since then, he has performed rock as well as folk music. His caring songs about everyday people have been particularly popular, bringing him a great following, abroad as well as at home.

Norman McLaren
Born 1914, Scotland

Film-maker Norman McLaren invented a new art form in his animated films. Instead of using a camera, he painted patterns directly onto the filmstock; and instead of using a tape recorder, he scratched drawings directly onto the film's soundtrack. His most famous film, *Blinkity Blank*, was made entirely with scratches.

McLaren grew up in Scotland, attending the Glasgow School of Art, but while studying art he spent his spare time making films. This attracted the attention of John Grierson,* who offered him a job in the British General Post Office Film Unit. In 1941 McLaren followed Grierson to the National Film Board, and it was there he developed his techniques with animated films. Over the years, he has won more than 150 awards, contributing enormously to the international reputation of the Film Board.

Robert McLaughlin
Born 1836, Tyrone, Ont.
Died 1921
The story of General Motors of Canada goes back to Robert McLaughlin, a farmer who was good at woodwork and turned his hand to making cutters and wagons. By 1876 he was running a carriage-making business in Oshawa, which grew rapidly when he invented a new form of steering gear for use on carriages.

His son Sam (Robert Samuel McLaughlin) took the family firm into the automobile age. In 1907 he founded the McLaughlin Motor Car Company, which produced a car fully designed in Canada, though it had an American Buick engine. To expand the business even further, Sam McLaughlin sold his company to General Motors in 1918, becoming president of the firm which was now called General Motors of Canada. He was chairman of the board until his death in 1972, when he was just over 100 years old.

John Bayne Maclean
Born 1862, Crieff, Ont.
Died 1950
Maclean's magazine is named after its founder, J. B. Maclean. He started his career as a newspaper reporter and then, in partnership with his brother, began to publish trade journals, including the highly successful *Canadian Grocer*. He founded *Maclean's* in 1905, calling it *The Busy Man's Magazine* for the first two years of publication. He also founded the *Financial Post*, *Chatelaine*, and a host of other periodicals which still provide Canada with a great variety of reading material, by, for, and about Canadians.

Hugh MacLennan
Born 1907, Glace Bay, N.S.
Two Solitudes and *The Watch that Ends the Night* are two of the best-selling novels written by Hugh MacLennan. Both won the Governor General's Award (as have three other MacLennan books) and both were stories set against a background of real-life Canadian events. *Two Solitudes* had particular impact when it came out in 1945, for it was about the conflict of French and English Canadians, the way the "two founding nations" were still in many ways two separate entities.

MacLennan was a teacher at Lower Canada College in Montreal when he wrote the book, and he later became a professor at McGill. In 1952 he was awarded the Lorne Pierce Medal for distinguished service to Canadian literature.

James Farquharson Macleod
Born 1836, Scotland
Died 1894
Colonel Macleod, more than anyone else, gave the North-West Mounted Police their stirling reputation for justice during their early years in the West. Trained as a lawyer as well as a soldier, he was among the first 300 who took part in the Great March West, and in 1876 he was made head of the NWMP.

Macleod became good friends with Chief Crowfoot,* and he often consulted with Crowfoot when deciding a case and then handed down a sentence which the Indian people would approve. He was painstakingly fair and he insisted that his men behave considerately too. Consequently, the Indians came to trust the Mounties. After Macleod retired from the NWMP, he stayed on in the West as a judge. So he was a permanent influence during the Indian people's very difficult years of great change.

John McLoughlin
Born 1784, Rivière du Loup, Que.
Died 1857

John McLoughlin was one of the larger-than-life figures of the fur trade, a giant grizzly bear of a man—tough, independent, stubborn, hot tempered. He started his career with the North West Company and then continued with the Hudson's Bay Company after the union of the two concerns in 1821. Appointed head of the HBC's Pacific Coast operations, McLoughlin had his main trading post on the Columbia River. This was a key position, since it was in the undefined border area, the Oregon Territory, which was claimed by the United States as well as by the HBC. But instead of making a strong British claim to the region (as James Douglas* later did in British Columbia), McLoughlin actually welcomed American settlers and helped them get established. This led to a bitter quarrel with Governor Simpson,* and McLoughlin left the HBC.

But the harm had already been done, for more Americans than British had moved into the Oregon Territory. When a boundary treaty was arranged in 1846, the United States could make a good claim to the region and ended up by getting it. McLoughlin settled there and became known as "the father of Oregon." He might also be known as "the man who lost Canada its southwest."

Marshall McLuhan
Born 1911, Edmonton, Alta.
Died 1980

"The medium is the message," said Marshall McLuhan. In the 1960s he set the world agog with his writings on the effects of mass communication, pointing out that media such as television have altered the way we see ourselves.

McLuhan was a university man with degrees from the University of Manitoba and Cambridge University in England, and for most of his life he taught at universities. Two of his most widely read books are *The Gutenberg Galaxy* (which won a Governor General's Award in 1962) and *Understanding Media*.

Ernest Campbell MacMillan
Born 1893, Mimico, Ont.
Died 1973

The great master of music once remarked, "I can't play for nuts and I've never written anything worthwhile, but I *can* conduct." This was the understatement of all time from the internationally famed conductor who was also an accomplished composer, pianist, organist—the man who contributed so much to Canadian music that he was given a knighthood, made a Companion of the Order of Canada, and showered with many other honours.

For many years, MacMillan was conductor of the Toronto Symphony Orchestra and the Toronto Mendelssohn Choir. He was also dean of the University of Toronto's Faculty of Music, chairman of the Canadian Music Council, and editor of *Music in Canada*.

Helen MacMurchy
Born 1862, Toronto, Ont.
Died 1953
At an international conference in 1949, Helen MacMurchy was named one of the ten leading women doctors in the entire western world.

Since her graduation in Toronto almost 50 years earlier, she had been involved in many areas of medicine: public health, mental health, child health. She had been editor of the *Canadian Nurse* journal and author of the popular "little blue books," which gave practical advice to Canadian women, telling them how to look after themselves and their babies. From 1920 to 1934 she was chief of the federal government's division of child welfare, and in 1924 she helped found the Federation of Medical Women of Canada.

Allan MacNab
Born 1798, Niagara-on-the-Lake, Ont.
Died 1862
Allan MacNab was a forceful member of the Family Compact, the small group of Tories who pretty well controlled Upper Canada during the early 1800s. For a while, he was speaker of the Legislative Assembly, but his power spread far beyond politics. He ran banks, railways, a steamship company, and was also a big landowner (he built himself a 72-room castle in Hamilton).

During the Rebellion of 1837, MacNab led the Loyalist militia which routed William Lyon Mackenzie's* rebel forces at Montgomery's Tavern, just outside Toronto. Pursuing Mackenzie to Navy Island in the Niagara River, MacNab then ordered an attack on the rebel supply ship *Caroline*, which was set on fire and sent plunging to destruction over Niagara Falls.

While making his way up the ladder of power, MacNab also used strong-arm tactics, wheeling and dealing in a way that was enthusiastic rather than scrupulously honest. Towards the end of his life, he headed the government of the Province of Canada. But his business affairs were in a terrible muddle and he died heavily in debt.

Archie MacNab
Born c.1781, Scotland
Died 1860
The Scottish laird Archibald MacNab came to Upper Canada in 1823, obtained a grant of land on the Ottawa River, brought out

Scottish families to settle it—and then proceeded to rule the area like a feudal baron. He made the settlers pay him quit-rents, wouldn't let them leave the land without his permission, and threw them in prison when they dared to complain. Although most of MacNab's actions were against the law, he had good friends among the Family Compact, and they tended to take his side.

This went on for more than 20 years before the settlers made any headway. They enlisted the support of Francis Hincks,* the Reform leader, who wrote up MacNab's doings in his newspaper, the *Examiner*. MacNab immediately sued Hincks for libel. But he lost the case and then lost his power over the settlers' lands. He left Canada and eventually died in great poverty in France. Meanwhile, Arnprior, the headquarters of his settlement, gradually grew into a town—a lasting reminder of the flamboyant laird of MacNab.

A. G. L. McNaughton
Born 1887, Moosomin, Sask.
Died 1966

General McNaughton was a man of many parts and many successful careers. A McGill graduate in engineering, he joined the army in 1914 and over the years rose to be chief of staff. In 1935 he was appointed president of the National Research Council, responsible for organizing scientific research, but he returned to the forces in World War II and served as commander of the 1st Canadian Army.

In 1944 Mackenzie King* appointed McNaughton to his cabinet as minister of national defence. After the war, McNaughton served as president of the Atomic Energy Control Board of Canada. And finally he moved onto the world stage, representing Canada at the United Nations.

Agnes Macphail
Born 1890, Proton Twp., Ont.
Died 1954

In 1921 Agnes Macphail was elected to the House of Commons—the first woman ever to sit in the Commons—and for 14 years she was the only woman there. In this lonely position, she was considered a curiosity. Every time she spoke, her remarks were reported in the papers, and there were constant jokes about the blue serge dress she generally wore. (She was not clothes-minded, and in any case she couldn't afford a large wardrobe.) A school teacher by profession, she had been elected by the United Farmers of Ontario (a people's party).

Throughout her years in Parliament, Agnes Macphail spoke for the underprivileged, championing the cause of striking miners as well as poor farmers, and starting some much-needed prison reform in Canada. Ordinary people loved her, but she was not particularly popular in Parliament. She once suggested that MPs should take a cut in salary.

John Macoun
Born 1831, Ireland
Died 1920

An enthusiastic naturalist, John Macoun had 48 species named after him, everything from plants to butterflies. In addition, he changed the route of the CPR, causing the railway to be built across the southern prairies, instead of via Edmonton and the Yellowhead Pass as had been planned.

Both Palliser* and Henry Hind* had condemned the southern prairies as "arid desert," unsuitable for settlers and therefore unsuitable for the railway line. But when Macoun went on expeditions in 1879 and 1880 he found lush grass, for there had been plenty of rain. He said that settlers could do very well there. This was good news for the CPR directors. The railway could be built more cheaply and quickly if it took the shorter, southern route. So although 10 years had been spent surveying the northern route, the directors announced in 1881 that the line would go via Calgary and Kicking Horse Pass. And so it did.

Duncan Macpherson
Born 1924, Toronto, Ont.

The political cartoons of Duncan Macpherson have been chuckled over from coast to coast for quarter of a century. He has a large international following too, for his cartoons have been reprinted in a great many overseas newspapers.

Macpherson studied in Boston and at the Ontario College of Art; and after working for *Maclean's* during the 1950s, he became cartoonist for the Toronto *Star*. Over the years, he caricatured most of the major political figures; and he made sketching tours in Cuba, Russia, China, and other countries, reproducing many of his sketches in books. He has won the National Newspaper Award six times.

Simon McTavish
Born 1750, Scotland
Died 1804

Nicknamed the Marquis, Simon McTavish was one of the great figures of the fur trade, and also one of the richest. Like many others, he learned the trade by going into the fur country and living among the Indian people.

In 1774 he set up his office in Montreal, where most fur-trading companies had their headquarters. McTavish realized that these small companies would make more profit if they joined together as one group, and with others he organized the North West Company. This combined fur-trading group became very successful. After his death, when his nephew William McGillivray* took over the leadership, it grew to rival the Hudson's Bay Company.

Antonine Maillet
Born 1929, Bouctouche, N.B.

Antonine Maillet is the voice of Acadia—its leading writer, who uses Acadian French to tell the story of her people's past, and to tell it to the world. She won France's most coveted literary award, the Prix Goncourt, for her dramatic book *Pélagie*. First published in 1979, and brought out in English in 1982, *Pélagie* is about the Acadians who were deported two centuries ago (see Charles Lawrence*). It tells the story of their gruelling 10-year journey back home, how they trekked with their ox carts all the way from Georgia to New Brunswick. Antonine Maillet is descended from those early Acadians.

She first gained nationwide attention with *La Sagouine* (1971), a monologue in which a wise-cracking old Acadian woman talks about her hard life. Staged as a one-woman show by actress Viola Léger, *La Sagouine* drew packed audiences in both French and English Canada. Maillet's other works include *Don l'Orignal*, which won a Governor General's Award.

Karen Magnussen
Born 1952, Vancouver, B.C.

Karen Magnussen won Canada's junior figure-skating championship in 1965 and gained the senior title three years later. But then disaster struck. In 1969, while training for the world championships, she suffered stress fractures in both legs. For three months her legs were encased in plaster. It looked as if she would never skate again.

But soon she was back in training and in 1970 she regained the Canadian title. She won the bronze medal at the 1971 world championships and the following year won the silver medal at the Olympics as well as at the world championships. And in 1973 she achieved every figure-skater's dream, carrying off the gold medal at the world championships.

Charles Mair
Born 1838, Lanark, Ont.
Died 1927

The poet and journalist Charles Mair was one of the founders of the Canada First movement, a patriotic organization formed by Ontario Protestants. They believed, among other things, that the prairies should be settled and controlled by English-speaking Canadians.

In 1868 Mair went to the prairies, to the Red River Settlement, and there he teamed up with Dr. John Schultz* who had similar views —pro-English and anti-Métis. Mair made such insulting remarks about Métis women that one woman drove him from her store with a horse-whip. In general, his behaviour helped to cause the ill-feeling which led to the Red River Rebellion. During the rebellion he was imprisoned by Louis Riel,* but he lived to fight again and served against Riel in the Northwest Rebellion.

Sieur de Maisonneuve
Born 1612, France
Died 1676

A seasoned soldier with a deep religious faith, Maisonneuve founded Montreal as a missionary outpost in 1642. He did so in spite of protests from the governor of New France, who said Maisonneuve was writing his own death warrant, for that whole region was controlled by the Iroquois. But Maisonneuve had been sent from France especially to set up a colony at Montreal, and he said he would do so "even if all the trees on the island were to change into so many Iroquois."

As it turned out, there were almost as many Iroquois as trees. During the 24 years Maisonneuve was governor of Montreal, the little settlement was attacked time and again. But Maisonneuve held out until finally so many soldiers and settlers arrived that there was no longer any fear of destruction.

Jeanne Mance
Born 1606, France
Died 1673

Our first secular nurse, Jeanne Mance came to Canada with Maisonneuve* and founded and ran Montreal's first hospital, the Hôtel Dieu. She was an early Canadian version of Florence Nightingale—cool-headed in the face of Iroquois attacks and wonderfully gentle with the sick and wounded. In Montreal's darkest hours, when it looked as if the tiny settlement would surely be destroyed, Jeanne Mance's courage shone like a light, stimulating even the most faint-hearted.

Maquinna
Birth unknown
Died 1795

Maquinna was the principal Indian leader of Nootka Sound when European seamen first arrived on Vancouver Island. In 1778 he welcomed Captain Cook.* Ten years later he let Captain Meares* build a house on shore. And he traded vigorously with the many ships that came flocking to Nootka Sound (from Spain and the United States, as well as from Britain).

A skilful diplomat, Maquinna played a key role in the negotiations early in the 1790s when Spain and Britain were on the brink of war over their rival claims to his territory. Both the Spanish captain Quadra and the English captain Vancouver* wined and dined Maquinna in their eagerness to get his support. But other seamen showed less respect, especially the Americans. Some of them used strong-arm tactics to get furs, shooting and looting, and raiding Indian villages.

Maquinna's successor (who was also called Maquinna) took revenge in 1803 by slaughtering the crew of the American ship *Boston*. Only two sailors were spared, and they were taken prisoner. One of them, John Jewitt, later wrote an account of the two years he spent as a captive of the Nootka.

Marie de l'Incarnation
Born 1599, France
Died 1672

Mother Marie de l'Incarnation came to Quebec in 1639 and started an Ursuline convent in a small house in the settlement. She was Canada's first great missionary nun. To begin with, she had only six other nuns to help her, but over the years she built up a network of well-organized convents, which ran schools for French and Indian children—some of the first schools in New France.

Mother Marie lived in a world of danger, for the French and Iroquois were almost constantly at war. But though her convents were at times attacked and her friends killed, she carried on her work, converting many of the Indians. She was one of the brave, determined spirits who helped build a strong Catholic society on the banks of the St. Lawrence.

Clara Brett Martin
Born c.1872, Toronto, Ont.
Died 1923

As the first woman lawyer in Canada (and in the entire British Empire), Clara Brett Martin had to fight all the way. When in 1892 she applied for permission to study law in Ontario, the Law Society said no. So she took her problem to the Ontario legislature, and after considerable lobbying from women's groups, the legislature passed a law saying that women could study law. This proved to be only the first step. For when Clara Martin completed her studies, the Law Society wouldn't "call her to the bar" as a barrister. Again she appealed to the legislature, which again took action, and in 1897 Clara Martin finally became a lawyer.

In New Brunswick, Mabel P. French had to go through a similar struggle before she was allowed to study law there in 1906. And when she moved to British Columbia some years later, she had to fight the same battle all over again. Between them, these two women successfully broke down the barriers, though it was not until 1941 that all of our provinces permitted women to study and practise law.

Lois Marshall
Born 1924, Toronto, Ont.

For many years, Lois Marshall was Canada's leading soprano, and she even performed in some operas, despite the fact that she had been lamed by polio as a baby. Until she was 12, she spent most of her time in hospital. But even then she liked to sing, sitting up in bed to entertain the nurses; and as soon as she left hospital, she started voice lessons.

Lois Marshall's first big chance came in 1947, when Sir Ernest MacMillan* picked her as a soloist for his annual performance of Bach's *St. Matthew Passion*. In the years that followed, her beautiful voice was heard in the world's major concert halls, and especially in Canada. She continues to perform from time to time, though she no longer does arduous concert tours.

Mungo Martin
Born c.1881, Fort Rupert, B.C.
Died 1962
Because of the Kwakiutl chief Mungo Martin, much of his people's culture has been saved, instead of being lost for ever.

Early in this century there was very little cultural activity among West Coast Indians, because the federal government had banned the potlatch, the central ceremony of Coast Indian life. Many traditional skills and art forms gradually died out, for there was no point in carving totem poles if you couldn't erect them with due honour, no point in learning traditional songs and dances if there was no occasion to perform them. By the time the potlatch law was repealed in 1951, very few people remembered the old traditions.

But Mungo Martin did. Though he had worked as a fisherman for most of his life, he had been a talented carver as a boy and had studied Kwakiutl ceremonials. In the 1950s he began to teach the younger generation the ancient skills—restoring old poles, building new ones, recording the traditional songs. He inspired a new awakening of the Kwakiutl culture.

He received many honours and even went to England for the presentation of one of his poles to the Queen. But the honour which pleased him most was the title bestowed on him by his own people: Naqapenkim. It means "ten times a chief" and is one of the highest titles in the Kwakiutl nation.

Hart Massey
Born 1823, Cobourg, Ont.
Died 1896
The multinational company now called Massey-Ferguson traces its origins to Hart Massey, who gave a great boost to farmers during the last century by producing some of Canada's earliest and best harvesting machines. His father Daniel had in fact started the business by making simple ploughs at his farm near Cobourg. But it was Hart and his son Charles whose combined talents carried the firm into the big leagues.

Establishing their headquarters in Toronto, they specialized in dramatic advertising, making each big sale an event; and gradually they built the family firm into the most successful farm-machinery company in the British Empire, with branches all over the world. They did so well that they could buy up competitors, including Alanson Harris's thriving company. For many years the firm was called Massey-Harris.

In the process of all this, Hart Massey became enormously wealthy, gaining enemies as well as admirers. Many people felt that he had grown rich on the backs of his workers. He was so mean, it was said, that when a labourer fell into a vat of paint and nearly drowned, Massey charged him for the spilt paint. Others praised him as a man who helped the poor and gave Toronto a magnificent concert hall, Massey Hall. The money left in his will supported many charities and provided for such buildings as the University of Toronto's Hart House, which was constructed under the auspices of his grandson, Vincent Massey.*

Vincent Massey
Born 1887, Toronto, Ont.
Died 1967
Vincent Massey was the first Canadian-born Governor General of Canada (1952-59). The grandson of Hart Massey,* he epitomized the grandeur associated with the family, which was expressed so neatly in the popular jingle:

Toronto has no social classes—
Only the Masseys and the masses.

Like his grandfather, Vincent Massey had as many detractors as admirers. His critics saw him as an untalented amateur who was given high office only because he was a Massey. His admirers saw him as a cultured, stately figure, just the person to represent them in public life.

He made an impressive ambassador to the United States in the 1920s—the first Canadian ever to be an ambassador—and he later served as high commissioner to Britain. He was also well known as a patron of the arts and was head of the Massey Commission (the Royal Commission on National Development in the Arts, Letters and Sciences) which led to the formation of the Canada Council, with its vigorous sponsorship of cultural activity.

His brother was the actor Raymond Massey (1896-1983).

Hannah Maynard
Born 1834, England
Died 1918

In 1862 Hannah Maynard opened a photographic studio in Victoria, B.C., and over the next 50 years she took literally thousands of pictures, many of them experimental photos like the self-portrait shown here. She was one of Canada's most original photographers, as well as one of the earliest.

She and her husband Richard had come to Canada in their twenties, and while he joined the gold rush, she learned photography and then practised it. Later he joined her in the business, while operating a boot and shoe store in the same building. But while Richard's true talents lay in making boots, Hannah's lay in creating extraordinary photos. One of the most extraordinary was a montage containing 22,000 tiny reproductions of children's faces.

John Meares
Born 1756, England
Died 1809

The sea captain John Meares was one of the first to take part in the West Coast fur trade, buying furs from the Nootka Indians and selling them at a profit in China. But though he was brave and adventurous, he was a notoriously shifty character and an accomplished liar.

In 1788 he "bought" Friendly Cove in Nootka Sound by giving Maquinna* a few sheets of copper. He then had his workmen build a house there and also a ship, the *North West America*, which was launched that same year. Meares was the first European to erect a house and launch a ship in the territory that is now British Columbia. He was also the first to bring in Chinese workmen, for some of his crew were carpenters he had hired in China.

Having established his base, Meares went off on another voyage, but while he was away the Spanish arrived and occupied Nootka. Meares sailed to Britain to complain, and there he told such stories of Spanish atrocities (most of them invented) that Britain prepared for war with Spain. However, the two countries eventually agreed on a peaceful settlement, which included a nice big payment for Meares to compensate him for his losses.

Arthur Meighen
Born 1874, Anderson, Ont.
Died 1960

Arthur Meighen was twice prime minister (1920-21 and for a few months in 1926). He was leader of the Conservative party for many years and made some of the best speeches ever heard in the House of Commons. Yet, after his second term in office, he couldn't even get into the Commons. The voters wouldn't elect him.

Remote and stern, Meighen was never very popular, even at the peak of his career. Although his abilities drew respect, he lacked the charisma to inspire affection. He was especially unpopular in Quebec, for he campaigned for compulsory military service during World War I, and many Quebeckers didn't see why they should fight in "Britain's war."

Meighen was fervently loyal to Britain and felt that whenever Britain was in trouble, Canada should say, "Ready, aye, ready! We stand by you." When he made this remark in the 1920s, a good many English Canadians agreed with him. But others were beginning to feel that Canada should not automatically get involved in every British war. As a young man, Meighen had seemed the great hope of the Conservative party. But he gradually lost the support of the Canadian people.

Honoré Mercier
Born 1840, St. Athanese, Que.
Died 1894

Honoré Mercier was premier of Quebec in the 1880s. A dapper man with elegant mustachios, he was a sparkling orator who could make his audiences laugh, weep, cheer, and always listen to what he said. Quebeckers adored him.

Mercier was leader of the Parti National, a pro-Quebec party which he had helped form. "Quebec is Catholic and French," he told his followers, "and it will remain Catholic and French." A devout Roman Catholic himself, Mercier enraged Protestants throughout Canada by awarding a large sum of money to the Jesuits, as payment for lands they had lost almost 100 years earlier. Later, he enraged Quebeckers, for it came to light that his government had accepted a large sum of money from a railway contractor (much as John A. Macdonald* had done in the Pacific Scandal). This was the end of Mercier's popularity. Disgraced and dismissed from office, he died a few years later.

William Hamilton Merritt
Born 1793, U.S.A.
Died 1862

William Merritt was one of the great figures in the story of Canadian transportation. He got the first Welland Canal built, enabling ships to sail between Lake Erie and Lake Ontario. And it was largely due to his efforts that the St. Lawrence canal system was completed, providing a navigable highway from the Great Lakes to the Atlantic Ocean. More than a century before the St. Lawrence Seaway was built, Merritt pointed the way.

He was the son of Loyalists who had settled at Twelve Mile Creek (today's St. Catharines, Ont.) near Niagara Falls. His first plan was very modest—to build a feeder canal to run the mills on his land—but this soon developed into a grander scheme, the Welland Canal. He formed a company with his neighbour George Keefer, raised money, hired engineers, and in 1829 the first two ships sailed through the canal. Over the years, Merritt became an influential businessman and politician, promoting railways as well as canals, so that a whole transportation network was built.

Monique Mercure

Born 1930, Montreal, Que.

In 1977 Monique Mercure won the best actress award at the Cannes Film Festival—the first Quebec actress ever to win this prestigious award. That same year she was also acclaimed best actress at the Canadian Film Awards. Both prizes were for her part in the film *J. A. Martin: Photographe*.

Raised in Montreal, Monique Mercure had wanted to be an actress since she was a small child, but she married young and didn't really get started on her career until she was 30. She has played in a wide range of productions, from Greek tragedies to tongue-in-cheek comedies, gaining a powerful reputation throughout the world.

Don Messer

Born 1909, Tweedside, N.B.
Died 1973

The oldtime music group called Don Messer and His Islanders was for many years the most popular of its kind in Canada. Messer was a violinist and musical director, and he formed the Islanders in 1939 to play on Charlottetown radio.

The group gradually attracted audiences across Canada and in 1959 began a weekly television program, *Don Messer's Jubilee*. This show was so popular that when the CBC finally cancelled it in 1969, there was a national outcry. Questions were even asked in the House of Commons. Messer had ardent fans south of the border too, and when he died one of his violins was placed in the Country Music Hall of Fame at Nashville in Tennessee.

Roland Michener

Born 1900, Lacombe, Alta.

As Governor General of Canada 1967-74, Roland Michener set the pace, literally. A great promoter of physical fitness, he went jogging every morning at a brisk pace.

Michener had always led an active life. He served in the air force during World War I, then worked as a lawyer and MP, and was for some years speaker of the House of Commons. He was in India, as Canadian high commissioner, when on General Vanier's* death he was called home to take up the position of Governor General.

In 1982, when Michener was 82, he scaled the mountain in Alberta that bears his name. Having been taken by helicopter up the lower slopes, he climbed the final 300 metres to stand triumphantly on the summit of Mount Michener.

Frederick Middleton
Born 1825, Ireland
Died 1898

General Middleton led the army that was sent to fight Louis Riel* during the Northwest Rebellion of 1885. Unlike Colonel Wolseley's* forces in the first Riel rebellion, Middleton's men sped west in about a week. The Canadian Pacific Railway was so nearly completed that they could do most of the journey by train.

Middleton was a British officer stationed in Canada, commander of the Canadian militia for most of the 1880s. After he returned to Britain, he had a rather different command: keeper of the Crown Jewels at the Tower of London.

David Milne
Born 1882, nr. Paisley, Ont.
Died 1953

David Milne devoted his whole life to painting. He believed that he must use his talents to the full and not waste them on other business. One of the few jobs he ever had was as a war artist in World War I. Milne generally lived deep in the country, and he seemed a romantic figure—a solitary artist, painting magnificent pictures, isolated from the rat race of everyday life. But he lived in the country because he couldn't afford to live in the cities.

Milne had an early success when in 1913 five of his paintings were included in a "modern art" exhibition in New York. But the main attractions at that show were the more startling paintings of Matisse and other French artists. When Milne held his own exhibition in Montreal in 1924, he didn't sell a single painting. Ten years later he found a sponsor in Vincent Massey* who bought a lot of his work, and by the time Milne died his talent was fairly widely recognized. But he was still struggling to make ends meet. Although the Massey family had bought 300 of Milne's pictures, they had paid only $5 per painting.

Jack Miner
Born 1865, U.S.A.
Died 1944

Jack Miner was Canada's famous bird man, the conservationist who established the Jack Miner Bird Sanctuary near Kingsville, Ont. He came to Kingsville with his family when he was 13 and at first made his living as a hunter, shooting moose, geese, ducks, and other wildlife. But by watching his prey so carefully, Miner came to admire them, especially the birds. So he decided to be their friend, and he made them a mud hole and put out grain for them. The geese came to know that his property was a safe resting place, and before long thousands were coming each year.

Then Miner began banding ducks and geese to find out where they migrated to and from. Strongly religious, he included a Bible text in the band. (Inuit who shot geese in the Arctic often found such messages as: "Keep yourselves in the love of God. Jude 1:21.") Because of Jack Miner's work, a great deal was learned about the migratory patterns of Canada geese. And today, thousands of birds still find a safe haven in the sanctuary he established.

Lord Minto
Born 1845, England
Died 1914
Lord Minto, who was Governor General 1898-1904, was a soldier by profession and he had served in the Northwest Rebellion. Military in manner, Minto was considered rather stiff, though this may have been because he had broken his neck in a riding accident. He was a keen jockey and rode four times in the British Grand National and won the French Grand National. As Governor General, he did much to promote all sports and gave Canada the Minto Cup for lacrosse.

Gaston Miron
Born 1928, Ste. Agathe des Monts, Que.
He has been hailed as Miron the Magnificent, "first bard of the Québécois nation." One of the world's leading French-language poets, Miron's reputation is high in France as well as Canada, though he writes in the language of Quebec, the day-to-day French of common speech.

Miron started writing when he was about 14 and published some of his first poems in *Le Devoir*. Many of his poems spoke up for an independent Quebec, and he was a hero to young Quebeckers during the 1960s. So well known was he as an ardent separatist that he was imprisoned during the October Crisis (see Laporte*). Miron has won several important literary prizes and has worked for many years as director of Les Éditions de l'Hexagone, a Montreal publishing company which he helped form in 1953.

W. O. Mitchell
Born 1914, Weyburn, Sask.
W. O. Mitchell invented Jake and the Kid—the elderly hired hand and the young boy whose doings and sayings have been the subject of wisely humorous radio and TV shows about a small Saskatchewan community called Crocus. The stories first appeared in *Maclean's* magazine during the 1940s, and they quickly became very popular. Although the town of Crocus didn't really exist, it seemed to be every small prairie community.

Mitchell has written a wide selection of other works, including a number of plays. One of his most celebrated works is the novel *Who Has Seen the Wind?* He has spent most of his life on the prairies and taught school in Alberta for a time during his early years.

Joni Mitchell
Born 1943, Fort Macleod, Alta.
Singer and songwriter Joni Mitchell was born Roberta Joan Anderson, daughter of a school teacher and a grocery store manager. Raised in Saskatoon, she studied art briefly in Calgary before moving to Toronto, where she wrote her first songs. But life was tough in Toronto as she tried to make her way by singing and playing the guitar in coffee houses.

Joni Mitchell's first big step was her performance at the Mariposa Folk Festival in 1965. Marrying the U.S. folksinger Chuck Mitchell that same year, she moved to the United States. Although her marriage soon fell apart, her career prospered. Joni Mitchell's unusual melodies, her flutelike voice, and the personal nature of her songs all combined to make her stand out from other singers. She has made more than a dozen LPs, which include such hits as "Chelsea Morning," "Woodstock," and "Both Sides Now."

Walter Moberly
Born 1832, England
Died 1915

Tough, stubborn, and a first-rate engineer, Walter Moberly explored in the Rockies in the 1860s, built part of the Cariboo Road, served as assistant surveyor general of British Columbia, and in 1871 was put in charge of the British Columbian surveys for the Canadian Pacific Railway.

Moberly wanted the railway to go through Eagle Pass, which he himself had discovered by watching eagles flying through the mountains. So keen was he on this pass that he quarrelled with Sandford Fleming,* who favoured the Yellowhead Pass. This led to Moberly's dismissal from the CPR project, and he moved to Winnipeg, where he built the city's first sewers. But he won his point in the end. For when the route of the CPR was changed (see Macoun*), Moberly's beloved Eagle Pass was one of those used. And the famous "last spike" was driven in there.

John Molson
Born 1764, England
Died 1836

Molson's ale was first made by John Molson, who arrived in Montreal in 1782 and a few years later started a small brewery. This was the beginning of a huge business empire, which was built up by Molson and his three sons, John Jr, Thomas, and William.

The Molson interests spread far beyond beer making. In 1809 John Molson launched the first steamship to ply the St. Lawrence between Montreal and Quebec. Called the *Accommodation*, it was also the first steamship to be built entirely in Canada. The Molsons soon added other ships to their fleet and developed a thriving steamship company. Their many other enterprises included whisky distilling, railway building, and Molson's Bank; and, in a later generation, ownership of the Montreal Forum and the Montreal Canadiens hockey team.

Guido Molinari
Born 1933, Montreal, Que.

Born of Italian parents and brought up in Montreal, the artist Guido Molinari opened his own *avant-garde* art gallery in Montreal when he was 22. He was soon recognized as a leading figure in the Montreal art world, and he went on to become the main spokesman for French Canadian artists throughout Canada. His style of painting is abstract and formal: stripes, triangles, carefully composed shapes, which are intellectually planned and very precise.

Lord Monck
Born 1819, Ireland
Died 1894

Lord Monck was the first Governor General of the Dominion of Canada. He was already in office at the time of Confederation. In 1861, Queen Victoria had appointed him "our Captain-General and Governor-in-Chief in and over our Province of Canada and . . . our Governor General of all our Provinces in North America."

On the day before Monck presided at Canada's birth as a nation, he wrote to his son: "I am obliged to go to Ottawa tomorrow for some business."

Marquis de Montcalm
Born 1712, France
Killed 1759

Montcalm was the general in charge of the French forces at the battle of the Plains of Abraham, the decisive battle in the struggle between Britain and France in North America.

A career soldier, he had been sent out from France in 1756, at the beginning of the Seven Years' War. At first he won victories against the British, but he did not follow up and strengthen his position as he was ordered to do by the French governor, Pierre de Rigaud de Vaudreuil. Constantly, he plotted against Vaudreuil and wrote letters of complaint to France. As a result, he was promoted to lieutenant general, which meant he ranked higher than Vaudreuil.

This was a disaster for French Canada, for Montcalm was not a clever soldier. During 1759 he made a series of tactical errors, allowing the British under General Wolfe* to sail up the St. Lawrence and besiege Quebec. Even then, Montcalm might have won, had he waited for reinforcements. But he went out and fought a pitched battle on the plains outside the fortified town of Quebec. His army was routed and he himself was mortally wounded.

A plaque on the site of the battle says that Montcalm was "gallant, good, and great" and that he was "defeated through no fault of his own." He was certainly gallant, extremely brave. But like Wolfe, he was a rather second-rate commander who has been glamorized through folklore into a superhero —a very different character from the man he really was.

L. M. Montgomery
Born 1874, Clifton, P.E.I.
Died 1942

Lucy Maud Montgomery was the author of *Anne of Green Gables*, the story of the red-headed orphan who finds happiness on a Prince Edward Island farm. The story was based partly on her own life, for her mother died when she was a small child and she was brought up by grandparents. But hers was not a happy childhood, and she escaped from it by writing—first, stories for children, then magazine articles.

Although they earned her a little money, success was a long time in coming. L. M. Montgomery was 33 before she wrote the "Anne" book which made her famous. From then on, she wrote many more novels, some of them sequels about Anne. The books have had immense popularity throughout the world and have been printed in a wide variety of languages, everything from Hungarian to Japanese.

Susanna Moodie
Born 1803, England
Died 1885

The writer Susanna Moodie immigrated to Upper Canada in 1832 and settled first near Cobourg and then near Peterborough, which was just a small settlement. She was the sister of Catharine Parr Traill* but didn't have her sister's positive outlook. Nor did she have the same brisk efficiency. She loathed being a pioneer.

Her book *Roughing It in the Bush* complained of just about everything: the climate, the gloomy woods, the low class and bad manners of neighbouring settlers; and the fact that "gentlefolk" like the Moodies couldn't possibly succeed as homesteaders. A later book, *Life in the Clearings*, was more cheerful, but that was about her life in Belleville after she had left the woods. There she occupied herself contentedly writing for magazines. Both books give a vivid picture of daily life at the time.

Mavor Moore

Born 1919, Toronto, Ont.

During his long and distinguished career, Mavor Moore has worked as actor, playwright, producer, director, all-round promoter of the arts, and in recent years as professor at York University and chairman of the Canada Council.

The son of actress Dora Mavor Moore, he wrote his first play when he was 11. In 1948 he launched the popular annual revue *Spring Thaw*. Over the years, he has written and performed in a wide range of productions, from tragedy to musicals and from radio to live theatre.

Mavor Moore's grandfather also played a prominent role in Canadian life. He was the economist Professor James Mavor, who helped bring the Doukhobors to Canada at the turn of the century.

James Wilson Morrice

Born 1865, Montreal, Que.
Died 1924

James Morrice was a landmark figure in Canadian art, for he was in the advance guard, moving from the nineteenth-century style of painting towards the "modern art" of the twentieth century. He was one of the first Canadian artists to gain a powerful international reputation.

Morrice lived most of his life in France but paid visits to Canada to hold exhibitions of his work, and he had a great influence on younger Canadian artists.

Norval Morrisseau

Born 1932, Fort William, Ont.

Brought up on a reserve near Lake Nipigon, Norval Morrisseau first began painting because he wanted to record the Ojibwa legends and make sure they were not forgotten. At first his fellow Ojibwas did not approve, for there was a taboo against making the legends public. But Morrisseau felt that Canada and the world ought to know about the richness of the Ojibwa culture.

Besides illustrating the legends, Morrisseau recorded the stories in a book, *Legends of My People*. He has since painted many other Indian subjects, bridging the cultures with his vibrant, colourful paintings.

Aaron Mosher

Born 1881, nr. Halifax, N.S.
Died 1959

One of the leading figures in the story of Canadian trades unions, Aaron Mosher left school when he was 15 and worked as a miner and as a freight handler. In 1908 he was made president of the newly formed Canadian Brotherhood of Railway Employees.

Mosher believed strongly that Canadian workers should have their own unions, rather than joining branches of American organizations. Nevertheless, in 1940, when Canadian and international groups joined together to form the Canadian Congress of Labour, he agreed to serve as president. He remained president throughout the life of the CCL.

Howie Morenz

Born 1902, Mitchell, Ont.
Died 1937

Howie Morenz was one of the fastest skaters and greatest stick-handlers who ever played hockey. He played with the Montreal Canadiens 1923-34, and during these years he three times won the Hart Trophy as most valuable player. Traded to the Chicago Black Hawks and then to the New York Rangers, he was back with the Canadiens for the 1936-37 season.

It was then that disaster struck. He was badly hurt in a game, suffering a broken leg and other injuries, and he died in hospital a few weeks later. The fans were appalled and thousands thronged to his funeral service in the Montreal Forum. Thirteen years after his death, in the Canadian Press poll of 1950, Morenz was voted Canada's greatest hockey player of the half-century.

Farley Mowat
Born 1921, Belleville, Ont.

Farley Mowat has gained celebrity in many areas: for his best-selling books, for his rumbustious character, for his championship of the Inuit, and for his efforts to save whales, seals, and wolves.

He started his writing career when he was 13, contributing a column on birds to a paper in Saskatchewan (where he spent part of his childhood). Because of his love for animals, he trained as a biologist, but changed course after becoming involved with the Inuit on a working trip to the North. Their desperate situation spurred him to write *People of the Deer*, an outspoken book that stirred up a lot of controversy. Four years later, in 1956, he published his first children's book, *Lost in the Barrens*. It won a Governor General's Award.

Mowat has since gone from strength to strength, gaining devoted readers across the world. His children's books alone have been translated into 29 languages.

Brian Mulroney
Born 1939, Baie Comeau, Que.

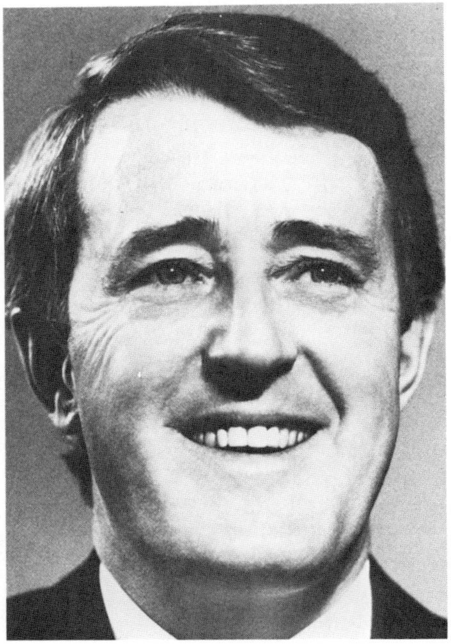

In 1983, at a party leadership convention, Brian Mulroney was elected leader of the Progressive Conservative Party of Canada.

Mulroney grew up in rural Quebec, the son of an electrician. He attended boarding school in Chatham, N.B., went on to St. Francis Xavier University, N.S., where he graduated in political science, and then gained a law degree from Laval University. This was followed by a successful career as a lawyer, as a legal specialist in labour disputes, and as a company president.

Although Mulroney was not an MP, he was a well-known public figure by 1976 when he first ran for the Conservative leadership. On that occasion he lost out to Joe Clark.* But at the 1983 leadership convention, it was Clark who lost to Mulroney on the fourth ballot.

Oliver Mowat
Born 1820, Kingston, Ont.
Died 1903

Oliver Mowat was premier of Ontario for 24 years (1872-96). This was a world record in the history of parliamentary government.

As a young man, Mowat had worked for John A. Macdonald* in his Kingston law office. He then spent most of his life working against Macdonald. He joined the Reform party, not the Conservatives. He championed provincial power, not federal power. He passed laws which Macdonald's government overruled, and then appealed successfully to the Privy Council in England to get the laws approved. By such actions during Canada's early years of nationhood, Mowat helped establish a truly federal system of government, in which the provinces had considerable power. He was appointed to the Senate when Wilfrid Laurier* became prime minister and he spent his last years as lieutenant governor of Ontario.

The writer Farley Mowat* is his great-great nephew.

Alice Munro
Born 1931, Wingham, Ont.
A two-time winner of the Governor General's Award for fiction, Alice Munro is one of Canada's most celebrated short-story writers. She writes about ordinary situations, the type of thing that might happen to anyone, and yet her stories are anything but ordinary. They have been called "precious gems"—dazzling little descriptions of the way people think and behave.

Alice Munro was raised in southern Ontario and later lived for many years in British Columbia. Most of her stories are set in Canada, especially in the Ontario countryside of her childhood. Two of her best-known books are *Lives of Girls and Women* and *The Moons of Jupiter*.

Emily Murphy
Born 1868, Cookstown, Ont.
Died 1933
Social worker, author, and clergyman's wife, Emily Murphy was the first woman in the British Empire to be made a magistrate. This was in 1916 when she was appointed to the women's court in Edmonton. Later that same year, Alice Jamieson was made a magistrate in Calgary. But the position of both women was challenged by Alberta lawyers, who argued that women were not legally "persons" and therefore could not hold public office.

Although the Supreme Court of Alberta ruled that women could hold public office, this was not necessarily the case throughout Canada. For instance, could a woman have a seat in the Senate? Emily Murphy decided to find out, and she and four others formally asked the Supreme Court of Canada for a judgement. Her fellow petitioners were Henrietta Muir Edwards, a founding member of the National Council of Women; Louise McKinney, a former Alberta MLA; Irene Parlby, an Alberta cabinet minister; and Nellie McClung.* To their dismay, the Supreme Court decided that women could not be senators.

But the Famous Five were not prepared to stop there. They appealed to the Privy Council in England, which in 1929 ruled that women were "persons" and were eligible for a Senate seat. This was a great step towards equal rights, and the following year Canada's first woman senator was appointed (see Cairine Wilson*).

Anne Murray
Born 1945, Springhill, N.S.

Singer Anne Murray grew up with her five brothers as a keen sports buff, intent on a sports career. She studied physical education at the University of New Brunswick and then taught it during 1966-67. But her other enthusiasm had always been music. By the time she started teaching, she had already sung at festivals and on radio, and in 1966 had sung in the chorus of the summer TV series *Singalong Jubilee*. This show was produced and hosted by Bill Langstroth, whom she later married.

By the end of 1967, singing had won out over teaching and Anne Murray was on her way to stardom. Her first big hit was "Snowbird," a song composed by Gene MacLellan (born 1939, Val d'Or, Que.). MacLellan was also a performer on *Singalong Jubilee* and he wrote several of the hits recorded by Anne Murray, including "Put Your Hand in the Hand."

Meanwhile, Anne Murray was performing in a wide range of shows. She soared to success during the 1970s, charming fans from Texas to Témiscaming with her husky voice and her "nice girl" appeal. She has won well over a dozen Juno Awards and a handful of Grammies, as well as numerous other awards.

Gordon Murray
Born 1894, Stratford, Ont.
Died 1976

Dr. Gordon Murray of Toronto General Hospital was one of the leading investigative surgeons of his time, constantly trying new methods, new approaches. He was the first Toronto surgeon to transplant a kidney and the first surgeon in the world to transplant a human heart valve. During World War II he invented an artificial kidney, which came into use in 1946. It was the first kidney machine in all North America.

Murray had graduated in Toronto in 1921 and then trained for six years under some of the world's greatest surgeons. He in turn trained others who became great surgeons.

John Wilson Murray
Born 1840, Scotland
Died 1906

John Murray was the Great Canadian Detective, a tough and very determined sleuth with steely eyes and a thick walrus moustache. He came to Canada by way of the United States, for his family had settled in New York, and he did his first detective work with the U.S. Navy. By the early 1870s, he was policing the Canada Southern Railway (which ran north of Lake Erie and into the United States); and he gained such a reputation that in 1875 he was appointed government detective for Ontario.

For the next quarter-century Murray relentlessly tracked down criminals in Ontario—and beyond. Once he pursued a suspect all the way to South America. When following a lead, he never gave up. Nor did he give in. On one occasion he was nearly strangled when struggling with a thief on a railway line. But he clung on to his attacker until help came.

Murray did his job so single-mindedly that he may well have put some innocent people behind bars. He was not the type of man to worry over subtleties. His duty, as he saw it, was to catch the suspects and get them tried and sentenced. And he did this with great success for many years.

Ma Murray

Born 1887, U.S.A.

Died 1982

Ma Murray, the feisty British Columbian newspaper woman, was awarded the Order of Canada in 1971. She was 84 at the time, still writing editorials and still sprinkling her writings with swear words whenever they just happened to happen. Some people were disgusted that she should be honoured with the Order of Canada. But most were delighted. For the irrepressible Margaret Murray had been entertaining readers for almost 40 years, ladling out large doses of common sense, along with her very definite views.

She and her husband George launched several papers, though she is most identified with the *Bridge River-Lillooet News*, which they started in 1934. She was the main force on the paper, for George had become a politician. After his death in 1961, she continued to publish the paper, stout-hearted as ever. Ma Murray may not have been *the* voice of the West, but she was a very strong voice; and an amusing one, offering "a chuckle every week and a belly laugh once a month" for half a century.

Andrew Mynarski

Born 1916, Winnipeg, Man.

Died 1944

Of all Canada's World War II heroes, one of the most heroic was Pilot Officer Andrew Mynarski, who stayed on in his blazing aircraft to try and rescue a fellow crew member.

All the crew had been ordered to bail out, but the rear gunner couldn't. He was trapped in his turret. Seeing this, Mynarski fought his way through the flames to try and free the gunner. It was a fruitless effort, and finally the gunner insisted that Mynarski must at least save himself. So he went back through the flames to the escape hatch. And there, though his parachute and clothes were on fire, he offered the trapped gunner a last gesture of encouragement—standing at attention and saluting, before jumping to safety.

Mynarski was so badly burned that he later died of his injuries. But the gunner, surprisingly, survived the crash and lived to tell of the pilot officer's amazing courage. In 1944 Andrew Mynarski was awarded a posthumous Victoria Cross.

James Naismith

Born 1861, Almonte, Ont.
Died 1939

The game of basketball was invented by James Naismith in 1891, when he was teaching physical education at the YMCA training school in Springfield, Mass. His director had asked him to think up an indoor game that would be more fun than P.T. and yet would still keep the students in shape between the football and baseball seasons. For the first games, Naismith used peach baskets nailed to the gymnasium balcony.

Naismith was the son of Ontario homesteaders, a McGill graduate in theology and a great believer in having a healthy Christian body as well as a healthy Christian mind. Later in life, he was appointed professor of physical education at the University of Kansas. And in 1936, at the Olympic Games in Berlin, he was a guest of honour when for the first time basketball was played as an Olympic sport.

Susan Nattrass

Born 1950, Medicine Hat, Alta.

She is Canada's shooting star, the girl with the golden gun. In 1982, for the sixth time, Susan Nattrass won the world championship in women's trapshooting. The previous year, she had been awarded the Lou Marsh Trophy as Canada's outstanding athlete.

Trained by her father, Susan Nattrass had her first big success at a handicap championship when she was 18, and the following year she beat 1,300 male competitors at a shoot in Nevada. Since then, she has proved time and again that she can outshoot all women and most men. In 1976 she was the first woman trapshooter ever to compete in the Olympic Games.

Susan Nattrass lives in Edmonton, which is also the home of Canada's champion male trapshooter, John Primrose (born 1942). Primrose has twice won the world trapshooting championship —the only Canadian man ever to win the title (in 1975 and 1983). He was given the honour of carrying the flag for Canada at the opening ceremonies of the 1982 Commonwealth Games.

Hilda Neatby

Born 1904, England
Died 1975

In 1953 Dr. Hilda Neatby stirred up a storm with her book *So Little for the Mind*, which criticized Canada's educational system, charging that public schools were not challenging students or offering them enough enrichment. She felt that there should be more emphasis on culture: more history, languages, arts, and music. In the controversy that followed, educators began to reassess what was taught, and how.

Hilda Neatby herself had received a very cultured upbringing, educated mainly by her scholarly parents on their remote Saskatchewan homestead. For much of her life she taught at the University of Saskatchewan, where she headed the history department 1958-69. Among her many activities, she served on the Massey* Commission, which led to the formation of the Canada Council.

Émile Nelligan

Born 1879, Montreal, Que.
Died 1941

One of the most brilliant poets of his day, Émile Nelligan was also the most tragic. The son of an Irish father and a French Canadian mother, he wrote his poems in French, but for a very brief period. By the time he was 20 he was seriously insane, and for the rest of his life he lived in mental institutions, too sick to write. He was too sick even to know when his first book of poems was published through the efforts of his friend and fellow poet Louis Dantin. His most famous poem is "Vaisseau d'Or" (The Ship of Gold).

Kate Nelligan

Born 1951, London, Ont.

Canada's Kate Nelligan won Britain's "best actress of the year" award in 1978 and was hailed as "the foremost English actress of her generation."

She had gone to England in her late teens to train as an actress, though she couldn't really afford it. Her family was not rich. She became so desperate during her second year in England that she wrote 150 letters to Ontario businessmen, asking for financial support. Richard Ivey, the insurance millionaire of London, Ont., came through with a weekly payment that enabled her to complete her training.

Nelligan had her first major role in a play in 1973 and went on to star in a wide range of productions, including the TV drama *Thérèse Raquin* and the movie thriller *The Eye of the Needle*. In 1983 she was a stunning success on Broadway, New York, in the play *Plenty*.

Wolfred Nelson

Born 1791, Montreal, Que.
Died 1863

As one of the leaders of the Lower Canadian Rebellion of 1837, Wolfred Nelson commanded the Patriotes in their victorious battle at Saint-Denis. Although born into a privileged British family, he had long sympathized with the underprivileged habitants, feeling that they were not getting a fair deal in the way Upper and Lower Canada were run.

Nelson was a doctor by profession, but also a politician. Before the rebellion, he had been elected to Lower Canada's assembly—a great triumph, considering that he ran against the attorney general of Lower Canada. For his part in the rebellion, he was banished to Bermuda, but was later allowed to return home and again served in the assembly.

As a member of La Fontaine's* government, he helped bring in the Rebellion Losses Bill (which caused Lord Elgin* so much trouble). But, typically, Nelson did not insist that his own family be repaid for losses suffered during the rebellion. Whether working as a politician or doctor, he always helped others, rather than himself. A marker on his grave reads, "Here lieth God's noblest work, an honest man."

Peter Newman

Born 1929, Austria

Peter Newman, author of *The Canadian Establishment* and other highly successful books, was editor of *Maclean's* magazine 1971-82. Of Czech and Jewish origin, he came to Canada with his parents during World War II, having fled his family home in Czechoslovakia when the Germans occupied the country.

The Newmans settled near Burlington, Ont., where young Peter went to school, later attending Upper Canada College. He completed his education at the universities of Toronto and McGill, and had his first job in journalism while still a student. During his years as editor of *Maclean's*, he built the magazine into a successful large-circulation weekly.

Margaret Newton

Born 1887, Montreal, Que.
Died 1971

Margaret Newton was a leading researcher in the battle against stem rust, the disease that kills wheat. She was a 1918 graduate of McGill University, having been one of the first two women students at Macdonald College—the first two ever to graduate in agriculture in Canada. She was appointed associate professor at the University of Saskatchewan and in 1925 joined the Dominion Rust Research Laboratory in Winnipeg.

By this time, Margaret Newton was a world authority on rust. She had discovered that the disease was not caused by one single organism. There were many different kinds of rust (just as there are different kinds of flu). This explained why, in some years, Red Fife and Marquis wheat had been stricken by the disease. And it led researchers to develop new wheat strains, in which the good milling qualities of Red Fife and Marquis were combined with the greater rust resistance of other varieties of wheat.

Cindy Nicholas

Born 1957, Toronto, Ont.

Cindy Nicholas started competitive swimming when she was five and had her first big success a few days before her seventeenth birthday. This was in August 1974 when she crossed Lake Ontario in 15 hours and 10 minutes—faster than any swimmer, male or female, had ever done before.

Cindy Nicholas went on to stack up a great list of record-breaking swims, including her 1977 two-way crossing of the English Channel. She broke several records on that occasion: first woman, youngest man or woman, and fastest swim. Altogether she has swum the Channel more than a dozen times. Meanwhile, she has graduated in both science and law, and has embarked on a career as a lawyer.

John Norquay

Born 1841, St. Andrews, Man.
Died 1889

The premier of Manitoba from 1878 to 1887 was big-hearted John Norquay, a giant of a man with great ambitions for the province. Like many others who were born and raised in the Red River Settlement, Norquay was a son of the fur trade—Scots on his father's side and of Métis descent on his mother's. His cousin (who was also called John Norquay) was a member of Riel's* provisional government during the Red River Rebellion.

Norquay himself did not figure prominently in the rebellion, but after it was over he ran for office and was elected to Manitoba's first legislature. A talented orator, he could speak in five languages: English, French, Cree, Saulteaux, and Sioux. He tried to represent all groups in the community, and this brought him wide popularity, though it did not make him popular with such extremists as John Schultz.*

As premier, Norquay enlarged the boundaries of Manitoba and worked to get the province greater control of its own affairs. He even tried to build provincial railways, but this angered the federal government so much that he had to resign. He died suddenly of appendicitis a couple of years later.

William Notman
Born 1826, Scotland
Died 1891

Many of the well-known historical photos of famous Canadians and famous Canadian events were taken by William Notman, the greatest of Canada's early photographers. The son of a Scottish artist, he set up a photographic studio in Montreal in 1856, and it did so well that he was able to establish branch studios in several other cities.

Photographs were still a novelty at the time and it was very fashionable to have one's portrait taken. Besides these formal photos, Notman and his sons made visiting cards with people's pictures on them. And they produced group portraits, taking separate photos of individuals and then combining them in one carefully arranged picture. Most important, they photographed significant scenes, thus giving a first-hand view of Canadian history while it was happening.

Alden Nowlan
Born 1933, nr. Windsor, N.S.
Died, 1983

Winner of the 1967 Governor General's Award for poetry, Alden Nowlan grew up the hard way. When he was 15 he went to work in a sawmill, and he then took a series of odd jobs before getting work on a New Brunswick newspaper. While earning his living as a journalist and news editor, he wrote stories and poetry in his spare time, bringing out his first book of verse in 1958. Eleven years later, with several books behind him, he was appointed writer-in-residence at the University of New Brunswick. He did much to encourage literary work in the Maritimes.

Lucius O'Brien
Born 1832, Shanty Bay, Ont.
Died 1899

Lucius O'Brien helped found the Royal Canadian Academy in 1880 and served as its first president. Educated at Upper Canada College, he worked as an architect and civil engineer before becoming a professional artist early in the 1870s.

O'Brien was chiefly a landscape painter, specializing in dramatic canvases of Canadian scenery. His best-known work is *Sunrise on the Saguenay*, which hangs in the National Gallery in Ottawa.

Daniel O'Donoghue
Born 1844, Ireland
Died 1907

Known as "the father of the Canadian labour movement," Daniel O'Donoghue was the first labour candidate ever elected to the Ontario legislature. He was a member of the legislature 1874-79.

A printer by trade, O'Donoghue had settled in Ottawa, where in his early years he helped organize local unions. He later became a leading figure in the Trade and Labour Congress of Canada, which was formed in the 1880s as a national organization. Year after year, O'Donoghue strove to get better conditions for Canadian workers. He was among the first to press for workmen's compensation laws and for safety measures to prevent on-the-job accidents.

Frank Oliver
Born 1853, Peel County, Ont.
Died 1933

Frank Oliver was one of the men who put Alberta on the map in 1905. He fought long and hard to get the province created. He was also one of early Edmonton's most vigorous boosters. When he arrived there aged 23, the town was little more than a collection of shacks —a few huts and tents huddled around a remote HBC post in the North-West Territories. By the time he died, Edmonton had long been the provincial capital, a busy city with cars and shops and thousands of people.

Even in his twenties, Oliver was a mover and shaker. As early as 1880 he founded the Edmonton *Bulletin*, an outspoken newspaper which struck at John A. Macdonald's* government for ignoring the West. From journalism, Oliver moved into politics.

For many years he was a Liberal MP in Ottawa, helping to shape western Canada while fighting for its interests. He was a cabinet minister under Laurier* and finally a railway commissioner, dying in harness at the age of 80.

Andrew Onderdonk
Born 1848, U.S.A.
Died 1905

The American engineering contractor Andrew Onderdonk built one of the most difficult sections of the Canadian Pacific Railway: 200 km of track in British Columbia, including the railway line through the Fraser Canyon.

As there were not enough workmen available in Canada, Onderdonk hired Chinese labourers, bringing thousands of men direct from China by ship. Between 1881 and 1884, more than 15,000 Chinese came to British Columbia. About 5,000 stayed on after the railway was completed, and others later came back to Canada, bringing their families with them. Although there were some Chinese living in B.C. before the railway was built, Onderdonk's construction workers formed the main core of the Chinese community that developed in the province.

Michael Ondaatje
Born 1943, Sri Lanka

The poet Michael Ondaatje has lived in three different countries. He spent his early childhood in Sri Lanka (Ceylon), was sent to England for his schooling, and came to Canada as a university student. He has since taught English at the University of Western Ontario and at York University.

Ondaatje has written several volumes of verse, two of which won the Governor General's Award. He has also written an autobiography and has made an experimental film about the poet bpNichol (who was born Barrie Phillip Nichol, Vancouver, 1944). A dedicated experimenter himself, bpNichol is Canada's leading exponent of what is called "concrete poetry." He too has won a Governor General's Award.

Bobby Orr

Born 1948, Parry Sound, Ont.

One of hockey's all-time greats, Bobby Orr seemed able to do everything better than any other player, and at top speed. Although he was a defenceman, he twice won the Art Ross Trophy as the NHL's top scorer. And he won every other available trophy too, including the Lou Marsh Trophy as Canada's outstanding athlete.

Orr played for the Boston Bruins 1966-75, and during those years he brought the Bruins out of the doldrums and led them to victory in two Stanley Cups. Many people who saw Orr in his heyday considered him the best player ever. But his heyday was relatively brief, for he was plagued by a knee injury that would not mend, despite a series of operations. After being in and out of hospital and then resting up for a whole season, Orr made a brief comeback with the Chicago Black Hawks in the fall of 1978. But his knee was still not right. He retired from professional hockey at the young age of 30, just when many of his contemporaries were at the height of their career.

William Osler

Born 1849, Bond Head, Ont.
Died 1919

William Osler was the most famous doctor of his day, a brilliant, vibrant figure who inspired others with his own enthusiasm for medicine. He was a professor at McGill aged 25, and he later taught at Philadelphia, at Johns Hopkins University in Baltimore, and finally at Oxford in England.

Osler changed the way medicine was taught in North America, emphasizing bedside instruction in hospital wards. He felt that medical students should meet patients and study their ailments personally, rather than doing most of their training in lecture halls and laboratories. He also caused changes in the type of treatment used in hospitals, pointing out that many of the traditional procedures did as much harm as good. An avid researcher, Osler wrote copiously on a wide range of subjects. His textbook, *The Principles and Practice of Medicine*, was translated into four languages, including Chinese.

J. Percy Page

Born 1887, U.S.A.
Died 1973

Raised in Ontario, J. Percy Page moved west as a young man, and for many years he was a teacher in Edmonton, where he coached the celebrated women's basketball team, the Edmonton Grads. Under his training, the Grads became world champions with a long record of success. Between 1915 and their disbandment in 1940, they won 502 of the 522 games they played. J. Percy Page also made his mark in politics, serving in the Alberta legislature, and he was lieutenant governor of Alberta 1960-66.

John Palliser
Born 1817, Ireland
Died 1887

John Palliser led a scientific expedition to western Canada 1857-60, gathering a mass of valuable information on this little-known region. He reported that much of the southern prairies (which became known as the Palliser Triangle) was very arid, unsuitable for farming.

Palliser was not himself a scientist. He was a well-born Irishman with a taste for adventure and a passion for hunting buffalo. One of his roles on the expedition was to shoot enough meat to keep his team of scientists fed. His scientists were Dr. James Hector, a Scottish geologist; Eugène Bourgeau, a French botanist; John Sullivan, a mathematician-astronomer; and Lieutenant Thomas Blakiston, who made magnetic observations, quarrelled with the others and left in a huff before the end of the expedition.

Besides studying the prairies, Palliser and his men explored the Rockies, looking for a pass which might one day be used by a railway. In 1858, Kicking Horse Pass was discovered and named by Hector, who was kicked in the chest there by his horse. This pass was used when the CPR was built, though the Palliser team advised against building a railway through the Rockies; they thought it would be too difficult. Hector later gained fame as an explorer in New Zealand. And Palliser, after travelling in various countries, settled on his Irish estate.

Louis-Joseph Papineau
Born 1786, Montreal, Que.
Died 1871

Papineau was the figurehead of the Rebellion of 1837 in Lower Canada, though he didn't intend armed revolt. When he realized that his followers were turning to violence, he fled across the border to the United States.

Papineau had long been head of the French cause in Lower Canada. As leader of the Patriote party and speaker of the Legislative Assembly, he had been striving to get the French population more say in the government of Lower Canada. But he did not favour responsible government. Although he admired American republicanism, he was in many ways an old-style seigneur. What he wanted was a French republic on the St. Lawrence with himself as president.

None of this came to pass. When Papineau returned to Canada after years of exile in France, his shining image was tarnished, for many Patriotes felt he had deserted them during the rebellion. He served in the Legislative Assembly for a while and then retired to Montebello, the mansion he had built on his family estate.

Duff Pattullo
Born 1873, Woodstock, Ont.
Died 1956

The Pattullo Bridge at New Westminster, B.C., is named after Thomas Dufferin Pattullo, who was the Liberal premier of British Columbia 1933-41. He had moved west as a young man, served as assistant gold commissioner in the Yukon, and then settled in Prince Rupert. Entering provincial politics in 1916, he was eventually voted in as premier at the worst possible time—at the height of the Great Depression.

Pattullo had won the election by promising "work and wages," and he tried to provide both by launching a public works' program to give jobs to the unemployed. The Pattullo Bridge was one of the projects in this program. But there were still thousands of unemployed, and in 1938 they marched through Vancouver and staged a sit-in which ended in a riot (see Steve Brodie*).

Pattullo increasingly lost popularity, even within his own party, until he was obliged to resign. Yet, through his policies, he had done much to lay the basis of British Columbia's future prosperity.

Howard Pawley

Born 1934, Brampton, Ont.

Howard Pawley became premier of Manitoba in 1981 when the New Democratic Party won the provincial elections. He had moved to Winnipeg when he was 17, together with his family, who were committed socialists. (His father had once run as a CCF candidate in Ontario.) The Pawleys were also strict Methodists, and Howard Pawley briefly considered being a Unitarian minister. But he studied law instead and in due course entered politics.

He was first elected to the legislature as an NDP member in 1969 and was a cabinet minister in Premier Schreyer's* provincial government. In 1979 he was elected leader of the Manitoba NDP, bringing his party into power in 1981 with a strong majority.

Lester B. Pearson

Born 1897, Toronto, Ont.
Died 1972

The prime minister of Canada 1963-68 was soft-spoken Lester Pearson, who was known for his affability as well as his ability.

In his early twenties, Pearson taught at the University of Toronto, having already served in World War I (and been invalided home when he was run over by a London bus). But soon he gave up teaching and embarked on his long career as civil servant and diplomat. He was ambassador to the United States 1945-46 and later negotiated Canada's entry into NATO, the western-defence alliance.

Elected to Parliament in 1948, Pearson was appointed minister of external affairs. In this position, he played an even greater part in world politics and served as president of the U.N. General Assembly 1952-53. A few years later, he helped solve the Suez Crisis in the Middle East by suggesting that a U.N. peacekeeping force be sent to the area. Pearson's quiet diplomacy in defusing the Suez Crisis gained him the Nobel Peace Prize in 1957.

As prime minister, he brought in several important measures, including the Canada Pension Plan. And he gave Canada a new flag, the present-day maple leaf flag. Yet his greatest role was before he became prime minister, when his skilful diplomacy gained for Canada its fine reputation as a world peacekeeper.

Brian Peckford

Born 1942, Whitbourne, Nfld.

In 1979 Brian Peckford became premier of Newfoundland, heading a Conservative government. He was educated at the Memorial University of Newfoundland and worked as a welfare officer during his student years. After graduating, he taught school until 1972 when he was elected to the provincial legislature. Two years later he was appointed to the cabinet.

As premier, Peckford has taken a strong stand in negotiations with the federal government, striving to retain control of Newfoundland's offshore petroleum resources, rather than letting Ottawa have control of them.

George R. Pearkes

Born 1888, England

George Randolph Pearkes began his working life as a homesteader on the prairies and ended it as lieutenant governor of British Columbia. In between, he served with the Mounties in the Yukon, joined the army in World War I and won the Victoria Cross, was a major general in World War II and head of Canada's Pacific Command; and after the war he served as an MP and minister of national defence. He was lieutenant governor of B.C. 1960-68, retiring at the age of 80.

Chief Peguis

Born c.1774, nr.Sault Ste. Marie, Ont.

Died 1864

It was largely because of Chief Peguis and his band of Salteaux Indians that the Selkirk* colonists managed to survive during their first difficult years in the Red River Settlement.

Peguis had moved westward in the 1790s, settling on Netley Creek, a branch of the Red River, and he befriended the Selkirk colonists from the moment the first group arrived in 1812. He gave them food in time of need and taught them how to hunt buffalo. He even housed some of them in his camp when they were being harried by the North West Company men.

Peguis became a good friend of the missionaries too, and in 1840 he was converted to Christianity. His grandson William Henry Prince, who was educated at St. John's College in Winnipeg, became a missionary and teacher.

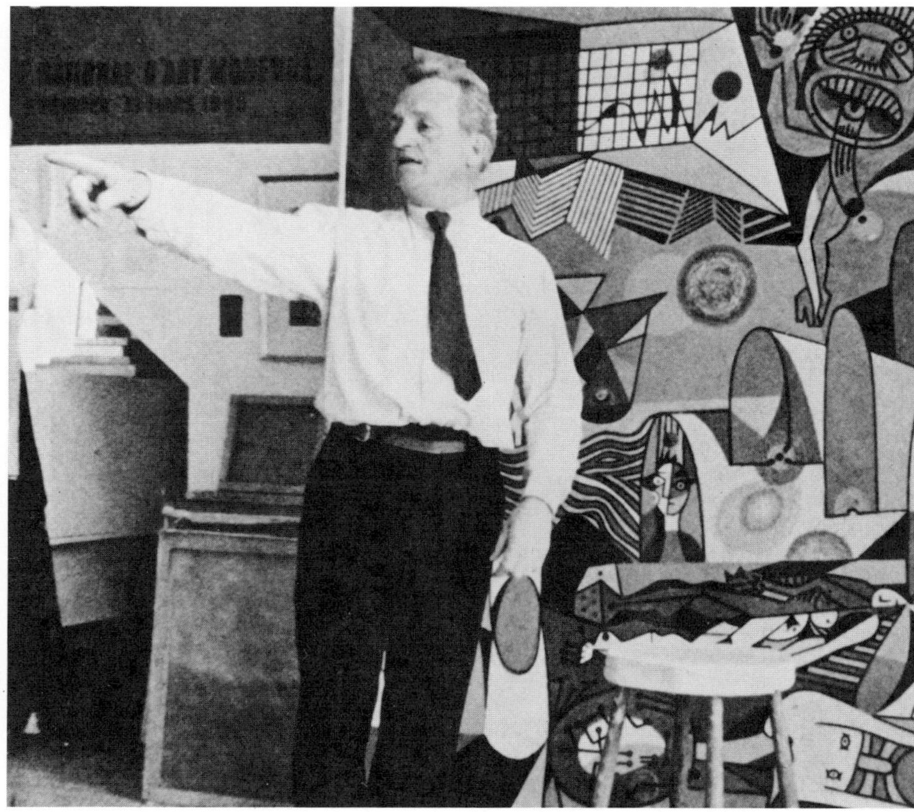

Alfred Pellan

Born 1906, Quebec, Que.

Alfred Pellan breathed new life into French Canadian painting—and, in due course, into all Canadian painting. He and Paul-Émile Borduas* introduced Surrealism to Canada, pointing artists away from traditional styles and towards abstract art.

Pellan was an outstanding artist even as a teenager. While still a student, he had one of his paintings bought by the National Gallery. After graduation, he won a scholarship to study in France, and it was there that he developed his expressionist style of painting. When in 1940 he finally returned to live in Canada, the exhibitions of his pictures caused great excitement. Here was a new way of seeing things, a new way of expressing what one saw. In 1943 Pellan was appointed to the teaching staff of the École des Beaux Arts in Montreal, a position he held until 1952. Over the years, he has continued to produce highly original paintings.

Wilfrid Pelletier
Born 1896, Montreal, Que.
Died 1982

The largest concert hall in Montreal's Place des Arts is named after Wilfrid Pelletier, a dynamic force in the music of Quebec province. He launched his career in New York, rising from pianist to conductor with the Metropolitan Opera, and in 1934 he returned to Canada to form and conduct the Montreal Symphony Orchestra.

Among his many activities, Pelletier helped found Montreal's Conservatory of Music so that promising young students could get expert training in their own province. As director of the conservatory 1943-61, he brought internationally famed musicians to come and teach the students. This led to a great flowering of musical talent among the younger generation of Quebeckers.

Pelletier had a worldwide reputation, and several countries awarded him their highest honours. In 1968 he received his own country's highest honour —Companion of the Order of Canada.

Thomas Peters
Born c.1738 (Africa?)
Died 1792

Thomas Peters was an early civil rights leader who courageously opposed injustice. A former slave from North Carolina, he fought for the British in the American Revolutionary War and came to Nova Scotia in 1784 along with 3,500 fellow black Loyalists.

Like the white Loyalists, the blacks who settled in the Maritimes were promised grants of land and three years' worth of provisions. But they received only three months' worth of provisions, and most got no land at all. Those who were granted land received tiny plots that were far too small to support them. And they weren't allowed to vote or to have the benefit of a trial by jury.

Peters had the courage to speak out against this situation, and in 1790 he went to Britain to make a formal complaint. There he was befriended by a group of reformers who were trying to start an African colony, in which blacks from North America could be landowners and have all the rights of British citizens. Peters thought this a great idea, and two years later he left Halifax with 1,200 others to settle in Sierra Leone. But life proved tough there too, and he died of fever a few months after his arrival.

Wilder Penfield
Born 1891, U.S.A.
Died 1976

One of the world's greatest brain surgeons, Dr. Wilder Penfield found a way of controlling epilepsy by removing the damaged brain tissue where the attacks were triggered. And he "mapped" the human brain, discovering which parts of it controlled which functions.

Educated in the United States and Britain, Penfield came to Montreal in 1928 to head a neurological department at the Royal Victoria Hospital and to teach at McGill. At the time, very little was known about how the brain worked. There was only one brain specialist in all Canada—Dr. Kenneth McKenzie, who had recently set up a brain surgery unit at Toronto General Hospital.

Penfield's interests went far beyond surgery, and in 1934 he founded the Montreal Neurological Institute so that doctors, surgeons, and other specialists could do co-ordinated research on the nervous system. Penfield was director of the institute until his retirement in 1960; and there, with his associate William Cone, he did his great pioneering work on the brain.

Oscar Peterson

Born 1925, Montreal, Que.

One of the giants of jazz, Oscar Peterson grew up in Montreal, and by the age of 16 he was playing the piano on Montreal radio. By the time he was 20 he was being heard nationally on such shows as *The Happy Gang*. A few years later he moved to the United States, where he formed his own trio, and during the 1950s he rocketed to fame, touring North America, Europe, the Far East, and making numerous records.

Although Canada has remained Peterson's home base, he continues to dazzle the world with his playing. He has received countless awards and in 1973 was made an Officer of the Order of Canada.

Piapot

Born 1816, southern prairies
Died 1908

The Piapot Reserve in Saskatchewan's Qu'Appelle Valley is named after the Cree chief Piapot (or Payepot), who settled there with his band in 1884. He had been allotted a reserve to the east of Regina, but after a terrible winter, during which almost half the band died, he led the survivors to the valley where he had hunted in his youth. There they could find fish and wild duck, and even a few deer, to supplement their small government rations.

Like all the prairie chiefs, Piapot had a difficult role to play looking after his people's welfare while their way of life was changing so drastically. He handled it very skilfully. Respected by government officials as a "trustworthy Indian," he often gained special favours for his band. Wisely, he declared his loyalty during the Northwest Rebellion, and this brought further favours.

But Piapot fell from grace in 1899 for allowing his young men to conduct a traditional ceremony which had been banned by the government. He was deposed by the Indian Department, though his band continued to regard him as chief until his death.

Mary Pickford

Born 1893, Toronto, Ont.
Died 1979

Known as "America's sweetheart," Mary Pickford was Canada's sweetheart too, the most popular movie actress of her day.

Born Gladys Smith, the daughter of a poor Toronto family, she was taken to the United States by her ambitious mother, and there in her teens she became a stage actress on Broadway and then a movie actress in Hollywood. By the time Mary Pickford was 20, she was famous throughout the world—the innocent-eyed heroine of silent films, often playing the part of the penniless waif she had been in early childhood.

But she was no longer penniless. She acted with Charlie Chaplin, had a much-publicized romance with Douglas Fairbanks (whom she married), and for more than 20 years was the star of the silver screen. She gave up movies after her divorce from Fairbanks in 1935.

Ivan Pillipiw
Born 1859, Ukraine
Died 1936
Ivan Pillipiw and his friend Wasyl Eleniak were the first Ukrainians to come to settle in Canada. They were poor peasants from the village of Nebyliv in Galicia, and there they heard of the free land being offered to immigrants. It seemed like a fairy tale: you could be your own boss in faraway Canada, without any landlord ordering you around. The two men decided to find out if the stories were true, and in 1891 they sailed to Montreal and then took the train west. They were amazed at what they saw: "There was land everywhere . . . all empty."

Eleniak took work in Manitoba while Pillipiw returned to the Ukraine to collect their families. His arrival home started an immigration fever as word spread of the opportunities in Canada. This brought Pillipiw into trouble with the authorities, and he was imprisoned for acting as a ticket agent to get people out of the Ukraine. However, many peasants did leave for Canada, and so did Pillipiw and his family in 1893. He settled in Alberta and died there aged 77 by falling out of a window at a wedding.

Pitseolak
Born 1904, Nottingham Island, N.W.T.
Died 1983
One of the most successful of the Cape Dorset artists, Pitseolak Ashoona grew up in the nomadic Inuit manner, moving from camp to camp in pursuit of the wildlife off which her family lived. After her husband died, she worked as a seamstress in Cape Dorset in order to provide for her children. She first took up art because it brought in more money than sewing. Since those early days, Pitseolak has gained wide fame for her prints and drawings, and her work has been hung in galleries across the world.

Another talented Pitseolak from Cape Dorset was Peter Pitseolak (1902-73) who was a photographer as well as an artist. Many of his photos are included in his autobiography, *People from Our Side*.

Gordon Pinsent
Born 1930, Grand Falls, Nfld.
Actor and author Gordon Pinsent was educated in Newfoundland and had his early acting experience in repertory companies. He became nationally known in the 1960s, when he starred in the popular CBC TV series *Quentin Durgens, MP*. This was followed by many other prominent roles in a wide range of productions, from films to Shakespeare plays.

As well as acting, Pinsent has written plays, screenplays, and novels. His book *The Rowdyman*, a Newfoundland story, was made into a film in which he starred. He also wrote and starred in the successful CBC TV series *A Gift to Last*, which was aired in the late 1970s. And in the 1980s he began to direct television drama. Among his many awards, he has been made an Officer of the Order of Canada.

Antoine Plamondon
Born 1804, Ancienne Lorette, Que.
Died 1895
Antoine Plamondon was known for his bad temper and good painting. Crusty and quarrelsome, he considered himself *the* portrait painter of Quebec City and was bitterly jealous of any other artists who dared trespass on his territory.

He had studied art in France, having had his early training from Joseph Legaré (1795-1855), who was the first Canadian-born artist to concentrate on landscape painting. Plamondon's speciality was portraits, and his most famous work is a wonderfully sensitive painting of a pretty young nun, Sister Saint-Alphonse. He was one of the founders of the Royal Canadian Academy and served as its first vice-president.

Jacques Plante
Born 1929, Shawinigan Falls, Que.
One of the best goalies in hockey history, Jacques Plante was also a superior skater and he used to wander far out of his net to handle the puck. He played for the Montreal Canadiens from 1952 to 1963, and during this period he pioneered the use of the goalie mask. At first he wore a mask only at practice sessions, but after receiving a hard shot in the face during a 1959 game, he took to wearing a mask whenever he was on the ice. Gradually other goalies began to do so too.

Plante was traded, and played for several teams after the Canadiens. He continued to play in the NHL until well into his forties.

Christopher Plummer
Born 1929, Toronto, Ont.
Film star Christopher Plummer grew up in Montreal, where he had his first parts in school plays and later acted in repertory. By the time he was 25 he was already acting on Broadway. He has starred in movies in Canada, Britain, Hollywood, even Russia, and has played in everything from musicals to Shakespeare plays. One of Plummer's best-known Canadian films was *Murder by Decree*. And one of his many leading roles was as Captain Von Trapp in *The Sound of Music*.

Peter Pond
Born 1740, U.S.A.
Died 1807
The trader Peter Pond was the first non-Native to travel into the Athabasca country of northern Alberta and Saskatchewan, a subarctic region that was rich in magnificent furs. This was in 1778.

Pond was a tough loner, surly and violent—he once killed a fellow trader and had a hand in the death of two others. Yet he was a man with a dream. Not content with opening up the Athabasca country, he longed to find a waterway from there to the Pacific. He drew maps of the way he thought the rivers ran (some of them amazingly accurate). Although Pond didn't explore to the Pacific himself, he inspired Alexander Mackenzie* to take up the challenge.

Steve Podborski
Born 1957, Toronto, Ont.
In March 1982, Steve Podborski was proclaimed king of the mountains, winner of the men's World Cup downhill skiing championship. He was the first man from North America ever to win the title, which was gained over a full season of racing.

Podborski had been on skis almost as soon as he could walk, going regularly to the ski slopes at Collingwood, Ont. In 1980 he won a bronze medal at the winter Olympics and in the 1980-81 season won three World Cup victories, coming second overall in the championship. His 1982 triumph crowned Canada's long-standing bid for the championship, which teammate Ken Read (born 1955) had come close to winning in 1978 and 1979.

Great things were expected of Podborski the following season, but in the spring of 1983 he suffered a bad skiing accident which put him out of the championships.

Pontiac
Birth unknown
Murdered 1769

The war chief of the Ottawas from Detroit, Pontiac was a supporter of the French during the Seven Years' War of 1756-63. Towards the end of the war, when it was obvious that the British had won, Pontiac and many other Indians launched their own war against the conquerors. This was because they feared they would lose their lands and would not have such favourable trading terms with the British as they had had with the French.

During the rising, Pontiac and his allies captured nearly all the posts west of Niagara. But the British brought in fresh troops, and before long peace treaties were made. Over the next few years, the British showed Pontiac particular respect, and in return he offered them his firm loyalty. Neither of these facts pleased Pontiac's former Indian allies, and a group of them hatched a plot and murdered him.

Jerry Potts
Born c.1840, U.S.A.
Died 1896

The son of a Blood Indian woman and a Scottish fur trader, Jerry Potts became a guide to the North-West Mounted Police when in 1874 they first arrived in the West; and for more than 20 years he served as a loyal, if unusual, member of the NWMP.

Potts was considered a bit of a "character," a man who spoke very little and drank far too much. Once, when the Mounties had captured some whisky traders (complete with their illegal liquor), Potts drank the evidence on the journey to Fort Macleod. But he was a first-rate guide, as the Mounties well knew. He taught them how to survive on the plains, and he often acted as a go-between, smoothing relations with the Plains Indians. When he died, he was buried with full military honours and with six members of the NWMP carrying his coffin.

Poundmaker
Born c.1842, nr. Battleford, Sask.
Died 1886

The Cree chief Poundmaker spent much of his life working for peace, yet he was imprisoned for being a warmonger. His great achievement was to end the age-old war against the Blackfoot Confederacy by forming an alliance with Crowfoot,* who made him an adopted son.

During the Northwest Rebellion, Poundmaker again tried to be peaceable, but without success. When he went to Battleford to ask for overdue rations, his followers went wild and looted the town. In reprisal, a Canadian force under Colonel William Otter attacked Poundmaker's band near Cut Knife Hill—and were roundly defeated by the Crees. There would have been a massacre if Poundmaker hadn't stopped his men from pursuing the retreating soldiers.

When brought to trial after the rebellion, Poundmaker insisted that he had "saved a lot of bloodshed." Nevertheless, he was sentenced to three years in prison. He was released a few months later because he was dying of TB.

Christopher Pratt

Born 1935, St. John's, Nfld.

Christopher Pratt was for many years the away-from-it-all artist, living in a clapboard house beside Newfoundland's Salmonier River. But as his fame increased, the world beat a path to his door—art collectors, art critics, reporters, all eager to meet the elusive Newfoundlander who produced such striking paintings.

Pratt had studied art under Alex Colville* at Mount Allison University, and his pictures are similar in style to Colville's, except that there is a cold starkness about them. His wife Mary also paints very powerful pictures. She couldn't concentrate on painting while she had four young children to look after, but in recent years she has been gaining a reputation which may yet rival her husband's.

E. J. Pratt

Born 1883, Western Bay, Nfld.

Died 1964

By the end of his life, E. J. Pratt was regarded as a type of unofficial poet laureate, winner of the prestigious Lorne Pierce Medal and a three-time winner of the Governor General's Award. He was famous for such narrative poems as "Brébeuf and His Brethren" and "Towards the Last Spike," as well as for his evocative lyrics about Newfoundland.

Although Pratt was a Newfoundlander heart and soul, he spent most of his life in Toronto, teaching English at Victoria College. There he passed on to his students his enjoyment of literature, along with his enjoyment of people and parties. He was a friendly spirit, very much part of the world around him.

Louis Quilico

Born 1925, Montreal, Que.

Canada's leading baritone and an internationally acclaimed performer, Louis Quilico is the son of an Italian father and a French Canadian mother. He began his singing career as a choir boy in Montreal and in 1953 won the radio competition Singing Stars of Tomorrow. Two years later he won the Metropolitan Opera Auditions of the Air. So began an operatic career that was to delight audiences from Paris to Parry Sound. His son Gino is also a baritone, and father and son have at times performed together in operas.

Al Purdy

Born 1918, Wooler, Ont.

Al Purdy has been writing poetry since he was 13—and has done a lot of other things too. In his early years, he earned his living at whatever job he could get, working in a mattress factory in Vancouver, driving a taxi in Belleville, Ont. He published his first book in 1944, paying for the printing himself, and eventually gained national attention in 1965 with the publication of *The Cariboo Horses*, which won the Governor General's Award for poetry.

Now one of Canada's best-loved poets, Al Purdy is known especially for the "Canadianness" of his work. He writes of Canadian people and places, often speaking up for the underdog.

Pierre Radisson
Born c.1640, France
Died 1710

Pierre Radisson was one of the founders of the Hudson's Bay Company. His partner in this venture was his brother-in-law, Médard Chouart des Groseilliers.

As a child, Radisson had been captured by the Iroquois and adopted by a Mohawk family. So he knew the Indian people well. This was a great asset for a *coureur de bois*, which he was at first. In 1659-60 he and Groseilliers went trading around Lake Superior, where the Indians told them about the vast number of beaver to be found farther north, near Hudson Bay. The two traders passed on this news to the French authorities, but little interest was shown. Even more annoying, they were taxed heavily on the furs they had obtained on their expedition.

In fury, they changed sides and teamed up with some British merchants. Throughout his life, Radisson flipped sides as easily as a coin, and somehow always managed to get away with it. The British outfitted a fur-trading voyage to Hudson Bay, which proved so profitable that in 1670 the Company of Adventurers was formed, later known as the Hudson's Bay Company.

John Rae
Born 1813, Scotland
Died 1893

Like Samuel Hearne,* John Rae was successful as an Arctic explorer because he learned from the Native people and adopted their ways. He travelled light, living off the land and finding his own food, which meant there was no limit to the distance he could go. Over the years, he charted hundreds of kilometres of Arctic coastline.

Rae was a Hudson's Bay Company man (he first worked for them as a doctor), and in the 1850s the HBC asked him to search for Sir John Franklin's* expedition, which had disappeared without trace. Though Franklin and his men were believed to have died in the Arctic, nobody knew where or how, and the British had offered a £10,000 reward to anyone who found proof of their fate. After much searching, Rae found proof—and received the reward. Ironically, the well-equipped Franklin party had died because they didn't have Rae's simple skills. They didn't know how to live off the land.

Raffi
Born 1948, Egypt

Canada's most popular children's entertainer started his career by singing for adults. In his early twenties, Raffi was one of the many folksingers trying to break into the music world in Toronto. But he could barely make enough to pay the rent.

Then one day his wife's mother asked him to sing at the nursery school she ran—and Raffi found his audience. Through the Mariposa in the Schools program, he went from school to school, giving highly successful concerts. He formed his own record company and brought out several albums, including *Singable Songs for the Very Young*, which quickly became Canada's top-selling children's album. In recent years, Raffi's fame has spread to the United States, and there too he tours small towns and large cities, delighting young and old alike.

James Reaney

Born 1926, nr. Stratford, Ont.

Poet and playwright James Reaney has won three Governor General's Awards. For his subject matter, he often draws on local history, as in the plays he wrote about the Donnellys.* Reaney grew up not far from Donnelly country—on a farm near Stratford—and he returned to southwestern Ontario after several years of teaching at the University of Manitoba. For many years now, he has been a professor at the University of Western Ontario. His large literary output includes a children's book, *The Boy with an R in His Hand*, which is a story about William Lyon Mackenzie.*

Kate Reid

Born 1930, England

An actress of tremendous power and presence, Kate Reid can hold an audience spellbound. She is one of the world's leading dramatic actresses.

She grew up in Oakville, Ont., and went to school at Havergal College in Toronto, later studying drama at the Royal Conservatory of Music. Over the years, she has starred frequently at the Stratford Festival, as well as at Charlottetown and many other theatre centres. She has also had successes on Broadway in such plays as *Who's Afraid of Virginia Wolfe?*

Although principally a stage actress, Kate Reid has had several film roles and has also performed in TV drama. She has received many honours and awards, including the Order of Canada.

Rocket Richard

Born 1921, Montreal, Que.

The Rocket, Maurice Richard, right wing of the Montreal Canadiens 1942-60, was one of the most exciting hockey players who ever caused the Forum crowds to yell themselves hoarse. One year, when he was suspended for striking a referee, the fans rioted in protest and did thousands of dollars' worth of damage in Montreal. Rocket Richard played in more than 1,000 games for the Canadiens, leading his team to victory in eight Stanley Cups. And in the 1944-45 season, he made hockey history by being the first player who ever scored 50 goals in 50 games.

His brother Henri Richard also starred with the Canadiens, playing for them 1955-75. Nicknamed the Pocket Rocket, Henri had a tough time at first because he was the younger brother, skating in the Rocket's shadow. But within five seasons of big-league hockey, he had already helped win five Stanley Cups.

Bill Reid

Born 1920, Victoria, B.C.

Bill Reid has revived the old Haida art forms in a new way, drawing on traditional legends and designs, but presenting them in a modern style. His work ranges from a massive carving of Raven to delicate rings and bracelets.

Reid is Scottish-German on his father's side and Haida on his mother's, and his art combines both cultures. While earning his living as a broadcaster, he studied European techniques of jewellery-making at Ryerson in Toronto. He also studied Haida techniques from his mother's father—a silversmith in the old tradition, who had learned his craft from one of the great Haida artists, Charles Edenshaw (1840-1920).

In the 1960s, Reid set up his own jewellery business, and in the past 20 years he has played a major part in promoting his people's culture. Such artists as Robert Davidson have drawn inspiration from his approach, leading Haida art in a new and exciting direction.

Louis Riel
Born 1844, St.Boniface, Man.
Hanged 1885

The Métis hero Louis Riel was leader of the Red River Rebellion (1869-70) and the Northwest Rebellion (1885). Deeply religious, he believed that God had chosen him to save the Métis people.

Riel was educated in Montreal and returned home at the age of 24, just when the federal government was arranging to buy the Northwest from the Hudson's Bay Company. With the change of ownership, the Métis feared that settlers would move into the area and take their lands. In trying to prevent this, Riel set up a "provisional government," thereby starting the Red River Rebellion. But he didn't see himself as a rebel. In fact, he sent three men to Ottawa to get approval for his measures. Instead of approval, the government sent an army under Colonel Wolseley* (for Riel had executed an Ontarian called Thomas Scott,* and English Canadians wanted revenge).

Riel fled, and for the next 14 years he lived as a fugitive and exile, mostly in the United States, though he spent some time secretly in mental hospitals in Canada. Then, in 1884, the people of the Saskatchewan valley asked him to come and be their spokesman, for there were again problems about land. This led to the Northwest Rebellion, after which Riel was tried for treason and hanged—to the fury of all French-speaking Canadians.

Riel's death, like his life, bitterly divided Canada. While French Canada honoured him as a martyr, English Canada viewed him as a villain. Many years passed before he was widely recognized as a sincere idealist striving for justice.

John Richardson
Born 1796, Queenston, Ont.
Died 1852

Adventurer, soldier, and writer, John Richardson was the author of *Wacousta*, a historical novel set in Canada at the time of Pontiac's* War. Richardson wrote several other novels, but none had the success of *Wacousta*, which has become a classic.

Richardson's own life was as dramatic as the stories he wrote. During the War of 1812 he was taken prisoner by the Americans. He later lived in Europe, fought for the royalists in Spain, and returned to Canada during the Rebellion of 1837 as a reporter for the London *Times*. This was not a success. Richardson was dismissed from the *Times* for praising Lord Durham.* Later ventures were equally ill-fated—running a newspaper in Brockville, policing the Welland Canal. Despite all his talents, Richardson died penniless.

Mordecai Richler
Born 1931, Montreal, Que.

The Apprenticeship of Duddy Kravitz is one of the best-selling novels by Mordecai Richler, whose books are read avidly throughout the world. Witty, sophisticated, and a master of satire, Richler writes rather dark comedy, telling stories that are sad as well as humorous. This is also the case in his children's story *Jacob Two-Two Meets the Hooded Fang*.

Richler was born and raised in Montreal's Jewish community, and this is the setting for many of his books. After studying at Sir George Williams University, he went to Europe and first had a story published in Paris when he was 19. Over the following years, he had a variety of jobs in broadcasting and film, often working as a scriptwriter. Several of his books have been made into films, and he generally takes an active part in their production. Richler has won numerous awards for his work, including two Governor General's Awards.

Susie Carson Rijnhart
Born 1864, Strathroy, Ont. (?)
Died 1908
Of all Canada's overseas missionaries, one of the bravest was Susie Rijnhart, a young doctor who accompanied her husband Petrus to Tibet in 1895. Tibet didn't welcome foreigners, and few missionaries had ever succeeded in entering the country. But both Petrus and Susie were kindly, understanding people, and they established a successful mission just inside the border. There they made good friends with the Tibetans and even taught the Gospel to a "living Buddha," one of the most powerful religious leaders in Tibet.

The Rijnhart's mission was so successful that they decided to venture into the heart of the country. This led to disaster. First their baby died. Then Petrus was murdered by bandits. Stranded alone in the snow among Tibet's hostile mountains, Susie had a terrible two-month journey to reach the nearest mission station in China. Yet this didn't frighten her off. She came home to Canada to drum up support for her mission and then returned to Tibet to carry on her work.

Jean-Paul Riopelle
Born 1923, Montreal, Que.
Jean-Paul Riopelle is famed throughout the world for his striking abstract paintings, many of them vibrant multicoloured pictures—a pattern of paint built up with a palette knife.

Riopelle had his first inspiration at the École du Meuble in Montreal, when he was a student of Paul-Émile Borduas.* He was one of the Automatists, the group of experimental artists led by Borduas. He was also one of the enthusiasts who signed Borduas's revolutionary pamphlet, *Refus Global*, which called for freedom from authority in life as well as art. In 1946 Riopelle went to France, and he has spent most of his time there since, though he maintains close ties with Canada.

John Robarts
Born 1917, Banff, Alta.
Died 1982
As premier of Ontario 1961-71, John Robarts was hailed as a "father of re-Confederation," because he helped to bring French and English Canadians closer together. At a time when the "two founding nations" seemed poles apart, he established good relations with two successive premiers of Quebec: Jean Lesage* and Daniel Johnson. In 1967 Robarts and Johnson hosted the Confederation of Tomorrow Conference, which tackled specific problems and did much to heal the rift between French and English Canadians. Robarts continued his efforts after retiring from the premiership, and in the late 1970s he was co-chairman of the Task Force on Canadian Unity.

In December 1977 he was appointed chancellor of Toronto's York University.

Charles G. D. Roberts
Born 1860, Douglas, N.B.
Died 1943

When Charles G. D. Roberts was 20, he brought out a book called *Orion, and Other Poems*. It made a very strong impression on other young poets, for it proved that English-speaking Canadians no longer had to look to England or the United States for their literary inspiration. Here was a home-grown Canadian writing very fine verse.

Of the poets inspired by Roberts, the most notable were his cousin Bliss Carman,* Archibald Lampman (1861-99), and Duncan Campbell Scott (1862-1947). As a group, they are called the Confederation Poets. Not only did they emerge as poets during the Confederation era, but they brought a new national spirit to Canadian poetry.

Roberts wrote a great deal of prose as well as poetry, gaining a wide following for his stories about animals. He taught literature in his youth and ended his life as one of our most celebrated writers of literature—showered with honours, including a knighthood.

Robbie Robertson
Born 1943, Toronto, Ont.

Robbie Robertson, lead guitarist of The Band, has been hailed as one of rock's finest players. At the age of 13, he was playing professionally around Toronto. When he was 15, two of his songs were recorded by American rockabilly singer Ronnie Hawkins, and the next year he joined Hawkins's backup band, The Hawks.

By 1960, all of The Hawks except drummer Levon Helm were Ontario-born musicians: bass guitarist Rick Danko (born Simcoe, 1942), organist Garth Hudson (born London, 1937), pianist Richard Manuel (born Stratford, 1943), and Robbie Robertson. They played together for more than 15 years, changing the group's name several times after leaving Hawkins. They first called themselves The Band in 1969. By then they had a tremendous international reputation and had performed frequently as Bob Dylan's backup band. This association caused many people to think they were an American group.

In 1976, The Band staged a farewell concert, which was the subject of *The Last Waltz* (1978), one of the most compelling rock films ever made. Since then they have continued to perform individually and with other groups.

Jean-François de la Rocque de Roberval
Born c.1500, France
Died 1560

The Sieur de Roberval was a thoroughly unpleasant character, cruel, crotchety, and overbearing. In 1542 he led the first colonizing expedition to Canada, much to the annoyance of Jacques Cartier,* who felt he should have been given the task.

Roberval's group of colonists included some of his friends and relations, as well as numerous prisoners from French jails; and one of his first acts was to dump a female relative on an island in the Gulf of St. Lawrence, because he had caught her having a love affair with one of the cavaliers. He then sailed on to found his colony at Cap Rouge, near the present site of Quebec City.

The whole thing was a disaster. Roberval's temper was such that he hanged people separately instead of pulling them together. Nor was he a good organizer. That winter, the settlers suffered from hunger and scurvy, as well as bitter cold. After a few months, Roberval gave up his dreams of empire and took the survivors home to France. They told such horror stories that more than 50 years passed before anyone else tried to found a colony in Canada (see Champlain*).

John Beverley Robinson
Born 1791, Berthier, Que.
Died 1863

A staunch Loyalist and Tory, Judge Robinson stood for law and order and "respect for rank and family." Educated at John Strachan's* school and then virtually adopted by Strachan, he was the most striking example of the power wielded by the Family Compact. During the 1820s he was government leader in the Legislative Assembly, and he was later chief justice of Upper Canada and also speaker of the Legislative Council and president of the Executive Council. His iron hand was on everything.

Robinson knew clearly what was right and what was wrong, and his actions were as firm as his beliefs. During the War of 1812 he condemned a group of men to death for siding with the Americans. As a result of these "Bloody Assizes" 8 men were hanged. He showed the same lack of mercy during the Rebellion of 1837 when he condemned Lount* and Matthews to be hanged.

These deaths still loom like dark shadows over Robinson's name. Yet he was sincerely doing what he thought best. Throughout his life, he worked to build a well-ordered society in Upper Canada.

John Robson
Born 1824, Perth, Ont.
Died 1892

Lured west by the Fraser River gold rush, John Robson became one of British Columbia's best-known citizens—a live-wire journalist and politician. He settled in New Westminster, where in 1861 he started mainland B.C.'s first newspaper. Called the *British Columbian*, the paper was highly critical of Governor James Douglas's* autocratic rule. Robson also criticized Judge Begbie,* and was imprisoned for a few days as a result. He took full advantage of this indignity, writing an article which began: "Fellow colonists, we greet you from our dungeon."

Robson worked ardently to get British Columbia made part of Canada, and after this was achieved in 1871 he was elected to the provincial legislature. He became premier of British Columbia in 1889. Three years later, during a visit to England, he caught his finger in the door of a cab and died of blood poisoning.

Thomas Roddick
Born 1846, Harbour Grace, Nfld.
Died 1923
Dr. Roddick, one of the leading medical men of his day, began his career aged 14 as a doctor's assistant in Nova Scotia. He went on to be dean of medicine at McGill, chief army medical officer during the Northwest Rebellion, and founder of the Medical Council of Canada. Based in Montreal for most of his life, he was especially noted as a surgeon.

In 1877 Roddick started to use the antiseptic methods recently pioneered in Scotland by Joseph Lister. This involved sterilizing instruments and dressings in carbolic acid, and spraying the patient with carbolic acid. Previously, surgeons had not recognized the importance of extreme cleanliness, and most of their patients had died of blood poisoning. But most of Roddick's patients survived. His success inspired other Canadian surgeons to follow Lister's methods.

John Rolph
Born 1793, England
Died 1870
During Upper Canada's turbulent years of rebellion and reform, one of the most turbulent figures was John Rolph, doctor, politician, and lawyer. He was one of the leading members of the Reform party and one of the most bitter enemies of John Strachan* and the Family Compact. Yet people were seldom sure where exactly Rolph stood, or even whose side he was on. During the Rebellion of 1837 he supported both sides at the same time, acting as spokesman for the governor while secretly plotting with the rebels.

The one constant in Rolph's life was his enthusiasm for medicine. He opened the first medical school in Upper Canada at the Talbot* Settlement in 1824, and he later started several more medical schools, including the famous Toronto School of Medicine. But even here his difficult character caused problems. In 1856 his whole staff walked out on him, taking many of the students with them. Nevertheless, Rolph was greatly admired as a teacher, and he has justly been hailed as the father of medical education in Upper Canada.

Bobby Rosenfeld
Born 1905, Russia
Died 1969
In the Canadian Press poll of 1950, Bobby Rosenfeld was voted Canada's outstanding all-round female athlete of the half-century.

Brought to Canada as a baby, she had grown up in Barrie, Ont., where she won her first trophy at a track meet in 1922. Two years later, she won the Toronto grass courts tennis title. And in 1928, at the Olympic Games, she won the silver medal in the 100-metre dash as well as bringing Canada a gold in the 400-metre relay. After giving up active sports, she was for many years a sports columnist for the *Globe and Mail*.

James Clark Ross
Born 1800, Scotland
Died 1862
In 1831, the British naval officer James Ross discovered the Magnetic Pole (the place to which a compass needle points when indicating north). This was during a four-and-a-half year stay in the Arctic on an expedition commanded by his uncle, Sir John Ross. The length of their stay was unintentional. Their ship was trapped in the ice.

Ross had first sailed to the Arctic with his uncle when he was 18, and he followed this up with four voyages under William Parry, another famous Arctic explorer. On one of these expedition's, Parry's ships sailed halfway through the Northwest Passage. And on an expedition in 1927, Parry and Ross came within 800 km of the North Pole. In 1848, Ross was put in charge of the first expedition that was sent to search for Sir John Franklin.* Although he couldn't find the missing explorer, his expedition added yet another link in the world's knowledge of the Arctic. (See also John Rae.*)

Sinclair Ross

Born 1908, nr. Prince Albert, Sask.

Sinclair Ross is the author of *As for Me and My House*, a novel about the loneliness of a windswept prairie community during the 1930s. This book is now considered to be one of Canada's greatest novels, but when it first came out in 1941 it attracted little attention. Ross earned his living by working in a bank, since he could not support himself as a writer. Only in recent years has his talent been widely recognized. He has written several other books, including *The Well* and *Sawbones Memorial*.

Gabrielle Roy

Born 1909, St. Boniface, Man. Died 1983

Gabrielle Roy was the first Canadian writer to win France's celebrated Prix Femina award. This was for her 1945 novel *Bonheur d'Occasion*, which was later translated into English as *The Tin Flute*. The book was a phenomenal success for a first novel, a best seller in the United States and Europe, as well as in Canada. Its strength lay partly in its realism. The main characters in the story lived in one of the poorest parts of Montreal, weighed down by all the grime and dismalness of life near the railway tracks. This was a great contrast to fashionable novels about the well-to-do, and it was an eye-opener to many Canadians.

Gabrielle Roy was not herself from such a poor background. In her early years, she worked as a school teacher and journalist. A three-time winner of the Governor General's award, she was widely admired as one of Canada's finest novelists.

Claude Ryan

Born 1925, Montreal, Que.

From 1964 to 1978, Claude Ryan was publisher of *Le Devoir*, the Montreal-based newspaper which had been founded by Henri Bourassa* early in the century. Since its origins, the paper had been one of the most powerful voices in Quebec, constantly speaking out on political issues. Ryan maintained this tradition with such integrity that Quebec politicians often based their policy on his editorials.

In 1978 he was invited to be leader of the Liberal party in Quebec. Quebec Liberals felt that he would be able to rally Quebeckers against the separatist government of René Lévesque.* But despite Ryan's efforts, he was not able to get the Liberals back into power, and he resigned from the party leadership in 1982. His major contribution as a politician was his role in the successful fight against Lévesque's separatist referendum.

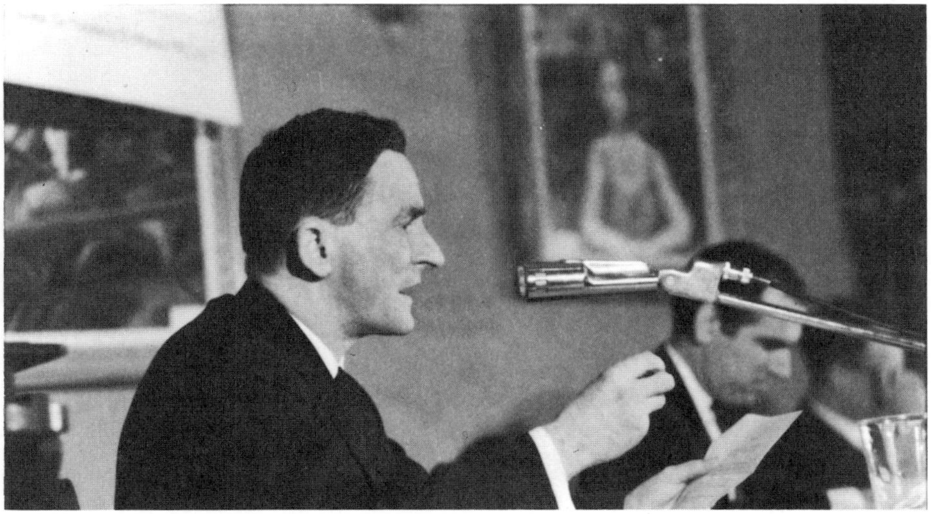

Egerton Ryerson
Born 1803, nr. Vittoria, Ont.
Died 1882

Egerton Ryerson was the organizer of Ontario's public school system. As superintendent of schools 1844-76, he brought in a series of measures, culminating in the School Act of 1871, which made free elementary education available to all Ontario children. He also improved the secondary schools, served as first principal of Victoria College in Cobourg, and worked in every way to provide a high standard of education in the province.

Ryerson was a Methodist minister who had gained attention early in life by championing the cause of Methodists and other "non-established" Christian groups; he stood up for their rights against the powerful Anglican churchman, John Strachan.* Besides speaking out firmly and often, Ryerson wrote numerous pamphlets and books, and served as first editor of the Methodist paper, the *Christian Guardian*. He also helped lay the basis of a publishing venture which eventually developed into the Ryerson Press. A committed crusader all his life, Ryerson was elected in 1874 to be the first president of the Methodist Church of Canada.

Charles de Salaberry
Born 1778, Beauport, Que.
Died 1829

The military commander Charles de Salaberry was a great hero of the War of 1812—"the hero of Châteauguay." It was there, south of Montreal, that he routed a large American force which had mounted an invasion into Lower Canada.

Salaberry was a regular army officer who had already fought in the West Indies and in the Napoleonic Wars. At the battle of Châteauguay he was commander of the Canadian Voltigeurs, a volunteer force that he had raised to fight off the Americans. After the war, he was appointed to the Legislative Council of Lower Canada.

Louis St. Laurent
Born 1882, Compton, Que.
Died 1973

Prime Minister St. Laurent was known as Uncle Louis—a kindly, courteous old gentleman. But he was much more than this. As Liberal prime minister 1948-57, he helped build Canada into a prosperous peacetime nation and made it a far more united country than it had been.

Under St. Laurent's government, three important projects were started: the St. Lawrence Seaway, the Trans-Canada Highway, and the transcontinental natural gas pipeline. There were also political changes: the first Canadian-born Governor General (Vincent Massey*) was appointed, and Newfoundland joined Confederation. Meanwhile, St. Laurent made sure that Canada played a useful part in world affairs. As a result of his policies, Canada gained a new respect in the eyes of the world.

Buffy Sainte-Marie
Born 1941, Piapot Reserve, Sask.
Singer and songwriter Buffy Sainte-Marie grew up in the United States with adopted parents, for her own Cree parents had died when she was a baby. During her childhood she felt very much of an outsider, and when she was 17 she returned to the Piapot Reserve and was formally adopted back into her tribe.

The Piapot Reserve remains her emotional home, but Buffy has travelled far afield while making her way as a musician. During her early twenties she was well known in New York's Greenwich Village, and before she was 30 she was an international star. She has made numerous records, many of them containing protest songs, such as "Now That the Buffalo's Gone." Through such songs, Buffy Sainte-Marie has been a powerful champion of the Indian people, pointing out the sufferings they have endured over the years.

Michel Sarrazin
Born 1659, France
Died 1734
New France's most famous doctor was the energetic Michel Sarrazin, who first arrived in Quebec in 1685. By the time he died almost 50 years later, he had done far more than serve as chief doctor and surgeon; he had added enormously to the scientific knowledge of the New World.

Sarrazin was an all-round scientist with a special interest in botany and zoology. Eagerly, he studied plants and animals, wrote scientific papers about them and collected specimens. He sent hundreds of seeds and plants to France so that they could be grown and studied there. He even tried to dissect a skunk, but the smell was too much for him. Another doctor, Jean-François Gaultier, continued Sarrazin's work in the 1740s. He made studies of the weather and the ecology, as well as plants.

Charles Edward Saunders
Born 1867, London, Ont.
Died 1937
Charles Edward Saunders developed the wheat called Marquis and several other wheat strains too. He was the son of Dr. William Saunders, the director of the government experimental farms in Ottawa, who, as part of his experiments, cross-fertilized various strains of wheat, hoping to produce one that would be suitable for the prairies. Charles Saunders was appointed Dominion Cerealist so that he could concentrate on this aspect of his father's work, and in 1904 he developed the first few heads of Marquis.

Marquis wheat was bred from Red Fife, but it ripened even quicker. This was very important to the many settlers who had been thronging west since the 1890s. All too often, their crop had been struck by frost before they could harvest it. Within ten years of Saunders's discovery, Marquis wheat was grown all across the prairies. As a result, Canada's wheat production more than doubled.

Jeanne Sauvé

Born 1922, Howell, Sask.

When Madame Sauvé was 12, her father showed her the bust of Agnes Macphail* in the House of Commons and told her that she too could be an MP one day. She did more than that. She became speaker of the House of Commons, the first woman to hold the position.

Brought up in Ottawa, the future politician was a "first" from earliest childhood, always top of the class, lead actor in the school play, president of the Young Catholic Students Association. As an adult, she became active in public affairs, while pursuing a career as a broadcaster and journalist; all of which she continued after her marriage to the politician Maurice Sauvé.

Jeanne Sauvé first ran for Parliament in 1972—and was elected. This was a major triumph, since Quebec voters had never before elected a woman. That year they also elected Monique Bégin (born 1936). Both women became cabinet ministers in the Liberal government. Monique Bégin's major portfolio has been health and welfare; Jeanne Sauvé's cabinet posts included communications and also science and technology. She was appointed speaker of the House of Commons in 1980.

R. Murray Schafer

Born 1933, Sarnia, Ont.

Canada has produced so many celebrated modern composers that there is one for almost each letter of the alphabet: Murray Adaskin, John Beckwith, Claude Champagne. . . .

Of all of them, one of the most famous internationally is R. Murray Schafer. He studied music in Toronto and then spent several years in Europe, where he supported himself as a journalist while studying medieval German as well as music. He has since become deeply interested in eastern languages and lifestyles. All of this is reflected in Schafer's compositions, which draw on a wide range of sources to get the effect he wants, using everything from the sound of the sea to Persian poetry. Some of his productions are multimedia experiences, rather than formal concerts.

An imaginative teacher as well as a musician, Schafer has written booklets for students, among them *Ear Cleaning* and *Rhinoceros in the Classroom*. He has also composed works for youth orchestras. One of the most moving is *Threnody* (Japanese children) which is based on the comments of survivors of the atomic bomb that was dropped on Japan in World War II.

Edward Schreyer

Born 1935, Beauséjour, Man.

In 1979 Edward Schreyer was sworn in as the twenty-second Governor General of Canada. He is the fifth Canadian-born Governor General and the first to represent the "third force" in Canada's multicultural mosaic—the many Canadians who are of neither French nor British ancestry. Ed Schreyer traces his descent from German-Austrian Canadians.

He is also the first social democrat to be Governor General. An elected politician since the age of 22, Schreyer became premier of Manitoba when he was only 33, heading the province's NDP government from 1969 to 1977. Two years later, when he was appointed Governor General, he was still only 43. He was the youngest person to hold the office since Lord Lansdowne* moved into Rideau Hall more than a century ago.

Catherine Schubert
Born 1835, Ireland
Died 1918
Catherine Schubert was the only woman among the Overlanders, the group that set out from the Red River Settlement in 1862, bound for the Cariboo gold fields. Thomas McMicking, the leader of the Overlanders, didn't want to take a woman. But Catherine insisted on accompanying her husband, and she brought her three young children along too.

Like the other Overlanders, the Schuberts had a terrible journey, trekking for months across the prairies and then struggling through the Rockies, where they ran out of food. To add to the difficulties, Catherine was heavily pregnant, so when they reached the North Thompson River, the Schuberts made a raft and headed for Fort Kamloops. They got there just in time. The next day, Catherine gave birth to a baby girl, the first white child born in the B.C. interior. The Schuberts settled in Lillooet, where Catherine ran a hotel, while her husband Augustus made frequent forays to the gold fields.

John Christian Schultz
Born 1840, Amherstburg, Ont.
Died 1896
Dr. John Schultz was one of the causes of the Red River Rebellion, and a very outspoken one too. He was unofficial leader of the small group of newcomers who had moved to the Red River Settlement from eastern Canada. A trader as well as a doctor, he owned the settlement's newspaper, and he used it to voice his views. Schultz's views were that the Métis were lazy and uncivilized, and that the region would best be settled and governed by English-speaking Protestants from Ontario.

The Métis already feared that this was going to happen, so they became all the more eager to take action. During the rebellion they captured Schultz, but he escaped, and in 1870 he visited Ontario where he helped stir up feeling against Louis Riel.* More than once during 1869-70, Schultz kept the flames of hatred burning when a peaceful solution might have been found. Yet his motive was loyalty to Canada. He later became an MP and in 1888 was appointed lieutenant governor of Manitoba.

Barbara Ann Scott
Born 1928, Ottawa, Ont.
During the 1940s, Barbara Ann Scott captured the hearts of Canadians—and much of the rest of the world too—as she skimmed so effortlessly over the ice, winning one figure-skating championship after another. Three times she was awarded the Lou Marsh Trophy as Canada's outstanding athlete of the year.

Barbara Ann Scott was 11 when she first skated her way into the headlines as the youngest person ever to win the Canadian junior championship. This was followed by the Canadian senior championship in 1944, the North American title in 1945, and the world title in 1947. In 1948 she again came top in women's figure-skating, winning the gold medal at the Olympic Games as well as in the world championships. With no more championships to conquer, she turned professional and performed in the Hollywood Ice Revue until her marriage in 1955.

Thomas Scott
Born c.1842, Ireland
Shot 1870

During the Red River Rebellion, Louis Riel* had Thomas Scott shot. This caused a furious outcry in English Canada—that a Roman Catholic Métis should murder a Protestant from Ontario. Scott immediately became a martyr-hero, a helpless victim who (according to his brother) was "a quiet and inoffensive young man."

In fact, Scott was a loud-mouthed thug. He had gone to the Red River in 1868, taking work as a road builder, and before long had threatened to drown his boss, who had refused him a rise in pay. During the rebellion, Scott treated several Métis very brutally; and when imprisoned by Riel, he hurled insults at his guards and attacked them. Riel ordered a court martial, which condemned Scott to death for insubordination (a capital offence among Métis buffalo hunters). But the main reason Riel had Scott shot was to "make Canada respect us." It had the opposite effect. English Canadians called Riel a murderer, and they never forgave him.

F. R. Scott
Born 1899, Quebec, Que.

Frank Scott has won two Governor General Awards—one for poetry and one for a book of essays on the constitution. This is not a contradiction, for Scott is both a poet and a lawyer, a former dean of law at McGill University. He was also one of the founders of the CCF (the socialist party which preceded today's NDP).

As a lawyer, Scott has watched over our rights and freedoms for many years, advising the government, speaking up for minority groups, and fighting law suits for people who were not getting a fair deal. As a poet, he has brought out anthologies as well as books of his own verse. He was co-editor of *The Blasted Pine*, a collection of satirical verse which he prepared with his friend and fellow poet A. J. M. Smith (born 1902).

Laura Secord
Born 1775, U.S.A.
Died 1868

Laura Secord, a Loyalist whose family had settled in Upper Canada, took a celebrated walk during the War of 1812. In June 1813, having learned that the Americans were planning a surprise attack, she walked from her home at Queenston to warn the Canadian forces at Beaver Dams. It took her the whole day. Late that night she gave the news to Lieutenant James FitzGibbon—who almost certainly already knew of the American plans. But he was too much of a gentleman to tell Mrs. Secord so, and anyway he was impressed by her brave effort.

After the war, the Secords were not well off, and Laura Secord wrote a series of petitions describing her walk and asking for a pension or a reward. FitzGibbon gallantly supported these petitions, the last of which was presented to the Prince of Wales (the future Edward VII) on his visit to Canada in 1860. This brought results, and at last, at the age of 85, Laura Secord received a reward of £100. Her perseverance gained her a place in Canadian history—and her face on chocolate boxes.

Meanwhile, another heroine, Abigail Becker,* never got her portrait on anything. Yet she showed very great courage and really did risk her life to save others.

Lord Selkirk

Born 1771, Scotland
Died 1820

The Earl of Selkirk tried to help Scottish crofters who had been turned out of their homes, by resettling them in North America. His first colonizing scheme was in Prince Edward Island, where he settled a group of Highlanders in 1803. He also helped establish a settlement at Baldoon in Upper Canada. Then he obtained a grant of land from the Hudson's Bay Company so that he could start a colony on the Red River. The first settlers arrived there in 1812 under the leadership of Miles Macdonell.*

The Red River Colony caused Selkirk terrible problems. The traders of the North West Company (the HBC's great rival) didn't want a settlement on the prairies, for it would harm their trade. They therefore tried to destroy the colony. After a group of settlers had been killed (see Cuthbert Grant*), Selkirk arrested William McGillivray* and other North-westers, holding them responsible for the affair. This only brought him more trouble because he had no authority to arrest anyone. He was made to pay a large fine. Over-burdened with his problems, he became ill and died.

Hans Selye

Born 1907, Austria
Died 1982

Hans Selye was known throughout the world for his studies of stress. As a young researcher at McGill in the 1930s, he set out to investigate the harm stress could do to people. This was a difficult project, since the damage wasn't obvious; it couldn't be pointed out clearly, like a wound or a disease.

Nevertheless, Selye persevered, and over the years he added vastly to the medical knowledge of stress—what it is, what it does, and how to cope with it. He wrote more than 1,700 scientific papers on his work and 38 books, including the best-selling *Stress Without Distress*. Meanwhile, he headed the Institute of Experimental Medicine and Surgery in Montreal.

Robert Service

Born 1874, England
Died 1958

Known as the Bard of the Yukon, Robert Service wrote "The Shooting of Dan McGrew" and other rip-roaring poems about the Klondike gold rush. He was not himself a gold miner. He was a shy young bank clerk who was sent to the Yukon early in the 1900s, after the gold rush was over. But the spirit of the gold rush lived on, and Service captured it brilliantly in his poems and also in his popular novel, *The Trail of '98*.

Service's books sold so well that he was able to give up his job in the bank and have some adventures of his own. He served as an ambulance driver in World War I, spent much of his life travelling, and finally settled in Europe, passing his last years in Monte Carlo and Brittany.

Ernest Thompson Seton

Born 1860, England

Died 1946

Ernest Thompson Seton wrote stories about animals, illustrating them with beautiful drawings. He had always been fascinated by animals, watching their behaviour closely, and many of his stories are based on real events. One of his most popular books is *Wild Animals I Have Known*, which was first published in 1898.

Seton grew up in Ontario, having been brought to Canada as a child. He trained at the Ontario College of Art and then lived a wandering life, spending long periods in the West. The last part of his life was spent mostly in the United States, where in 1902 he founded the Woodcraft League, a forerunner of the Boy Scouts movement. He served for a few years as chief of the Boy Scouts of America. His daughter Anya Seton became a popular American novelist.

Jack Shadbolt

Born 1909, England

Jack Shadbolt, the well-known Vancouver artist, came to Canada when he was three and grew up in Victoria. For many years he taught at the Vancouver School of Art, but since 1966 he has devoted his full time to painting. Many of his pictures are of West Coast subjects. One of his most famous is *Winter Theme No.7*, an impression of moored boats, presented in a dramatic pattern of light and colour.

Alfred Shadd

Born 1870, nr. Chatham, Ont.

Died 1915

In the early 1900s, one of the most respected figures in Melfort, Sask., was Alfred Shadd, western Canada's first black doctor. He had arrived in the region as a school teacher in 1896, causing quite a sensation, for most of the inhabitants had never seen a black person before. But Shadd quickly settled into the community. He already had some medical training at this time, and he soon became known as a man who could cope in an emergency, a friend in need.

There was certainly need for a local doctor, so Shadd went to Toronto to graduate in medicine. He then set up a practice in Kinistino, the settlement where he had taught school. In 1904 he moved to nearby Melfort, where he served as coroner as well as doctor, and helped found the town's hospital. He also ran a farm, became first president of the Melfort Agricultural Society, was owner-editor of the local newspaper and warden of the Anglican church. Meanwhile, he took part in almost every community activity, from starting a tree-growing program to marching in the Orangemen's parade. When Shadd died suddenly of appendicitis, thousands of people came to mourn. His funeral procession was more than 3 km long.

Jacob Shantz

Born 1822, Kitchener, Ont.

Died 1909

The first groups of Russian Mennonites settled in western Canada in the 1870s, and they did so largely because of the efforts of Jacob Shantz. He was a member of the German Mennonite community that was already established in Ontario and was a leading citizen of Kitchener (then called Berlin). On behalf of the Canadian government, he travelled time and again to Manitoba to help settle the Russian immigrants along the Red River. Sometimes he lent them money to buy farming implements.

Shantz later helped start Mennonite settlements in Alberta, moving there himself in the 1890s. With his family and various friends, he founded the town of Didsbury, Alta.

Shawnawdithit
Born c.1800, Nfld.
Died 1829

This young woman was the last of the Beothuk Indians of Newfoundland. Ever since the Europeans had first arrived in the sixteenth century, the Beothuks had been a doomed people. Many had died of the unfamiliar diseases —smallpox and tuberculosis. Others had been killed off. (At one time it was considered good sport to go on hunting parties and shoot Beothuks.)

By 1825, Shawnawdithit was the only member of her race still living. She was taken in by a Newfoundland family, given the name Nancy, and employed as an unpaid servant. But some people were kind to her, particularly the explorer William Epps Cormack.* He encouraged her to talk about her past and to draw pictures of Beothuk life. He was also hoping to convert her to Christianity. But she died of tuberculosis before this could be achieved.

Don Shebib
Born 1938, Toronto, Ont.

Don Shebib's 1970 movie *Goin' Down the Road* brought him worldwide acclaim as a film director. It was a story everyone could relate to: the adventures of a couple of Maritimers who left home to make good in the big city . . . fell on hard times and ended up by making bad. The film was popular with audiences as far away as the Soviet Union, where it was the first Canadian feature film ever shown in Russian cinemas.

Shebib had studied cinema in Los Angeles, and he already had a long experience in films and TV by the time he made *Goin' Down the Road*. He has since made several other features, including *Heartaches* (1981), as well as doing TV dramas for the CBC. His films have a strong, gritty character, and they have brought him a great reputation, though little financial success. Nevertheless, Shebib remains committed to making his films in Canada, rather than seeking his fortune abroad.

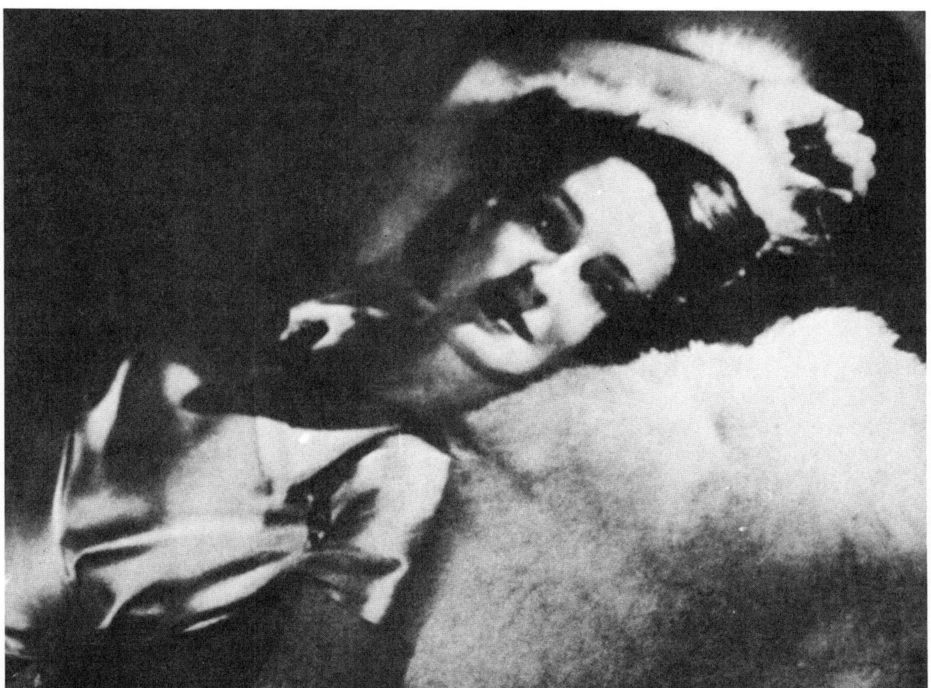

Norma Shearer
Born 1900, Montreal, Que.
Died 1983

Norma Shearer was one of the many Canadians who gained fame in Hollywood. Raised in Montreal, she began her film career in New York and then moved on to California, where she was one of the top-ranking stars of the 1920s and 1930s. A fine actress, she received six Academy Award nominations, one of which brought her an Oscar for her role in *The Divorcee*.

In the late 1930s, a younger Canadian-born actress became a Hollywood idol—sweet-singing Deanna Durbin (born 1921, Winnipeg). And the 1940s saw the emergence of the beautiful dancing girl and heroine of westerns, Yvonne de Carlo (born 1922, Vancouver). There have been many others, both before and since, from Mary Pickford* to Geneviève Bujold.*

Joe Shuster
Born 1914, Toronto, Ont.
Superman owes his origins to Joe Shuster, the Toronto boy who moved with his family to the U.S. in 1923, teamed up with writer Jerry Siegel, and in 1938 produced the first Superman story for *Action Comics*. The pictures were by Joe Shuster, the words by Jerry Siegel.

For about ten years, Shuster continued to draw Superman strips, but he didn't own the character so didn't make a fortune when his hero became so popular. As Shuster grew older, his sight began to fail and he retired to a nursing home in California. Meanwhile, Superman continues to flourish—and so does his girlfriend, Lois Lane, as played on the screen by another Canadian, Margot Kidder (born 1948, Yellowknife, N.W.T.).

Clifford Sifton
Born 1861, nr. London, Ont.
Died 1929
As minister of the interior in Wilfrid Laurier's* cabinet from 1896 to 1905, Clifford Sifton was responsible for settling the West. He sorted out which lands were available and then launched a huge immigration campaign, advertising in Britain, the United States, and continental Europe. As a result of his efforts, settlers flocked to the prairies.

Sifton had grown up in Brandon, Man., where he worked as a lawyer before going into politics. As a cabinet minister, he was the Liberal party's most efficient organizer, though he didn't agree with all Laurier's policies. He was against the West having government-supported schools for French-speaking children. And he was against Laurier's free-trade arrangements with the United States. He finally broke with Laurier and supported the Conservative leader Robert Borden* in the 1911 elections. Although Sifton himself withdrew from Parliament that year, his vigorous support helped Borden win the election.

His brother Arthur Sifton was also a politician: premier of Alberta 1910-17 and then a cabinet minister in Borden's government.

Jay Silverheels
Born 1919, Brantford, Ont.
For more than 20 years, Jay Silverheels starred in both film and television, playing the role of Tonto, the Lone Ranger's faithful companion.

A Mohawk Indian from the Six Nations Reserve, he was born Harold Jay Smith, the son of Major George Smith who was the most decorated Canadian Indian soldier of World War I. Young Harold Smith gained early success as a runner, and it was because of this that his grandfather, a Mohawk chief, formally renamed him Jay Silverheels.

From excelling in track-and-field, Silverheels moved on to hockey, boxing, and lacrosse, becoming one of the leading athletes on the Six Nations Reserve. In 1939 he went to Hollywood to play in a lacrosse match as part of a Canadian all-star team, and there he later gained a job as a movie extra. For several years he played very minor roles and then auditioned for Tonto, the part he was to play with such success. In 1982 Jay Silverheels had a star dedicated to him on the Hollywood Walk of Fame. His star was placed beside that of singer Frank Sinatra. Silverheels is the first Indian to have a star on the Walk of Fame.

René Simard
Born 1961, Chicoutimi, Que.
During the 1970s, René Simard took the world by storm—a boy pop star, who sang everything from disco to "Ave Maria."

The son of a choirmaster, Simard first gained attention at the age of nine, when he won a singing prize on TV. By the following year, he had performed at Montreal's Place des Arts and had brought out two records. Already he was a superstar at home. When he was 13, he was chosen to represent Canada at the International Song Festival in Japan. He won first prize. The Japanese went crazy over the exuberant Simard. So did the French when he appeared in Paris. And so did just about everyone else. He performed in the United States with such stars as Bing Crosby and Liberace, and in 1977-79 gained ardent fans in English-speaking Canada, when he hosted *The René Simard Show* on CBC television.

Meanwhile, his younger sister Nathalie has also been having a successful singing career. By 1980, when she was still only 11, she had already made three LPs.

John Graves Simcoe

Born 1752, England
Died 1806

John Graves Simcoe was the first governor of Upper Canada (1791-96) and the founder of York, today's Toronto. As governor, he did much to strengthen the colony. He built roads so that troops could be moved through the forests quickly, and he encouraged settlement by offering land cheaply. There were hardly any settlers when he arrived, for most of the European population was in Lower Canada. By the time Simcoe left, many pioneers were busily at work, clearing the forest and farming the land in Upper Canada.

Governor Simcoe and his wife Elizabeth shared the hardships of the pioneers. They lived in a drafty tent while York was being built, and they were often short of supplies. Even so, Elizabeth Simcoe behaved very much as the governor's lady. She entertained visitors in her tent, gave balls and tea parties, often went sketching, and also kept a diary which gives a fascinating glimpse of her unusual life.

Guy Simonds

Born 1903, England
Died 1974

General Simonds commanded the Canadian forces during one of their great victories in World War II, the battle of the Scheldt. This was in 1944, when the 1st Canadian Army fought a bitterly tough campaign to capture the German-held Scheldt Estuary and its port of Antwerp in Belgium. Once the Scheldt was in Allied hands, supplies could be brought in to support the advance on Germany, which led to the end of the war in Europe.

Simonds was a career soldier who had grown up in Canada and attended the Royal Military College in Kingston. Aged 39 he became Canada's youngest general. He was known for his brilliant military tactics, which were at their most brilliant during the Scheldt campaign. He held several positions in the army and from 1951 to 1955 served as chief of staff in Ottawa.

Léopold Simoneau

Born 1918, St. Flavien, Que.

One of the finest Canadian tenors of this century, Léopold Simoneau gained an international reputation as a Mozart singer, especially in opera, and as a singer in French roles.

He studied singing in Montreal, where he met the soprano Pierrette Alarie, whom he married. In the 1940s, when he first had major roles in operas, Pierrette Alarie often performed opposite him.

A teacher of singing as well as an operatic performer, Simoneau held staff positions at Montreal's Conservatory of Music and at the Banff School of Fine Arts, among other places. And in the 1960s, when working for Quebec's ministry of arts and culture, he prepared a report which led to the creation of the Opéra du Québec in 1971.

George Simpson
Born 1787 (?), Scotland
Died 1860
Ruthless and domineering, George Simpson was known as the Little Emperor of the Hudson's Bay Company. He came to Canada in 1820, a spirited little HBC officer with good connections among the board of directors in England and with a determination to acquit himself well in the field. He acquitted himself so well that six years later he was made governor of all the HBC territories, from Labrador to the Pacific Ocean. And in 1839 he was given the imposing title of Governor-in-Chief.

Simpson devoted his whole life to the Hudson's Bay Company, to its aggrandizement and therefore his own. He increased profits by cutting the voyageurs' wages and by bringing in other economies. And he increased efficiency by insisting on hard work and high standards. Almost every year, he made rapid canoe journeys across the territories—often travelling at record speed—so that he could see for himself how trade was being conducted. Although callous and overbearing (even his wife had to do as he said), Simpson was a superb administrator, one of the great businessmen of his age.

He died as he had lived, in the grand manner. He was struck down by apoplexy shortly after entertaining the Prince of Wales in Montreal.

John Sissons
Born 1892, Orillia, Ont.
Died 1969
Judge Sissons was called Ekoktoegee by the Inuit. This means "one who listens." Sissons did listen very attentively in his efforts to understand the Inuits' problems.

From 1955 to 1966, he was judge of the first territorial court that was set up in the Northwest Territories, though his "court" was often an igloo or the cabin of his aircraft. He flew all round the Territories, taking his robes and a Canadian flag with him so that he could hold formal trials wherever they were needed.

The Inuit knew they would get a fair deal whenever they saw Sissons limping down from his aircraft. (He had polio as a child). But the officials in Ottawa thought him a nuisance—too keen to take the Native people's side. Earlier in his life, as lawyer and MP in the Peace River country, Sissons had won a case which protected Indian treaty rights. And now, as judge, he sometimes let murderers off if they hadn't committed murder according to Inuit law. Painstakingly fair, he brought well-balanced justice to the Inuit during the years when they were adapting to Canadian ways and Canadian laws.

Gordon Sinclair
Born 1900, Toronto, Ont.
The well-known broadcaster first made his mark as a journalist, writing for the *Toronto Daily Star*. His wandering assignments included a trip to India in 1932, and soon after his return he wrote the book *Footloose in India*, which promptly became a best seller. Sinclair had also been doing some broadcasts on CFRB radio, and in the 1940s he was given his own program, *Let's Be Personal*. This did not please his *Star* bosses, who objected to their reporters having other jobs. So Sinclair shook the *Star* dust from his feet and settled in on his long and lively career with CFRB.

As well as radio, there was television. Since his first appearances on CBC's *Front Page Challenge* in 1957, Gordon Sinclair has been one of Canada's most forthright television personalities. Meanwhile, he has continued to write books, including *Will the Real Gordon Sinclair Please Stand Up* and *Will Gordon Sinclair Please Sit Down*.

Laurie Skreslet

Born 1949, Calgary, Alta.

Laurie Skreslet was the first Canadian to scale Mount Everest, the world's highest peak. He reached the summit on October 5, 1982, accompanied by two Nepalese guides: Sungdare Sherpa (who had twice before climbed to the summit) and Lhakpa Dorje Sherpa. Two days later, Pat Morrow (born 1952, Invermere, B.C.) also climbed to the top of Everest. He was accompanied by Sherpas Lhakpa Tshering and Pema Dorje.

Both Canadians had a long experience of high-altitude climbing. Skreslet had first been attracted to mountaineering on an Outward Bound course in 1970, and only one year later he scaled the highest mountain in Peru. Morrow, a professional photographer, has also conquered some formidable peaks, including China's highest mountain.

During the Everest climb, four members of the Canadian Mount Everest Expedition met their deaths on the mountain at the treacherous Khumbu Icefall. This tragedy cast a dark shadow over the expedition. Yet it did not weaken the resolve of Skreslet and Morrow, whose courage and tenacity took them to the very top of the world.

Josef Skvorecky

Born 1924, Czechoslovakia

Josef Skvorecky is a writer of such distinction that in 1982 he was nominated for the Nobel Prize in Literature. Yet in his native Czechoslovakia, people can be arrested for owning one of his books. Since Skvorecky immigrated to Canada in 1968, the Czech authorities have wiped his name from their records, as if he never existed. His novels are considered "subversive," because they do not give the official Communist viewpoint. Nevertheless, many Czechs continue to read his books—in secret.

Skvorecky grew up in Czechoslovakia during the Nazi occupation of World War II and the Communist takeover after the war. In spite of the political situation, he did get some of his stories published. Two of his best-known books are *The Cowards* and *The Bass Saxophone*, both of which are about love, jazz, and politics. Skvorecky himself was a keen jazz player, even though that type of music was banned by the Nazis. Since settling in Canada, he has continued to write novels, while working as a university professor in Toronto.

Joshua Slocum

Born 1844, Annapolis County, N.S.
Drowned 1909

In April 1895, Joshua Slocum put to sea in the *Spray*, a 12-metre sailing ship which he had built from an old hulk. His aim—to sail alone round the world. Three years and two months later, he had done it. He was the first person to sail round the world on his own.

Slocum was a seasoned mariner by the time he did this voyage. He had already been five times round the world, but with a crew. His first wife Virginia had been his chief crew member until she died. She loved the sea as much as he did and had given birth to all their children on board ship. Slocum's second wife wasn't so keen on seafaring, so he took to sailing alone. Even in his sixties, he was still doing so. He was on a one-man voyage to the Amazon when he and the *Spray* disappeared without trace. He was presumed drowned, for he had never learned to swim.

Ambrose Small

Born 1863, Adjala Twp., Ont.
Vanished 1919

The disappearance of Ambrose Small is one of Canada's most intriguing mysteries. He was a self-made millionaire, owner of the Grand Opera House in Adelaide Street, Toronto, and of a chain of theatres across the country. On December 2, 1919, he sold his theatre chain, receiving a cheque for $1 million as the first instalment of the sale. He then had a celebratory lunch with his wife and lawyer, and in the late afternoon he met at the opera house with his lawyer to finalize arrangements. The lawyer left just before 5.30, waving goodbye to Small in the doorway. That was the last time anyone saw Ambrose Small. Was he murdered? Did he purposely disappear? Nobody knows, though people are still expecting his body to be found.

Joey Smallwood

Born 1900, Gambo, Nfld.

Joseph Smallwood is known as "the only living Father of Confederation." This is because in 1949 he brought Newfoundland into Confederation as Canada's tenth province. In many ways, he represents the spirit of Newfoundland, a lifetime champion of its people.

Smallwood started his career as a journalist, and in the Depression he worked as a radio broadcaster, giving chatty talks under the name Joe the Barrelman. During this period, he was also an active organizer of labour unions. He was therefore already a well-known public figure when, after World War II, he formed the Confederate party and pressed for union with Canada. After Newfoundland joined Canada, Smallwood headed the province's Liberal party, serving as premier from 1949 to 1972. His years as premier saw great changes which affected almost every aspect of life in his beloved Newfoundland.

Goldwin Smith

Born 1823, England
Died 1910

Goldwin Smith was the intellectual prima donna of the post-Confederation years, a brilliant and very learned man who awed many people and infuriated others. A former professor of history at Oxford University, he settled in Toronto in 1871 and immersed himself in journalism. He wrote mostly for political and literary publications, some of which he aided with cash donations. The *Week* and the *Bystander* (which he founded) were two of the papers most identified with him.

Goldwin Smith proved to be a formidable political journalist. With his sharp mind, sharp tongue, and even sharper pen, he shafted his enemies (including George Brown*) with pitiless accuracy. For a time he was a member of Canada First, but then he left this nationalist movement and swung in the opposite direction, saying that Canada would do best to join the United States.

Whatever his views, people listened to Goldwin Smith. A well-known author as well as a journalist, he was widely recognized as one of the leading intellectuals of the period.

Titus Smith

Born 1768, U.S.A.
Died 1850

Titus Smith was Nova Scotia's pioneer botanist, the son of Loyalists who settled at Preston in 1783. He worked periodically as a land surveyor, but his main passion was plants.

In 1801 he was chosen to make an exploratory survey of the interior (which was virtually unknown at the time). He spent about a year and a half in the interior and produced a number of reports which were remarkable for their botanical information. He became known internationally for his interpretations of Nova Scotian flora. Towards the end of his life, he served as secretary of the Central Board of Agriculture.

Mary Agnes Snively

Born 1847, St. Catharines, Ont.
Died 1933

Mary Agnes Snively spearheaded the movement which transformed Canadian nursing in the late nineteenth century, making it a respectable profession. Since the earliest days of New France, there had been many dedicated nurses, but most were nuns working in Catholic hospitals. In other hospitals, nurses were all too often the type of women Florence Nightingale described as "fat drunken old dames." Uneducated, untrained, and poorly paid, they were the lowest type of servant.

Miss Snively was one of our first qualified nurses, having trained at Bellevue Hospital, New York. On her graduation in 1884, she was appointed lady superintendent at Toronto General Hospital. She stayed there 25 years, during which time she built up a first-rate school of nursing. Strict and very exacting, she set high standards. Many of her nurses later started training courses in other hospitals, not only in Canada but throughout the world. Meantime, Miss Snively helped found the Canadian Nurses' Association and served as its president.

Sandy Somerville

Born 1903, London, Ont.

In the Canadian Press poll of 1950, Sandy Somerville was voted Canada's outstanding golfer of the half-century. The son of a chewing-gum manufacturer, he started playing golf when he was five, and between 1926 and 1937 he won the Canadian amateur championship six times. In 1932 he won the U.S. amateur championship, the first Canadian ever to do so.

Michael Snow

Born 1929, Toronto, Ont.

The fibreglass geese in Toronto's Eaton Centre were designed by Michael Snow, one of Canada's most original multimedia people. Although principally a painter and sculptor, Snow has also performed as a jazz musician and as a filmmaker; and in the 1960s he gained wide fame for a cutout figure called the Walking Woman.

The Walking Woman always had the same outline, but she appeared in different colours, sizes, and materials—and not only in Snow's pictures and films. There were tall, flat, silver figures of the Walking Woman near the Canadian pavilion at Expo 67. There were cutouts of the Walking Woman pasted on signboards in the New York subway. She appeared on T-shirts, on wallpaper, in advertisements. The Walking Woman seemed to be taking over. And this was what Snow intended: to make art a part of life.

Robert Stanfield
Born 1914, Truro, N.S.
Robert Stanfield was leader of the Conservatives in both provincial and federal politics. He graduated from Dalhousie University, winning the Governor General's medal, then gained a law degree at Harvard and worked for a while as a lawyer before taking up politics. Stanfield served as premier of Nova Scotia from 1956 until 1967, when he resigned in order to take over as leader of the federal Conservative party in Ottawa. In this position, he was leader of the Opposition in the House of Commons 1967-76.

Lord Stanley
Born 1841, England
Died 1908
Lord Stanley was Governor General 1888-93. He presented Canada with the Stanley Cup, the silver trophy which is competed for each year by the teams of the National Hockey League. Now the most important award in professional hockey, it was originally given to encourage amateur hockey.

Steven Staryk
Born 1932, Toronto, Ont.
Steven Staryk, the celebrated violinist, was appointed concertmaster of the Toronto Symphony Orchestra in 1982. He had previously been concertmaster of other prestigious orchestras, including the Royal Philharmonic in England.

Staryk was raised in Toronto, the son of poor Ukrainian immigrants, but his mother had great ambitions for him and he began violin lessons when he was six. By the age of 18 he was a professional musician, playing with the Toronto Symphony and other orchestras. Since then, he has performed and taught music all over the world, from Ottawa to Japan.

Canada has produced a number of very fine violinists, among them Harry Adaskin (born 1901) who was one of the founders of the famous Hart House String Quartet, with which he played for many years.

Sam Steele
Born 1849, Purbrook, Ont.
Died 1919
Many of the films and fables about the Mounties were based on the flamboyant Sam Steele, a huge man with the build of a buffalo and the heart of a lion. He was one of the first 300 Mounted Police who took part in the Great March West, and for almost 20 years he policed the prairies, driving out the American whisky traders, keeping peace among the Indians, and controlling the hard-living construction workers who came west to build the Canadian Pacific Railway.

When in 1898 the Klondike gold rush brought gun-toting adventurers to the Yukon, Steele was sent there to restore order. A couple of years later he was sent to another trouble spot, to the Boer War in Africa, where he led a corps of mounted riflemen into battle.

And during World War I he trained the 2nd Canadian Division and took it to England. During his action-packed life he rose from private to major general, and by the time he died he was Sir Samuel Steele.

Vilhjalmur Stefansson
Born 1879, Gimli, Man.
Died 1962

My Life with the Eskimo and *The Friendly Arctic* are two of the books written by Vilhjalmur Stefansson, one of the greatest of all Arctic explorers. The son of Icelandic immigrants, he was educated in the United States, where he studied anthropology at Harvard University. He embarked on his first Arctic expedition in 1906, and from then until 1918 he was almost continually in the Canadian Arctic, exploring, discovering, mapping, and especially studying the people of the region.

Unlike most of the earlier explorers, Stefansson lived and travelled with the Inuit. He learned their skills, learned how to hunt caribou and seal, learned how to survive in the Arctic. In his books and lectures he continually stressed that people can survive in the North, that it is not a hostile wilderness. The books of his adventures, as well as his more formal scientific works, greatly added to the world's knowledge of the Arctic.

Henry Bird Steinhauer
Born c.1818, nr. Rama Indian Reserve, Ont.
Died 1884

Henry Steinhauer was an Ojibwa Indian and a Methodist minister. He took his name from an American who paid for his education.

Steinhauer was enrolled at Upper Canada Academy (the future Victoria University) from which he graduated in 1839 at the head of his class. He spent the rest of his life working as a missionary to the Indian people, first in Ontario and Manitoba, and then for many years among the Crees in the region that is now Alberta. One of his daughters married the Methodist missionary to the Blackfoot, John McDougall. And one of his great-grandsons, Ralph Steinhauer, was lieutenant governor of Alberta 1974-79.

George Stephen
Born 1829, Scotland
Died 1921

George Stephen made a fortune and then risked losing it by undertaking to build the Canadian Pacific Railway. The CPR was a gamble: to build a line north of Lake Superior, across the prairies, and through the Rockies. Some people said it was impossible. Certainly, the cost would be enormous. But Stephen had already succeeded with other railway projects, and he had made his fortune by daring to take such risks.

Stephen's main ally and fellow investor was his cousin Donald Smith (Lord Strathcona*). Together they teamed up with other railway builders, and at the beginning of 1882 they put William Van Horne* in charge of constructing the line. Three years later they ran out of money and were facing ruin. They were saved by the Northwest Rebellion in the spring of 1885. By then, so much track had been laid that troops could be rushed west in about a week. As a result, the government loaned Stephen's company the funds it needed, and in November that year the CPR was triumphantly completed.

William Stephenson
Born 1896, Point Douglas, Man.
War hero, inventor, millionaire, and master spy—William Stephenson seemed to have at least nine lives. As a soldier and then a fighter pilot in World War I, he survived a gas attack, shot down 20 enemy aircraft, and was himself shot down and taken prisoner. As a radio pioneer after the war, he developed a way of sending photographs by wireless. This work was done in partnership with the British scientist T. Thorne Baker, and it enabled newspaper pictures to be transmitted instantly across the world. The first officially sent by this method (a photo of two skiers) was printed in the British *Daily Mail* on December 27, 1922.

This invention alone would have been enough to bring Stephenson fame as well as fortune, but it was in World War II that he took on his most celebrated role. Under the code name Intrepid, he was head of Winston Churchill's intelligence operations in the western hemisphere. A book about his adventures, *A Man Called Intrepid*, was written by his fellow Canadian and near-namesake, William Stevenson.

Stephenson was knighted by the British, and at home he was named a Companion of the Order of Canada. In 1982, at the age of 86, he was made honorary colonel commandant of the intelligence branch of the Canadian Armed Forces.

Emily Stowe
Born 1831, Norwich, Ont.
Died 1903
A woman of battering-ram determination, Emily Stowe blazed the trail on two fronts. She founded Canada's first suffrage group and was a driving force in the struggle to get women the vote. And she was the first Canadian woman to be a doctor. This was in 1867 when she set up a practice in Toronto, having that year graduated from the New York Medical College for Women. At the time, no Canadian medical school accepted women. Nor could Dr. Stowe even get licensed as a doctor in Canada. She practised illegally until 1880, when she was finally granted a licence.

Her daughter Dr. Augusta Stowe-Gullen was the first woman to get a medical degree in Canada (1883) having been allowed to study at the Toronto School of Medicine. Augusta's ordeal there among the male students convinced her mother of the need to start a Canadian medical school especially for women. Two were founded in 1883: one in Toronto by Emily Stowe, and one in Kingston by Jennie Trout* (who was the first Canadian woman actually licensed as a doctor in Canada).

John Strachan
Born 1778, Scotland
Died 1867

Bishop Strachan was a key member of the Family Compact, a staunch Loyalist and Tory who stood for the Anglican church and the established order of things. He believed that Upper Canada should be ruled by a few high-minded men, and was therefore strongly against the Reform party, which wanted responsible government.

The Reformers thought Strachan high-handed rather than high-minded. He had arrived in York in 1812 and had quickly become very influential. He was on both the Legislative and Executive councils, and also ran a boys' school where he taught the sons of the elite. Appointed head of the Board of Education, he founded King's College as an Anglican university; and when a Reform government made it a secular college, he started another Anglican university, Trinity College.

Strachan was brave as well as public-spirited. During the War of 1812, he fearlessly told off the American general who captured York; and he worked unstintingly during the cholera epidemics of the 1830s. Yet he was 61 before he was made bishop of Toronto. Until then he was archdeacon. His unyielding character may have delayed his promotion. However, as Bishop Strachan, he outlasted most of his opponents, living to the age of 89.

Teresa Stratas
Born 1938, Toronto, Ont.

Teresa Stratas, who has sung in all the world's great opera houses, was born on her parents' dining-room table in their flat above a Chinese laundry in Toronto. Her parents were poor Greek immigrants, struggling to make a living by running a small restaurant; but they bought a piano for their children and encouraged them in music.

Stratas was singing at Greek functions in her teens, and as soon as she started formal voice lessons, her talent was quickly recognized. Known for her dramatic acting as well as for her beautiful soprano voice, she soared to success, becoming one of the superstars of New York's Metropolitan Opera.

Lord Strathcona (Donald Smith)
Born 1820, Scotland
Died 1914

Donald Smith was a central figure in most of the dramatic events of his time. Having toughed it out for 30 years as the Hudson's Bay Company man in Labrador, he was made head of the HBC in Canada and in 1869 was sent to the Red River to negotiate with Louis Riel.* There, his courage and firmness helped to keep the Red River Rebellion from getting too out of hand. After the rebellion, he became an MP, and this led to his next significant role. By refusing to vote for John A. Macdonald* during the Pacific Scandal, he caused Macdonald's government to resign.

Smith's next role was as builder of the Canadian Pacific Railway.

Although not officially a partner in the CPR company, he was deeply involved from the outset; and like his cousin George Stephen,* he risked all his money by backing the project. On completion of the railway, he was given the honour of driving in the famous "last spike." From then on, honours came thick and fast. He was made a knight, appointed president of the Bank of Montreal, chancellor of McGill University, Canadian high commissioner to Britain . . . and in 1897 was made Lord Strathcona.

Marlene Stewart Streit

Born 1934, Cereal, Alta.

At the age of 17, at the Ontario amateur golf championships, she beat the reigning champion, the celebrated Ada Mackenzie.* So began the rise to success of Marlene Stewart (who became Marlene Streit on her marriage). She was one of the finest amateur golfers, male or female, who ever played the game. She won the Canadian, British, Australian, and U.S. national amateur titles, and twice was awarded the Lou Marsh Trophy as Canada's outstanding athlete of the year.

Since Marlene Streit's heyday, several other Canadian women have also excelled on the links, most notably Sandra Post and Cathy Sherk, both of whom have made their name in professional golf.

David Suzuki

Born 1936, Vancouver, B.C.

Through his radio and TV programs, David Suzuki has brought science to the people of Canada in a way that can be easily understood. He is especially known for such popular TV series as *The Nature of Things*.

Suzuki had a difficult start in life. Like other Canadians of Japanese origin, he was interned in a camp during World War II (see Takashima*), even though his parents were Canadian-born. After the war, the family settled in Ontario, where Suzuki continued his education, completing it with a Ph.D. at the University of Chicago.

In 1969, at the age of 33, he was appointed professor of zoology at the University of British Columbia, and there he embarked on a research project on the common fruit fly—the aim being pest control. Through his genetic studies of the fruit fly, Suzuki found that he could breed a strain that died in hot weather. This brought him a wide international reputation, but it also caused him to worry about the effects scientists can have on the world. Science, he felt, was too important to be left to the experts. So he set out to explain it to the public.

Donald Sutherland

Born 1934, Saint John, N.B.

One of the world's "leading men," Donald Sutherland began his acting career at Hart House Theatre when he was a student at the University of Toronto. He then went to England to study acting, and it was there that he first made his name—in theatre and on television. He achieved stardom when playing the irrepressible Hawkeye Pierce in *M*A*S*H*, the 1970 film that inspired the TV series. Since then, the lanky Maritimer has starred in many Hollywood movies, as well as in such CBC TV productions as *Bethune*.

Anna Swan
Born 1846, Mill Brook, N.S.
Died 1888

She was called the Nova Scotian Giantess. Childhood was no fun for Anna Swan. She was 142 cm tall by the time she was five, and she went on growing. She couldn't fit behind the desks at school, couldn't buy big enough shoes. But at 16 she began to enjoy life, for the American showman P. T. Barnum asked her to join his New York Museum. Anna made good friends with the people there and was paid well for letting the public look at her.

Touring with the company, she met and married a man called Martin Bates. And who was he? He was the Kentucky Giant. They were billed as "the tallest couple in the world." Anna's height was 228 cm and Martin's 219 cm.

Alexandre-Antonin Taché
Born 1823, Rivière du Loup, Que.
Died 1894

As bishop and then archbishop of St. Boniface, Alexandre Taché worked in the West for almost 50 years. He understood the problems of the Métis, and before the Red River Rebellion he warned the Canadian government that trouble was brewing. Something had to be done very quickly to assure the Métis that settlers wouldn't take their lands. But Taché's warnings were ignored. Nothing was done in time.

Unfortunately, he was away from the Red River when the rebellion started, but he later helped to restore calm. And by acting as a go-between for the government, he arranged for Louis Riel* to leave Canada. Taché had known Riel for years and had been responsible for his education, sending him to school in Montreal.

Taché's uncle also played a prominent role in Canadian affairs. He was Sir Étienne-Paschal Taché who headed the government of the Province of Canada in the years before Confederation.

Shizuye Takashima
Born 1928, Vancouver, B.C.

Shizuye Takashima is the author of *A Child in Prison Camp*, which describes her experiences during World War II. She was one of thousands of West Coast Canadians who were turned out of their homes during the war and interned in camps. They were interned by the Canadian government because they were of Japanese ancestry—and Canada was at war with Japan. In the surge of anti-Japanese feeling, people forgot that such families as the Takashimas were in fact Canadians, many of them very loyal Canadians. They were all regarded as dangerous aliens, even children like Shizuye who had never known any country but Canada.

She spent three years at a camp high in the Rockies, along with her sister and parents, but not her brothers. The boys were sent to camps in eastern Canada. After the war, the family gradually came together again, settling in Toronto where Shizuye studied art. She has since become a successful artist.

Thomas Talbot
Born 1771, Ireland
Died 1853

Port Talbot, the Talbot Road, and St. Thomas in southwestern Ontario were all named after Thomas Talbot, the eccentric colonizer of the region.

Talbot had been private secretary to Governor Simcoe* and he had many influential friends in England. So when he applied for a grant of land, he was given it: a huge stretch along the north shore of Lake Erie. There, early in the 1800s, he founded the Talbot Settlement, brought in settlers, established townships, and got roads built. Meanwhile, he ruled the settlement as if it was his private empire. He kept the township plans in pencil so that he could erase the names of any settlers who displeased him—and, of course, kick them off the land.

As the years passed, Talbot had to behave more democratically. But he remained an oddity. Sometimes he would only speak to his settlers through a window. Nevertheless, he was a major force in getting much of southwestern Ontario cleared and settled.

Jean Talon
Born c.1625, France
Died 1694

Jean Talon was the first person to be appointed intendant of New France—a chief administrator, working beside the governor as much as under him. In this powerful position, Talon did wonders for the small colony. When in 1665 he arrived in Quebec, New France was facing ruin, shaken by years of warfare against the Iroquois. When he left in 1672, the colony was well ordered and organized, and in many ways self-sufficient. And the population had doubled to more than 7,500.

Talon brought in hundreds of immigrants and encouraged them to have children by giving rewards to large families. He penalized the unmarried by forbidding single young men to fish, hunt, or take part in the fur trade. Meanwhile, he started many industries, including a shipyard, and he gave farming such a boost that peas, hops, and barley were actually exported. In addition, he sent out explorers who claimed vast areas of North America for France. Although many people thought Talon far too high-handed, he achieved more in a few years than anyone else was to do in the next hundred years.

Elaine Tanner
Born 1951, Vancouver, B.C.

The record-breaking swimmer was nicknamed Mighty Mouse and hailed as the best performer in the entire history of the Commonwealth Games. This was at the 1966 games when 15-year-old Elaine Tanner won four gold medals and three silver, breaking two world records. She was awarded the Lou Marsh Trophy as Canada's outstanding athlete of the year—the youngest person ever to receive the honour.

Like all top athletes, Mighty Mouse had worked hard for her success. In her early teens, she used to get up at six each morning to take swimming lessons before school. Her last major international appearance was at the 1968 Olympic Games, where she won two silver medals and a bronze.

Eva Tanguay
Born 1878, Marbleton, Que.
Died 1947

Eva Tanguay was the "I Don't Care" girl. That was the name of the song in the show *The Chaperons* which in 1904 made her a smash-hit in the United States. By 1912 she was the most highly paid actress in America. And she didn't care. She roared through the Roaring Twenties, singing risqué songs, quarrelling with fellow actors, with managers, with almost every business associate—and wowing the public.

The tempestuous Tanguay was the daughter of a respectable Quebec doctor, and her first stage appearance, aged eight, had been thoroughly respectable: playing Cedric in *Little Lord Fauntleroy*. But her medium was vaudeville and musical comedy. There she sparkled, a brilliant but brief flame. She lost her fortune in the Wall Street crash of 1929, lost her health, began to lose her sight. By the time she died, she was virtually forgotten.

Joseph-Israel Tarte
Born 1848, Lanoraie, Que.
Died 1907

As both politician and journalist, Israel Tarte was one of the most prominent French Canadians during the latter part of the nineteenth century. He had a reputation for being very upright, very Catholic, very Conservative. But after Louis Riel* was executed, Tarte left the Conservatives in fury and in due course he joined the Liberals. He was made a cabinet minister when Wilfrid Laurier* came to power, and he served as Laurier's second-in-command until 1902, when he was dismissed from the cabinet for scheming against his leader. Tarte then became a Conservative again, attacking the Liberals both in Parliament and in his newspaper *La Patrie*.

Elzéar Taschereau
Born 1820, Ste. Marie de la Beauce, Que.
Died 1898

Elzéar Taschereau was the first Canadian to be made a cardinal, an honour bestowed on him in 1886. At the time, he was archbishop of Quebec.

Taschereau was greatly admired by many Catholics. He was known for his work in education; he had been superior of the Quebec Seminary and first rector of Laval University. He was also known for his bravery, having risked his life ministering to Irish immigrants during an epidemic. Most of all, he was known for his liberal-minded attitudes. By tradition, the church had forbidden Catholics to vote for the Liberal party (which in those days was considered dangerously revolutionary). At first Taschereau went along with this, but then he said that Catholics could vote as they liked. This made the future far more promising for Liberal politicians like the young Laurier.*

Angella Taylor
Born 1958, Jamaica
Canada's fastest woman sprinter of all time, Angella Taylor has set several world records. She came to Toronto in her teens, and when she was first at high school she planned to train as an auto mechanic. But she trained as a runner instead, embarking on a rigorous regimen of situps and knee raises and running and jogging, 12 hours a day, 6 days a week.

Angella Taylor's training paid off. She won a silver and a bronze medal at the 1979 Pan American Games and then sprinted to victory in the 1982 Commonwealth Games, winning two gold medals for Canada: in the women's 100-metre dash (in which she set a new Commonwealth record) and the 400-metre relay.

Cyclone Taylor
Born 1883, Tara, Ont.
Died 1979
Fred Taylor was nicknamed "the Cyclone" early in his career, when as a rushing defenceman, he played for the Ottawa Senators. He was one of the most brilliant of all hockey stars.

In 1910 he joined the newly formed Renfrew Millionaires, and this caused a fierce rivalry with the Senators, who looked on Cyclone Taylor as a turncoat. To rile them, he once boasted that he would skate backwards through their defence and then score a goal against them. And he did just that. He played rover and centre after his first years as defenceman and moved to the Vancouver Millionaires in 1912, staying with them until his retirement in 1921.

Ken Taylor
Born 1934, Calgary, Alta.
Early in 1980, Canada's ambassador to Iran, Kenneth Taylor, suddenly became the number-one hero in the United States. At the beginning of November the previous year, the Iranians had stormed the American embassy in Tehran, and they held 53 Americans hostage. But unknown to them (and to the public), six Americans had escaped capture and found sanctuary at the Canadian embassy. For more than three months, some of them were secret houseguests of Ambassador Taylor and his wife Pat, and some were living secretly with the first secretary and his wife, John and Zena Sheardown.

Meanwhile, Taylor was getting Canadian passports made for the fugitives; and at the end of January the head of embassy security, Sergeant Gauthier, escorted the six "Canadians" to Tehran airport and saw them safely out of the country.

By the time the news of the escape was made public, Taylor and his remaining staff had also left Iran so that there could be no reprisals. He has since been appointed Canadian consul general in New York. Americans have showered honours upon him, and there has also been recognition at home. He and the other Canadians who were most deeply involved in the hostage drama have all been awarded the Order of Canada.

E. P. Taylor
Born 1901, Ottawa, Ont.
One of Canada's millionaires, E. P. Taylor started his career working for an investment company and gradually built up a huge financial empire which included breweries, food products, farm machinery, and the powerful group called the Argus Corporation. He also set up a racing stable, the National Stud Farm. One of his horses, Northern Dancer, was the most successful thoroughbred in Canadian racing—the first Canadian horse ever to win the Kentucky Derby (in 1964).

Tecumseh
Born 1768, U.S.A.
Killed 1813
Together with General Brock,* Tecumseh was the great military leader in the War of 1812, a first-rate organizer as well as an inspired military commander.

He was a Shawnee chief from Ohio, who had come into conflict with the U.S. government over ownership of Indian lands. During the War of 1812, he allied himself with the British, bringing other tribes into the war against the Americans. As brigadier general of the Indian troops, Tecumseh played a major part in the early victories of the war, including the capture of Detroit. He was killed at the battle of Moraviantown on the Thames River in October 1813.

Kateri Tekakwitha
Born 1656, nr. the Mohawk River
Died 1680
At the St. François-Xavier Mission at Caughnawaga, near Montreal, is a shrine to Kateri Tekakwitha, who is also known as the Lily of the Mohawks. This gentle, sweet-natured woman was the first Indian to be named "venerable" (which is the first of three steps towards being made a saint).

Kateri had been converted by Jesuit missionaries and was baptised a Christian on Easter Day, 1676. Her conversion did not please her fellow Mohawks, who attacked her bitterly for forsaking her hereditary religion, and threatened to kill her. But Kateri's Christian faith remained strong, though her body was very frail. She was only 24 when she sickened and died.

In death, she was seen to be remarkably beautiful. She had been scarred by smallpox as a child, and now the scars seemed to have vanished. This was regarded as a miracle, the result of her piety. For centuries, pilgrims have come to pray at the shrine of the Lily of the Mohawks.

Veronica Tennant
Born 1947, England
Veronica Tennant started ballet lessons in England when she was four, and was totally committed to ballet by the age of nine when her family moved to Toronto. When the National Ballet School opened in Toronto, she was one of the first students accepted. On graduating in 1964, she was appointed a principal dancer with the National Ballet and soon drew rave reviews for her moving performances as Juliet in *Romeo and Juliet*.

Further successes followed, and it looked as if Veronica Tennant would continue to thrill audiences with her dramatic dancing. But during a rehearsal in 1977 she tore the ligaments in her left knee. The injury was so severe that she was not expected to walk properly again, let alone dance. Yet in less than two years she was back on stage, giving even more powerful performances than before. She is especially famed for the drama she brings to her roles, including a more recent and even more dramatic interpretation of Juliet.

David Thompson
Born 1770, England
Died 1857
A weak-eyed Welshman, with a kindly nature and a great devotion to his Métis wife and children, David Thompson cut an unlikely figure as an explorer. Yet he surveyed and mapped more territory than any other geographer of his time.

Thompson had learned surveying and astronomy as a Hudson's Bay Company clerk (he was apprenticed to the HBC at the age of 14); but he later transferred to the North West Company, as it offered more opportunity for exploring. Year after year, he travelled through the West. He surveyed the source of the Mississippi, found his way through the Rockies (accompanied by his wife and children); and in 1811, by tracing the Columbia River its full length, he discovered the great waterway to the Pacific which Alexander Mackenzie* had searched for in vain.

Thompson is now recognized as one of the world's great geographers, but he had few rewards during his lifetime. In his last years, he was not only desperately poor, but blind. And when he died, only his friends and family mourned. Or even noticed.

John Thompson
Born 1844, Halifax, N.S.
Died 1894
Sir John Thompson was Conservative prime minister 1892-94. He was offered the position a few years earlier but turned it down, for he was a convert to Roman Catholicism and he thought the staunch Ontario Protestants would rise up in anger if a Catholic headed the government. But when Sir John Abbott* suddenly became ill and had to retire, Thompson agreed to take over as prime minister.

There was no angry outcry, for people respected Thompson. He was a straight-ahead type of person, strong-minded, quick to make decisions, very efficient. A lawyer by profession, he had been a judge and then minister of justice. But he wasn't long enough in office to have great impact. On a visit to Britain, he died suddenly at Windsor Castle.

Roy Thomson
Born 1894, Toronto, Ont.
Died 1976
Roy Thomson started work at the age of 14 as a clerk earning $5 a week. By the end of his life he was Lord Thomson of Fleet, one of the world's greatest press barons, owner of a chain of newspapers which included the London *Times* as well as numerous Canadian papers.

Thomson's financial empire had its beginnings in 1931 when he bought a radio transmitter and licence, and set up a radio station at North Bay, Ont. Soon he was able to start more radio stations and in 1934 to acquire his first newspaper, the Timmins weekly *Press*, which he turned into a daily paper. More radio stations followed and more papers, and gradually he spread his net abroad. His financial empire has been inherited by his son Ken Thomson, and it now includes North Sea oil fields, department stores, and many other concerns.

Tom Thomson
Born 1877, Claremont, Ont.
Died 1917

Tom Thomson was a leading spirit among the artists who became known as the Group of Seven. But he was not one of the seven, for he died before they formally named themselves and held their first exhibition. Had he lived, it would have been a Group of Eight.

Thomson worked for several years as a commercial artist at Grip Ltd., the Toronto engraving and graphic design firm where J. E. H. MacDonald* was in charge of design. Led by MacDonald, the artists went on weekend sketching trips, and constantly they discussed their ideas about painting Canadian scenery in a new way. Their work was encouraged by a wealthy doctor, James MacCallum, who in 1913 began to support Thomson so that the young artist could concentrate on painting. During the winters, Thomson lived in a studio provided by MacCallum; and during the summers, he went to Algonquin Park to paint the rugged scenery.

When Thomson was not painting, he was fishing. This was his other great passion. He died mysteriously on a lone fishing trip near Canoe Lake in Algonquin Park. His upturned canoe was found on July 8, 1917. His body was found eight days later. "Accidental drowning" was the verdict, but Thomson had a deep cut on his head, and there have been many different theories as to how exactly he met his death. One theory even suggests murder.

Tom Three Persons
Born c.1887, southern Alberta
Died 1949

At the first Calgary Stampede in 1912, the crowds went wild as they watched Tom Three Persons riding a wild-eyed bucking bronco called Cyclone. Some of the world's best cowboys had taken on Cyclone, and all had been thrown. Tom Three Persons stayed on. Amid the cheers of the crowds, he was declared winner of the world bronco-riding title.

Three Persons was a Blood Indian from Stand Off in southern Alberta, and he became a successful rancher, raising cattle and also supplying broncos to local rodeos. Towards the end of his life, he was badly injured by a colt which he had tried to stop from breaking out of a corral.

Benjamin Tibbets
Born 1813, Youngs Cove, N.B.
Died 1853

Benjamin Tibbets invented a compound steam engine which made ships run faster and better on less fuel. The first of his engines was installed in 1845 in a paddle-wheeler called the *Reindeer*. Although a few compound steam engines had already been designed in other parts of the world, Tibbets's model gave a great boost to the shipping industry in the Maritimes.

A man of many talents, Tibbets was a musician and artist as well as inventor. But he suffered from tuberculosis and died relatively young. He died in dramatic circumstances at his father's house near the St.John River. A ship powered by one of his engines had caught fire, lighting up the sky; and as it burned to ashes, Tibbets breathed his last breath.

Samuel Leonard Tilley
Born 1818, Gagetown, N.B.
Died 1896

As New Brunswick's leading politician during the 1860s, Samuel Leonard Tilley was one of the "big seven" Fathers of Confederation. Tilley was ahead of most New Brunswickers in his eagerness for Confederation. He lost an election on the issue in 1865, but rallied support and got his party back into power in time to take part in the final arrangements in England.

At the London Conference of 1866 he came up with a suggestion of what to call Canada. The "kingdom" of Canada had been considered, but such a term could offend the United States. Tilley quoted Psalm 72: "He shall have dominion also from sea to sea." This gave Canada its title, "dominion," and its motto, *a mari usque ad mare* (from sea to sea).

It was no accident that Tilley could quote the Bible at will. He was a very strict Christian and far more pure-living than many of his fellow politicians. After Confederation he served in the federal government as a cabinet minister, and he also served twice as lieutenant governor of New Brunswick.

Harold Town
Born 1924, Toronto, Ont.

Painter, printmaker, sculptor, speaker, writer, actor . . . Harold Town is an artist in the all-round sense, a man who is always creating in some way. He studied at the Ontario College of Art and was one of the abstract artists, Painters Eleven, who exhibited together in the 1950s. The two main organizers of this group were William Ronald and Jock MacDonald (see p. 221); and one of the most outstanding artists in the group was Jack Bush (1909-77). Bush was famed for his bold, colourful abstracts, and like Harold Town he has had his work hung in some of the world's major galleries.

Catharine Parr Traill
Born 1802, England
Died 1899

Catharine Parr Traill wrote *The Canadian Settler's Guide*, a type of survival manual, telling settlers in Upper Canada how to grow corn, how to make their own soap, and what to do if their cabin caught fire. The guide is still fascinating to read, for it gives a first-hand picture of pioneer life in Upper Canada.

The capable Mrs. Traill was herself a pioneer. In another book, *The Backwoods of Canada*, she described her first years in the bush country near Peterborough. She always found time to write, however busy she was at soap-making or wool-dyeing. She had published her first book in England at the age of 16, a collection of children's stories, and some of her later works were also for children. They had wonderfully Victorian titles, such as *Lady Mary and Her Nurse*.

Her brother Samuel Strickland was also a writer and backwoods pioneer, and so was her sister Susanna Moodie,* though not a particularly happy one.

Michel Tremblay

Born 1942, Montreal, Que.

In the late 1960s, Michel Tremblay made the great leap from little-known playwright to national celebrity with the performance in Montreal of his play *Les Belles-Soeurs*. He again hit the headlines in the 1970s when the play was staged in English in Toronto.

This same play had been rejected by the Dominion Drama Festival in 1966, and for two and a half years Tremblay had peddled it round Montreal, trying to get some company to put it on. It was considered too "different." Written in *joual*, it was a depressing story about depressed women, not at all the type of drawing-room comedy people were used to. Today, *Les Belles-Soeurs* is seen as a landmark event in Quebec theatre, because it started a new and realistic type of drama.

In the past years, Tremblay has produced a wide variety of work. Born into a poor Montreal family, he is now considered one of Quebec's greatest playwrights, if not the greatest playwright in all Canada.

Jennie Trout

Born 1841, Scotland
Died 1921

Jennie Trout was the first Canadian woman ever licensed to practise as a doctor in Canada. She received her licence in 1875 on passing the registration exams of Ontario's College of Physicians and Surgeons. This was the crowning triumph of her long struggle to become a doctor.

Her parents were settlers near Stratford, Ont., and there she had grown up. But she had to go to the United States to train as a doctor (to the Woman's Medical College of Pennsylvania), for no Canadian university admitted women medical students. To make life easier for the next generation of students, Dr. Trout founded the Women's Medical College, Kingston, in association with Queen's University in 1883. Meanwhile, she ran a splendid establishment in Toronto which offered novel "galvanic" electrical treatment. A gentle yet determined character, Dr. Trout was an inspiration to many younger women who were eager for a career in medicine. (See also Emily Stowe.*)

Pierre Elliott Trudeau

Born 1919, Montreal, Que.

In 1968 Pierre Trudeau became prime minister of Canada, embarking on a term as nation's leader that was to last more than 15 years, with only one brief period out of office (see Joe Clark*).

Raised in Montreal, Trudeau studied law and then spent several years travelling, going as far afield as China. During the 1950s he was a political journalist, writing for the left-wing *Cité Libre*, and in 1961 he was appointed a professor of law at the University of Montreal.

He first entered Parliament as a Liberal in 1965 and two years later was made minister of justice. Then came what has been called Trudeaumania, when he was swept into office as the swinging bachelor prime minister of the swinging sixties. He gained even more popularity when in 1971 he married 23-year-old Margaret Sinclair (from whom he has since separated).

Trudeau's years as prime minister have seen some important pieces of legislation, including the patriation of Canada's constitution (see Laskin*). At a stirring ceremony in Ottawa in 1982, Queen Elizabeth II, as Queen of Canada, proclaimed the new constitution in force.

Charles Tupper
Born 1821, Amherst, N.S.
Died 1915

Charles Tupper was successively a doctor, a politician, premier of Nova Scotia and one of the "big seven" Fathers of Confederation; then a federal MP, a cabinet minister, Canadian high commissioner in England . . . and, finally, prime minister of Canada. He was prime minister for just a few months in 1896, the last Conservative to hold the office before Wilfrid Laurier* swept the Liberals into power.

As might be expected, Tupper was a vigorous man, lusty and energetic. He was known as the Cumberland Warhorse because of his staunch fighting abilities during the political battles of the day. But Tupper was more like a bulldog than a horse. For many years, he acted as John A. Macdonald's* guard dog. (Any attack from the Liberals was guaranteed to bring on a furious barking from Tupper.) His fierce loyalty was backed by ability. Strong in mind and spirit, Charles Tupper was one of the key figures of the Confederation era.

Wallace Turnbull
Born 1870, Saint John, N.B.
Died 1954

Working in a woodshed at his home in New Brunswick, W. R. Turnbull invented the variable-pitch propeller, which was hailed as the most important invention in the history of aeronautics. Previously, all propellers had been fixed at one angle. With Turnbull's propeller, the blades could be adjusted (much as one changes gears on a car) so that they were at one angle for take-off and at another angle for level flight. This allowed heavier loads to be carried, and it led to the development of the air transport industry.

Turnbull spent more than ten years developing the variable-pitch propeller, which was first flight-tested in 1927. He made the early tests in a wind tunnel he built in his woodshed laboratory. It was the first wind tunnel in Canada. His numerous inventions increased Canada's reputation as one of the world's leading pioneers in aviation. The Saint John airport, Turnbull Field, is named in his honour.

Philip Turnor
Born c.1751, England
Died 1800

The most important thing about Philip Turnor is that he trained David Thompson.* Turnor was a first-rate surveyor—the first person to be especially appointed surveyor by the Hudson's Bay Company—and in 1789-90 he and Thompson were both at the fur-trading post of Cumberland House at the same time. During the long winter months, Turnor taught the 19-year-old Thompson mathematics, surveying, and astronomy. As a result, Thompson had the basic knowledge that enabled him to develop into one of the world's great map-makers.

Meanwhile, Turnor himself also surveyed and charted. Between 1778 and 1792 he travelled throughout Rupert's Land, putting much of it on the map in pen and ink.

Lord Tweedsmuir
Born 1875, Scotland
Died 1940

Canada's fifteenth Governor General first gained fame as John Buchan, author of *The Thirty-Nine Steps* and other adventure stories. He was not born a lord. He was the son of a clergyman and was made Lord Tweedsmuir in 1935, on being appointed Governor General.

Joseph Burr Tyrrell
Born 1858, Weston, Ont.
Died 1957
The greatest Canadian land explorer of his day, Joseph Tyrrell trekked across the empty areas of the West and North. He worked for the Geological Survey of Canada, and in 1883 he not only found a huge coal seam in the Red Deer Valley; he also found dinosaur skeletons there. Ten years later, he and his brother James crossed the Barren Lands of the Northwest Territories—the first white men to do so since Samuel Hearne.* Like Hearne, they did most of the journey on foot.

Tyrrell left the Geological Survey in 1898 and became a highly successful mining engineer, at first in the Yukon and then as president of the Kirkland Lake Gold Mining Company in Ontario. One of his many achievements was to unearth David Thompson* from obscurity; he published Thompson's journals and thus made Canada and the world aware of the early geographer's amazing accomplishments.

Ian and Sylvia Tyson
Ian born 1933, Victoria, B.C.
Sylvia born 1940, Chatham, Ont.
Ian Tyson and Sylvia Fricker met as folksingers in Toronto, teamed up as "Ian and Sylvia," became central figures in the folk revival of the 1960s, married, had success after success . . . and eventually parted and continued to have success individually.

Both have written songs that were international hits, such as Ian's "Four Strong Winds" and Sylvia's "You Were on My Mind." And both have had their own CBC shows as well as countless other engagements. Not least of their achievements is that they were among the first to sing Gordon Lightfoot's* songs, bringing his music to a wide audience.

James Boyle Uniacke
Born c.1800, Halifax, N.S.
Died 1858
In all the British Empire, James Uniacke was the first politician to be premier of a colony under the system of responsible government.

Previously, there had been representative government. Although people could elect members to represent them in their assembly, it was the governor and his appointed council who ruled. But under responsible government, the ruling was done by a cabinet chosen from the party which had the most members elected to the assembly. The governor had to accept the decisions of these elected leaders, even if he didn't agree with them. And, of course, he also had to accept them as leaders. This is what happened in Nova Scotia in February 1848, when Uniacke's Liberal party took office as a result of winning an election.

Uniacke was a lawyer by training, and with Joseph Howe* he had long been pressing for responsible government in Nova Scotia. One month later, the Province of Canada also achieved responsible government, when La Fontaine* and Baldwin* formed their Great Ministry. The winning of this right laid the foundation of the system of parliamentary democracy that we have today.

George Vancouver
Born 1757, England
Died 1798

The British naval officer George Vancouver came to the West Coast with two ships, and between 1792 and 1794 he and his men surveyed and mapped the entire mainland coast of British Columbia. Vancouver also conducted lengthy negotiations with Captain Juan Francisco de la Bodega y Quadra, who was in command of the Spanish settlement at Nootka Sound. At the time, both Spain and Britain had rival claims to the Pacific seaboard. But the Spanish gave up Nootka Sound in 1795.

Vancouver had originally visited the region in 1778. As a young midshipman under Captain Cook,* he had been one of the first Europeans ever to land on Canada's West Coast.

Georges Vanier
Born 1888, Montreal, Que.
Died 1967

General Vanier was the second Canadian-born Governor General and the first French Canadian to hold the position. He was in office 1959-67.

A stately, silver-haired old gentleman, Vanier had long been a hero to many Canadians. As a young man during World War I, he helped organize the "Van Doos," the famous French Canadian regiment, known for its spirit and fighting power. When leading his men into battle, Vanier was so seriously wounded that he had to have his leg amputated. Undaunted, he continued to serve Canada in many different ways and was ambassador to France for some years. As Governor General, he tried to get the different peoples of Canada to live together in a more friendly manner.

William Van Horne
Born 1843, U.S.A.
Died 1915

William Van Horne built the Canadian Pacific Railway, and he did so in an amazingly short time. He took over as general manager in January 1882, when only a few sections of track had been laid. Less than four years later, in November 1885, the last spike was driven on a railway line that wound north of Lake Superior, across the prairies, and through the Rockies.

Many others also took part in this impressive achievement, but Van Horne was the driving force. He was known as the Boss of Everything and Everybody. Blunt and outspoken, he was constantly on the job, inspecting the track, urging the men on, and swearing lustily as he roared out praise or blame. He drove himself as hard as his men, catching only a few hours' sleep each night.

Having built the CPR, Van Horne spent the rest of his life promoting it, building branch lines and hiring artists to paint the scenery it disclosed. In more than one way, he opened the West to Canadians.

Frederick Varley
Born 1881, England
Died 1969

Of all the Group of Seven artists, Frederick Varley was the one who concentrated most on portraits. Some art critics feel that he was Canada's greatest portrait painter. He came to Canada in 1912, worked as a commercial artist in Toronto, and then signed on as a war artist in World War I. In 1933 he founded the British Columbia College of Arts, together with Jock MacDonald (1897-1960) whom he had inspired to take up painting.

Jock MacDonald had started his career as a fabric designer, and he painted strong, colourful abstracts. He and Varley had a lasting impact on Vancouver artists, though their art school closed after a couple of years. Both men then left Vancouver and went their separate ways. They both ended up in Toronto, where MacDonald taught at the Ontario College of Art and was a strong influence on younger artists, a key figure in the art world.

Philippe de Rigaud de Vaudreuil
Born 1643, France
Died 1725

A decisive man of action, Vaudreuil was one of New France's greatest generals. He fought the Iroquois in their own manner, using guerrilla tactics, and led several successful expeditions against them during the 1690s. These campaigns brought to an end the long-standing warfare between the French and the Iroquois. Frontenac* was governor of New France at the time.

Vaudreuil himself was appointed governor in 1703, holding the position until his death. During this period, he made peace with many Indian tribes so that the fur trade could carry on unmolested. And he defended New France's borders from the British, using the same tactics he had employed against the Iroquois. Instead of fighting a defensive action, he carried the war into enemy territory, harassing the New England settlers with a series of guerrilla raids.

One of his sons, Pierre de Rigaud de Vaudreuil, also became governor of New France. Pierre was the last governor, for he was in office when Wolfe* defeated Montcalm* at the battle of the Plains of Abraham.

Madeleine de Verchères
Born 1678, Verchères, Que.
Died 1747
Marie-Madeleine de Verchères was one of Canada's youngest heroines—14 years old when she defended her family seigneury against an Iroquois attack. Her parents were away from home at the time, and the two soldiers left on guard panicked. So Madeleine took charge of the people in the fort. Seizing a musket, she shouted, "Let us fight to the death for our country and for our holy religion!" She then ordered the soldiers and her younger brothers to keep up a regular fire, giving the impression that the seigneury was filled with soldiers. Spurred on by her courage, they held out for eight days until help finally came.

Peter Verigin
Born 1859, Russia
Killed 1924
Called Peter the Lordly, Verigin was the first leader of the Doukhobors in Canada. In 1899 several thousand Doukhobors arrived in Canada, fleeing from persecution in tsarist Russia. Verigin was at the time a prisoner in Siberia, but in1902 he was allowed to leave Russia, and he became head of his people's religious communities in Saskatchewan.

The Doukhobors had been promised that in Saskatchewan they would be allowed to carry on their traditional way of life; but they came into conflict with the authorities when they began to do so. This was partly because they would not take an oath of allegiance (for it was against their religion to do so). The government confiscated their lands, whereupon Verigin set up a community in British Columbia, taking most of his people with him.

The B.C. community prospered, though there were again problems with the authorities—and also bitter disputes among the Doukhobors themselves. Verigin's death has never been fully explained. In the fall of 1924, the railway carriage in which he was travelling suddenly blew up.

Jon Vickers

Born 1926, Prince Albert, Sask.

Jon Vickers, the operatic superstar, had a hard time getting into professional music. At first, he earned his living by working in chain stores in the West. He then became a hardware salesman, as this gave him more time for singing engagements.

After winning a scholarship to the Royal Conservatory of Music in Toronto, he at last began to attract notice, and in 1956 he was offered a three-year contract at Covent Garden in England. Vickers hasn't looked back since. He performs mostly abroad at such celebrated opera houses as New York's Metropolitan and Milan's La Scala.

Gilles Vigneault

Born 1928, Natashquan, Que.

Poet, songwriter, singer, and broadcaster, Gilles Vigneault has been called "Quebec's true ambassador abroad." Much of his work is inspired by the folk songs and countryside of Quebec, which he brings to Canada and the world in songs and poems, in records and books, in concert performances and overseas tours.

Vigneault originally earned his living as a library assistant and teacher, and first sang his own songs in public in 1960. A few years later, he gained wide acclaim with his chanson "Mon Pays," which was sung by Monique Leyrac* at the International Song Festival in Poland in 1965. A book of his poems published that same year won a Governor General's Award. Vigneault has won many other awards and honours, and has had several films made about him.

Gilles Villeneuve

Born 1950, Chambly, Que.
Died 1982

The finest racing driver Canada has ever produced, Gilles Villeneuve won six Grand Prix races all told, competing against the world's fastest drivers.

From early childhood, Villeneuve had been fascinated by cars; he knew how to drive long before he was old enough to get a licence. When he was 16, he began racing snowmobiles, and it was in this sport that he first made his name, winning two Canadian championships and a world title. From snowmobiles, Villeneuve moved on to Formula Atlantic motor racing and then to Formula One, the Grand Prix. He drove his first Grand Prix races in 1977, and the following year he was taken as a regular on the Ferrari team. In all, he drove in 67 Grand Prix.

He was killed in a high-speed crash during a practice session for the Belgian Grand Prix.

Horatio Walker

Born 1858, Listowel, Ont.
Died 1938

Horatio Walker was one of the most successful artists of his day. He painted quiet pastoral scenes of farmers and farm animals, which were extremely popular. His friend Homer Watson (1855-1936) also specialized in pastoral landscapes, one of which was bought as a present for Queen Victoria.

The two artists had very similar careers. Both were Ontario farm boys, both gained fame early in life, both studied in the United States, and both were influenced by the work of the French artist, Millet. The main difference between them was that Horatio Walker was a better businessman than Homer Watson. Walker did phenomenally well, gaining top prices for his pictures, while Watson died broke.

James Morrow Walsh
Born 1843, Prescott, Ont.
Died 1905

A dashing dare-devil with great bravado, James Walsh was one of the first recruits to join the North-West Mounted Police. In 1876, when the Sioux fled to Canada following the battle of Little Bighorn, he played a key role in keeping them peaceful. Fearlessly, he rode into their camps to lay down the law or to make an arrest, regardless of the hundreds of armed Sioux surrounding him. This drew the admiration of their chief, Sitting Bull.

Walsh became friendly with Sitting Bull, and he tried to get the Americans to pardon the chief and allow him to return home. This did not please the authorities, and Walsh had to resign from the Mounties. But he was taken on again during the Klondike gold rush, when he served as police superintendent in the Yukon.

Dorothy Walton
Born 1908, Swift Current, Sask.
Died 1981

In the Canadian Press poll of 1950, Dorothy Walton was voted one of Canada's six most outstanding female athletes of the half-century. She excelled at a wide range of sports, including tennis, and won 54 local, provincial, and western Canadian tennis titles between 1924 and 1931. But she gained even more renown as a badminton player. In 1939 she won the All-England badminton championship, which was in effect the world title. She held the title until 1947.

In the 1950s she made her name in a different field. As a leading member of the Consumers Association of Canada, she fought for lower prices and for a better quality of consumer goods.

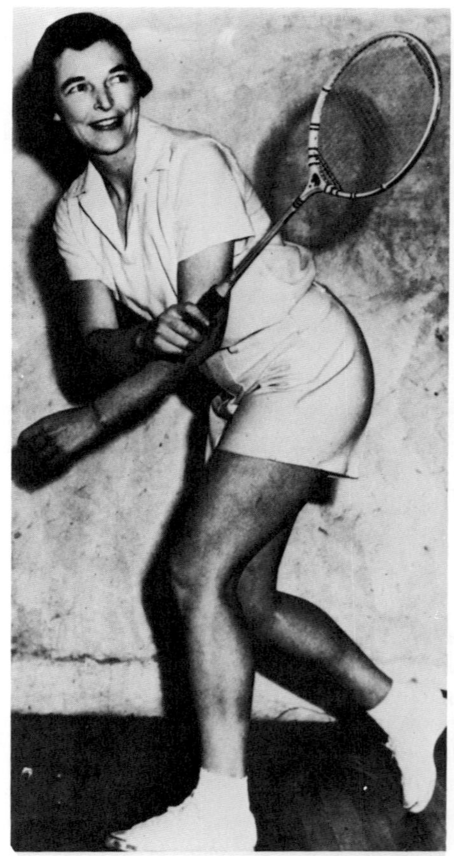

Angus Walters
Born 1882, Lunenburg, N.S.
Died 1968

Angus Walters was captain of the *Bluenose*, the famous sailing ship that was called "queen of the North Atlantic fishing fleet." Designed by William J. Roué of Halifax and launched in 1921, the *Bluenose* won five international races over the years and countless Canadian ones. In 1933 Walters took the ship to Chicago for the Century of Progress Exposition, and in 1935 he sailed her to England for the Silver Jubilee celebrations of George V.

After spending most of his life on fishing schooners, Walters sold the *Bluenose* to a West Indian company in 1942 and spent his last years farming in Lunenburg. The *Bluenose* was later wrecked off Haiti. But a replica was built in 1963, so the elegant schooner still sails our waters. She jingles in our pockets too—on the backs of 10-cent coins.

John Ware

Born 1845, U.S.A.
Died 1905

Around the turn of the century, John Ware was a legendary figure in the West, a black rancher who could tame the wildest horses. Born a slave in South Carolina, he became a cowboy in Texas after slavery was banned in the United States, and in 1882 he came to Canada on a cattle drive. He liked what he saw and decided to stay, marrying a 19-year-old black girl from Calgary, Mildred Lewis.

Ware ran a small ranch on the Sheep Creek near Calgary, later moving to a larger location near the Red Deer River. He was tough, as he had to be, for there were very few blacks in the Canadian West and there was a lot of prejudice. Ware won through by a mixture of good humour and feats of daring. Admired as a champion steer-wrestler, he was also liked as a person—praised as "one of the best-natured and most obliging men in the country." Many ranchers felt a deep sense of loss when Ware was killed by his horse, which tripped and rolled on him.

Whipper Billy Watson

Born 1917, Toronto, Ont.

One of the great attractions of Toronto's Maple Leaf Gardens used to be Whipper Billy Watson, the "good guy" wrestler that the crowd cheered (as against the "bad guy" who got booed). Like all great wrestlers, he was a superb show-man as well as a toughie.

He was born William Potts and excelled in a number of sports, including marathon swimming, before he found his niche as a professional wrestler. He twice gained the light-heavyweight world title, once in 1947 and again in 1956. In his 31 years in the ring (from the 1940s through to the 1970s), he fought more than 7,400 bouts. Since his retirement, he has helped to sponsor charitable causes such as Easter Seals.

Wayne and Shuster

Born 1918 and 1916, Toronto, Ont.

Comedians Johnny Wayne and Frank Shuster met in high school in Toronto and both went on to University College, where they performed together in the college revue. This drew the attention of an advertising agent for radio shows, and it launched Wayne and Shuster on their joint career of inspired buffoonery, first with CFRB radio in Toronto and then with the CBC.

During World War II they gained great popularity with *The Army Show*, and their appearances on *The Ed Sullivan Show* after the war brought them popularity throughout North America. Long-time favourites on both television and radio, Wayne and Shuster are especially celebrated for such skits as their take-off of the assassina-tion of Julius Caesar.

John Weinzweig
Born 1913, Toronto, Ont.
For more than 40 years, John Weinzweig has been a key figure in Canadian music. The son of Polish immigrants, he was the pioneer Canadian modernist—the composer who broke away from traditional sounds and used the 12-tone scale and other innovations. Inevitably, his works drew as much criticism as praise. "He rode out the storm of criticism alone," wrote R. Murray Schafer,* who was one of his pupils.

Weinzweig taught for many years at the University of Toronto's Faculty of Music, where his students included Murray Adaskin, Harry Freedman, and Harry Somers, all of whom have long been highly acclaimed composers themselves. Not least of Weinzweig's achievements was his role in forming the Canadian League of Composers. Because of the league, Canadian composers were able to work together in their efforts to accustom the public to "modern" music.

Charlotte Whitton
Born 1896, Renfrew, Ont.
Died 1975

The first woman to be mayor of Ottawa, Charlotte Whitton was both peppery and peppy. She was determined not to let men talk down to her. When a visiting lord mayor of London looked at the rose she was wearing and asked, "If I smell your corsage, will you blush?" she immediately replied, "If I pull your chain, will you flush?"

Because of her forthright character, Charlotte Whitton's years in office were rather stormy, yet she served two periods as mayor of the capital (1951-56 and 1961-64). She worked in the civil service before becoming mayor and for a time was director of the Canadian Welfare Council. She was also a journalist for the Ottawa *Citizen*, author of several books, and above all a stirring example to the women of her day. For she proved that a woman could perform very effectively in jobs that were normally done by men.

Christopher Widmer
Born 1780, England
Died 1858
Known for his bad language and good surgery, Dr. Christopher Widmer has gone down in history as "the father of medicine in Upper Canada." He was a brusque and businesslike army surgeon—very outspoken and with no bedside manner. Settling in York after the War of 1812, he worked as both doctor and surgeon, formed medical committees and examining boards, taught the few medical students, and oversaw the birth of York's tiny hospital (which grew to become the Toronto General). Virtually all Upper Canada's medical affairs were guided by Widmer.

Rudy Wiebe
Born 1934, nr. Fairholme, Sask.
Rudy Wiebe writes spellbinding, word-spinning novels based on historical themes. One of his best-known books is *The Temptations of Big Bear*, which won a Governor General's Award. Another is *Peace Shall Destroy Many*, the story of a group of Mennonites who immigrated to Canada from Russia in the late nineteenth century.

Wiebe is himself a Mennonite, the son of Russian immigrants who settled in Saskatchewan in the 1920s. Raised on the prairies, he attended universities in Canada and abroad, and is now a professor at the University of Alberta. Through his fiction, he explores the world he knows best: the land and people of western Canada.

Healey Willan
Born 1880, England
Died 1968
Healey Willan wrote the anthem "O Lord, Our Governour," which was sung in Westminster Abbey in 1953 at the coronation of Queen Elizabeth. He was one of the greatest Canadian composers of all time, known especially for his church music, though he also wrote symphonies, sonatas, and several operas. *Deirdre* is his most celebrated opera.

Willan had started his career as a church organist in England, and for many years he was organist and choirmaster at the Anglican church of St. Mary Magdalene in Toronto. Meanwhile, he worked as a teacher of music, notably at the Royal Conservatory of Music and the University of Toronto.

James Miller Williams
Born 1818, U.S.A.
Died 1890
James Williams was the pioneer of our petroleum industry. An Ontario manufacturer of carriages and railway cars, he turned to oil exploration after Abraham Gesner* discovered how to refine petroleum.

Williams's first attempt at searching for oil was not successful. The well he dug flooded with water. But then he dug a 20-metre well near Oil Springs, Ont., and there he struck oil. This was in 1857, and it was the first commercial oil well in all North America. That same year Williams built an oil refinery, the first in Canada. And within two years he took another step forward —drilling for oil. He dug down to bedrock and then drilled into the rock itself. Williams was one of the first people in the world to use this method.

Percy Williams
Born 1908, Vancouver, B.C.
Died 1982
For a few brief years, Percy Williams was the fastest sprinter in the world. He spurted to fame in the 1928 Olympics, winning two gold medals: for the 100-metre dash and the 200-metre. An overnight hero, he was given a tumultuous reception when he returned home to Vancouver.

Over the next couple of years, Williams went on running and went on winning. But at the British Empire Games in 1930 he pulled a muscle in his thigh, and though he won the race, his leg was never really right again. After competing unsuccessfully at the 1932 Olympics, he decided to call it quits. So he opted out of sport and into business.

Another famous track star was Saskatchewan-born Harry Jerome (1940-82). During his career, he tied two world sprint records and won a bronze medal at the 1964 Olympics.

John Williamson
Born 1907, Montfort, Que.
Died 1958
John Williamson was the discoverer of one of the world's richest diamond deposits. A geology graduate from McGill University, he went to Africa when he was 26, searching for adventure as much as riches. And he found unimagined wealth on the dusty plains of Tanganyika (now Tanzania). The mine he opened there at a place called Mwadui yielded as much as $10 million worth of diamonds a year.

Besides developing his diamond mine, Williamson built a beautiful settlement for his workers, complete with schools, a hospital, swimming pools, and well-watered lawns. This was a great contrast to South African mines, where black labourers lived in barracks and weren't allowed to have their families with them. Williamson is remembered warmly in Tanzania.

Lord Willingdon
Born 1866, England
Died 1941
Lord Willingdon was Governor General in the late 1920s. Like most of his predecessors, he was posted to other countries as well as Canada. He served in China, took a goodwill mission to South America, and for five years was Viceroy of India.

Bertha Wilson
Born 1923, Scotland
In 1982 Bertha Wilson was appointed to the Supreme Court of Canada, the first woman ever to be made a judge of the Supreme Court. An arts graduate from Aberdeen in Scotland, she had come to Canada with her clergyman husband in 1949. While living in Halifax, she took a law degree at Dalhousie and in 1959 joined a Toronto law firm. In 1976 she was appointed a judge on the Ontario Court of Appeal, where she soon gained a name for her fearless decisions.

Carbide Willson
Born 1860, Princeton, Ont.
Died 1915
Long before he earned his nickname, Thomas Willson was an enthusiastic inventor. As a teenager, he experimented in the basement of his parents' Hamilton home, trying all sorts of projects. During one period of his life, he even tried to make diamonds. But he is most famous for his discovery, in 1892, of how to make carbide (a substance) and acetylene (a gas) from a mixture of lime and coal tar. This laid the basis of today's mammoth carbide industry.

Besides giving the world this new industry, and operating his own carbide and acetylene works, Carbide Willson established the first Canadian hydro-electric plant. It was at Merritton between St. Catharines and Niagara Falls. Willson was ahead of most Canadians in recognizing the value of hydro-electric power, and it was largely due to his efforts that Canada asserted its right to use Niagara Falls power. Some Americans were already using Niagara power, and had it not been for Willson, all hydro-electricity from Niagara Falls might today be owned and managed by American corporations.

Cairine Wilson
Born 1885, Montreal, Que.
Died 1962
Cairine Wilson was the first woman appointed to the Senate (in 1930). A staunch Liberal and the daughter of a Liberal senator, she was a member of the Liberal women's committee that had worked for Mackenzie King.* Among her many activities as a senator, she was chairman of a committee which helped refugee children from France during World War II.

Eric Wilson
Born 1940, Ottawa, Ont.
The boy detective Tom Austen and his sister Liz were dreamed up by Eric Wilson, author of such fast-moving adventure stories as *Terror in Winnipeg* and *The Ghost of Lunenburg Manor*. Wilson himself had some interesting adventures while establishing himself as a writer. His part-time jobs included being a bulldozer operator in the Arctic and a counsellor at a Saskatchewan camp for handicapped children. A graduate of the University of British Columbia, he is a teacher as well as a novelist.

James Wolfe
Born 1727, England
Killed 1759

General Wolfe was killed in action during the battle of the Plains of Abraham, which took place just outside Quebec in 1759 during the Seven Years' War. The battle was a decisive victory for the British forces, signalling the end of New France and the beginning of British rule in Canada. This, together with Wolfe's death, has caused him to be celebrated (among English Canadians) as a great and gallant hero. But in fact Wolfe was not an outstanding general. He couldn't get on with his officers, couldn't make up his mind, and sometimes made the wrong decision in the end.

Like his French opponent Montcalm,* Wolfe was a career soldier. He had served in Scotland at the battle of Culloden, and more recently in Canada at the siege of Louisbourg. Early in 1759, he was given command of the forces which set out to capture Quebec. His success in this venture was largely due to luck, to the strategy planned by his brigadiers, and to Montcalm's mistakes.

Two of the brigadiers so disliked Wolfe that they refused to be included in the romanticized memorial portrait of his death. Like Montcalm, Wolfe was not clever with people. But, like Montcalm, he did have great bravery.

Henry Wise Wood
Born 1860, U.S.A.
Died 1941

A farm leader from Missouri, Henry Wise Wood settled in Alberta at the age of 45 and spent the rest of his life working for prairie farmers, their vigorous organizer and spokesman. In 1916 he was elected president of the United Farmers of Alberta, and many people thought he would become premier of Alberta when in 1921 the UFA won the provincial election. But Wood preferred to work for the farmers in other ways.

One of his great achievements was to get prairie wheat pools organized so that farmers could have some control over how their grain was handled and marketed. Before these co-ops were formed, western farmers had to accept whatever price they were offered for their crop. The first of the grain co-operatives was the Alberta Wheat Pool, formed in 1923, and Wood served as its president until he was almost 80. Over the years, he had great influence on the lives of people throughout the prairies, as he guided their fortunes and looked after their interests.

Garnet Wolseley
Born 1833, Ireland
Died 1913

Colonel Wolseley led the 2,000-man Red River Expedition that was sent west in 1870 during the first Riel* rebellion. His soldiers had a desperately tough journey in the heat of summer, plagued by mosquitoes and torrential rains. Travelling mostly by water routes, they had to haul all their boats, supplies, and cannons over 47 portages between Lake Superior and the Red River.

Wolseley was an experienced campaigner who had already served as a British officer in India and the Crimea. Later in life, he led another epic expedition when he was sent to rescue General Gordon during the siege of Khartoum in Africa. He wound up his career as Lord Wolseley, commander-in-chief of the British army.

George Woodcock

Born 1912, Winnipeg, Man.

George Woodcock has written more than 50 books, on just about every subject and of just about every type—poetry, plays, biography, history, everything from studies of Canadian literature to the story of explorers in Tibet. Each year he brings out two or three books, as well as writing numerous pieces for magazines and newspapers.

Woodcock lives in Vancouver but spent his childhood and youth in England, where he became an active member of the London literary world. He returned to Canada in 1949 and taught at the University of British Columbia 1956-63. During this period he founded the magazine *Canadian Literature*, and he served as its editor for almost 20 years. In 1966 he won a Governor General's Award. One of his best-known books is *Canada and the Canadians*.

J. S. Woodsworth

Born 1874, nr. Islington, Ont.
Died 1942

James Shaver Woodsworth was the principal founder and first leader of the Co-operative Commonwealth Federation (CCF), the socialist party which was formed in 1932 and which later merged with other groups to become today's New Democratic Party.

Woodsworth had started his career as a Methodist minister, but his work in the slums of Winnipeg and other cities caused him such heartache that he became increasingly committed to social reform—and increasingly at odds with his church. In 1918 he finally resigned from the ministry and went to work in the Vancouver docks. Over the next few years he helped organize labour movements throughout the West, playing a prominent role in the Winnipeg General Strike. And in 1921 he was elected to Parliament as a labour candidate.

Woodsworth remained an MP for the rest of his life, continually pressing for better conditions for Canada's working people. It was largely because of his perseverance that old age pensions were introduced, as well as many other much-needed benefits. He was Parliament's conscience, widely respected for his lifelong efforts to improve the lot of millions of ordinary Canadians. A convinced pacifist, he resigned from the leadership of the CCF after the outbreak of World War II. He was succeeded by a fellow founder of the party, M. J. Coldwell (1888-1974).

Joseph Workman

Born 1805, Ireland
Died 1894

A kindly man with a wise sense of humour, Dr. Workman brought a new attitude to the treatment of the mentally sick.

Mental patients had at times been nursed sympathetically in the past, but reforms were badly needed by 1854 when Workman was appointed superintendent of Toronto's Insane Asylum. As in England, mental institutions had become more like prisons than hospitals. Patients were chained up, kept in filthy conditions, underfed and often beaten. During the 21 years Workman was superintendent, he changed the whole approach. He cleaned up the hospital, started a program of games and readings, and gave the patients a degree of freedom that shocked many Torontonians. Workman even spent his evenings with the patients, trying to cheer them up.

One of his assistants was a young medical student, Charles K. Clarke, who later became a leading Toronto doctor, and professor of psychiatry at the University of Toronto. Clarke took Workman's methods one step further, giving the patients professional treatment as well as kindness. He laid the foundation of psychiatry as a medical science in Canada. The Clarke Institute of Psychiatry is named after him.

Letitia Youmans

Born 1827, nr. Cobourg, Ont.
Died 1896

Letitia Youmans was the leading light of Canada's Woman's Christian Temperance Union (WCTU). Her aim was to prevent drunkenness and all the harm it caused, and to get laws passed prohibiting the sale of liquor. By travelling around the country and meeting women's groups, Mrs. Youmans got branches of the WCTU started in many parts of Canada. And in 1883, when a national WCTU was formed, she became its first president.

Besides campaigning for prohibition (which eventually came into force in most parts of Canada during World War I), the WCTU was also very active in the suffrage movement, helping to win Canadian women the right to vote.

George Young

Born 1910, Toronto, Ont.
Died 1972

George Young was nicknamed the Catalina Kid, because he was the first person to swim the tide-swept Catalina Channel from Catalina Island to the Californian mainland. He made the marathon swim in 1927 when he was 17, crossing the 32-km channel in less than 16 hours and beating more than 100 champions from all over the world. Because of the tides, his actual swim was almost 50 km.

The Catalina Kid was given a hero's welcome when he returned home to Toronto, and he was the star attraction later that year when the Canadian National Exhibition staged its own marathon swim. But this time Young had to be pulled from the water after only 8 km. He didn't win another marathon swim until 1931, by which time the public had given up on him. Yet it was largely because of George Young and his early success that the CNE swims became so popular. In the Canadian Press poll of 1950, he was voted Canada's outstanding swimmer of the half-century.

Neil Young

Born 1945, Toronto, Ont.

In 1972 Neil Young sold one million copies of his song "Heart of Gold." Less than ten years earlier, his career as a singer and songwriter was struggling along so badly that he had taken a job in the stockroom at Coles bookstore.

His luck changed in 1966 when he bought a second-hand hearse ("big enough to hold a band") and set off for California. There, with Stephen Stills, he formed the Buffalo Springfield, which became one of America's first supergroups.

Between 1969 and 1974, Neil Young performed with the group called Crosby Stills Nash and Young. During these years, all his albums received gold-record sales awards. Whether singing hauntingly quiet songs or breaking the sound barrier as a rock guitarist, he has had hit after hit, gathering millions of fans throughout the world.

Jan Zurakowski

Born 1914, Russia

Canada's famous test pilot grew up in Poland, where he took to the air at an early age. Zurakowski flew gliders as a high school student and first piloted a plane at the age of 15. A few years later he joined the Polish air force, but escaped to Britain to join the Royal Air Force when Germany invaded Poland in 1939. He made his first test flights while serving with the RAF in World War II.

Immigrating to Canada in 1952, Zurakowski became the first pilot to fly a Canadian-designed aircraft faster than the speed of sound. This was on December 18, 1952, during a test flight in the CF-100 jet fighter.

He also test flew the Avro Arrow (a supersonic fighter) until the government decided to save money by stopping development of these planes. Zurakowski's daring pioneering flights brought great prestige to the Canadian aircraft industry.

Credits

Many individuals and organizations have responded most kindly during the search for pictures. Special thanks go to the National Gallery of Canada, the Public Archives of Canada, the Canadian Broadcasting Corporation, the Glenbow Archives, Fitzhenry & Whiteside, and McClelland and Stewart. Every effort has been made to trace and attribute correctly the sources of the illustrations used, and to obtain all necessary permissions and copyright clearances. Should there be any omissions or errors, the author and publisher will be glad to hear of them.

The following abbreviations are used below:

CBC	Canadian Broadcasting Corporation
CP	Canapress Photo Service
Glenbow	Glenbow Archives
NFB	National Film Board of Canada
PABC	Provincial Archives of British Columbia
PAC	Public Archives of Canada
SHF	Canada's Sports Hall of Fame

F. Abbott Dagmar Stegelmann. **J. Abbott** PAC PA-26319. **M. Abbott** PAC C-9479. **Aberdeen** PAC C-2158. **Aberhart** PAC C-9448. **Agar** PAC/Antray photo, C-60002. **Albani** PAC C-49491. **A. Allan** Courtesy of CBC. **H. Allan** PAC C-26668. **Almighty Voice** Glenbow NA-2310-1. **André** Courtesy of St. Joseph's Oratory/Br. Dennis photo. **Anka** Graham Pilsworth. **Arbuckle** Illustrations of Hearne and Henday. **Archer** Courtesy of Violet Archer. **Archibald** PAC PA-26321. **Arden** Courtesy of Elizabeth Arden of Canada. **Atwood** Courtesy of the University of Toronto/Robert Lansdale photo. **C. Baker** Courtesy of Tembo Music/Hans Ulrich Lichtenberg photo. **Casey Baldwin** University of Toronto Archives. **K. Baldwin** Courtesy of CKSL Radio, London, Ont./Robert Nelson photo. **Banting** Banting and Best Institute. **Billy Barker** PABC 2428. **W.G. Barker** PAC PA-6505. **Barr** Saskatchewan Archives Board R-A 2521. **Barry** Courtesy of the Federation of Medical Women of Canada. **Baumann** Athlete Information Bureau. **Beaverbrook** PAC PA-6467. **Beck** PAC C-26070. **Begbie** PAC C-36048. **Béliveau** PAC/David Bier Studios, C-29510. **A.G. Bell** PAC C-28214. **M. Bell** PAC/SHF PA-50353. **R.B. Bennett** PAC C-7733. **W.A.C. Bennett** PABC 70606. **Benoit** Courtesy of Mme. Benoit. **Bernier** PAC C-25960. **Berton** Courtesy of CBC/Fred Phipps photo. **Bessette** Courtesy of Québec Amérique/Kéro photo. **Bethune** PAC/NFB PA-114782. **Beurling** Dept. of National Defence. **Big Bear** PAC C-1876. **Bigelow** Courtesy of Dr. W.G. Bigelow. **Bigot** PAC C-3751. **Birney** Courtesy of University of Western Ontario/Plum Studios. **Bishop** PAC PA-105928. **Black** PAC C-23354. **Blades** Courtesy of Ann Blades/Joan Malcolmsen photo. **Blais** Courtesy of McClelland and Stewart. **Blake** Archives of Ontario 14054-21. **Blakeney** Courtesy of Mr. Blakeney's Office. **Bland** Courtesy of Art Gallery of Ontario/artist Lawren Harris. **Bombardier** Courtesy of Bombardier Inc. **Borden** PAC C-46314. **Borduas** Self-portrait, National Gallery of Canada. **Bottrell** Courtesy of Performing Rights Organization. **Bourassa** PAC C-5110. **Bourgeoys** PAC C-8986. **Bowell** PAC PA-25663. **Boyd** Courtesy of CBC/Jorge Waterhouse-Hayward photo. **J. Boyle** Courtesy of Joe Boyle Repatriation Committee. **Brant** National Gallery of Canada/artist W. Berczy. **Brébeuf** PAC C-1470. **Broadbent** Courtesy of NDP/Photo Features Ltd. **Broadfoot** Courtesy of Dave Broadfoot. **Brock** PAC C-11222. **A. Roy Brown** Canadian Government Photo Centre, RE 18431-24. **G. Brown** PAC C-9553. **Kootenay Brown** Glenbow NA-678-1. **Brûlé** PAC/artist C.W. Jefferys, C-73635. **Burka** PAC/SHF/D.G. Newman photo, PA-50342. **E.L.M. Burns** PAC/C.E. Nye photo, PA-115498. **Tommy Burns** PAC C-14092. **By** PAC/artist C.W. Jefferys, C-73703. **Byng** PAC PA-1283. **Cabot** PAC/artist C.W. Jefferys, C-70249. **Caouette** PAC/Canada Wide photo, C-87201. **Carignan** Courtesy of CBC Photo Library, Montreal. **Carleton** PAC C-14500. **Carman** PAC C-25816. **Carr** PAC C-20368. **Carter** Glenbow NA-2771-1. **G.E. Cartier** PAC C-6166. **J. Cartier** PAC/artist Théophile Hamel C-11226. **Cartwright** PAC PA-25960. **Casgrain** PAC PA-126768. **Casson** Courtesy of Royal Canadian Academy. **Champlain** PAC/artist C.W. Jefferys, C-73716. **Charlebois** Balvis Rubess. **Chisholm** PAC/DND PA-115641. **Clancy** PAC/Hockey Hall of Fame, PA-49032. **Clark** Courtesy of Progressive Conservative Party of Canada, CP/Peter Bregg photo. **Cockburn** Courtesy of Finkelstein Management Co. Ltd. **Cohen** Dagmar Stegelmann. **Colicos** Courtesy of Jerry Lodge Agency. **Colombo** Courtesy of John Robert Colombo/Ellen Tolmie photo. **Colville** Courtesy of Art Gallery of Ontario/Diane McConnell photo. **Conacher** PAC/SHF PA-50708. **Connors** Courtesy of CBC. **Cook** PAC/artist C.W. Jefferys C-73567. **Cornwallis** PAC/artist C.W. Jefferys, C-125. **Cranston** Courtesy of International Management Group. **Crawford** PAC C-6720. **Creighton** PAC/Robert Lansdale photo, PA-123984. **Crerar** PAC PA-43102. **Crowfoot** Glenbow NA-29-1. **Cummings** Courtesy of CBC/Harold White photo. **Cunard** PAC PA-124022. **Currie** PAC PA-1575. **Cyr** PAC C-86343. **Dafoe** Courtesy of Winnipeg Free Press. **Davies** PAC C-31986. **Davin** PAC C-4651. **Davis** Courtesy of Government of Ontario. **Dawson** PAC PA-25520. **De Cosmos** PAC PA-25397. **De la Roche** PAC C-5482. **Denny** Courtesy of RCMP. **Deschamps** Courtesy of CBC Photo Library, Montreal. **Dewdney** PAC PA-118778. **Dextraze** PAC/DND/Paul Tomelin photo, PA-128847. **Dickins** PAC C-57675. **Diefenbaker**PAC C-17646. **Dionne** PAC/Nea Services, C-36305. **Dollard** PAC C-7695. **Donnelly** Martha Staigys. **Doucet** CP. **J. Douglas** PAC C-3316. **T.C. Douglas** PAC C-36221. **Drapeau** Courtesy of Mayor's Office, Montreal. **Dressler** Balvis Rubess. **Dubé** PAC PA-100966. **Dufferin** PAC C-2124. **Dumont** PAC C-15282. **S.J. Duncan** PAC C-46447. **W. Duncan** PAC C-36058. **Dunlop** Metropolitan Toronto Library Board. **Duplessis** PAC C-19522. **Durelle** SHF. **Eaton** David Shaw. **Edwards** Glenbow NA-450-1. **Elgin** PAC C-6737. **Engel** Courtesy of Marian Engel/Paul Orenstein photo. **Erickson** PAC PA-114590, Toronto Star Collection. **Fairclough** PAC/D. Cameron photo, PA-129249. **Ferguson** PAC/NFB/Chris Lund photo, PA-111381. **Fessenden** PAC PA-93160. **Findley** Courtesy of Nancy Colbert & Associates/Robert Lansdale photo. **Fleming** Courtesy of Confederation Life/artist Rex Woods. **Forrester** Courtesy of CBC/Norman Chamberlin photo. **Forsey** PAC PA-120736. **Fowke** Dagmar Stegelmann. **Fox** Canada Wide Feature Service Ltd./Fred Thornhill photo. **Franca**

Courtesy of National Ballet of Canada/Ken Bell photo. **Fraser** PAC/artist C.W. Jefferys, C-70270. **Fréchette** PAC PA-123941. **Frontenac** PAC/artist C.W. Jefferys, C-73710. **Frum** Courtesy of CBC. **Frye** Courtesy of University of Toronto/Robert Lansdale photo. **Fulford** Courtesy of CBC/Norman Chamberlin photo. **Gagnon** Courtesy of Showbiz International. **Galbraith** CP/Doug Ball photo. **Gallant** PAC PA-114591. **Gallie** Courtesy of Toronto General Hospital. **Galt** PAC C-11066. **Garneau** PAC C-6721. **Gascon** Courtesy of Stratford Festival. **Gay** David Shaw. **Gélinas** PAC/NFB/Ronny Jacques photo, PA-122724. **Dan George** Courtesy of CBC/Fred Phipps photo. **Gerussi** Courtesy of CBC/Jorge Waterhouse-Hayward photo. **Gilbert** Courtesy of Confederation Life/artist J.D. Kelly-H.B. Goodridge. **Gimby** PAC C-26756. **Gladstone** Glenbow NA-1524-1. **Gorman** PAC/SHF PA-50382. **Gould** Courtesy of CBC/Robert C. Ragsdale photo. **Gouzenko** CP. **C. Grant** PAC/artist C.W. Jefferys, C-73663. **G.M. Grant** PAC C-50192. **L. Greene** Courtesy of Lorne Greene. **N. Greene** PAC/SHF PA-50385. **Grenfell** PAC C-68717. **Gretzky** Bob Mummery photo. **Grey Owl** Archives of Ontario S.144482. **Groulx** PAC C-16657. **Grove** Courtesy of McClelland and Stewart. **Guibord** Martha Staigys. **Gun-an-noot** PABC 12931. **C. Gzowski** Archives of Ontario S.17159. **P. Gzowski** Globe and Mail/Davis photo. **Haliburton** PAC C-6087. **Hall** PAC C-18743. **Hamel** Self-portrait, courtesy of Musée du Séminaire de Québec. Also by Hamel: portrait of Jacques Cartier. **Hanlan** PAC C-25324. **L. Harris** PAC C-85902. By Lawren Harris: portrait of Salem Bland. **R. Harris** Self-portrait, Permanent Collection, Confederation Centre Art Gallery and Museum, Charlottetown. Also by Robert Harris: portraits of John A. Macdonald and Oliver Mowat. **Harron** Courtesy of CBC. **Hart** Courtesy of Royal Winnipeg Ballet/David Cooper photo. **Hatfield** Courtesy of Premier's Office, N.B. **Hawley** CP/GnM Derek DeBono photo. **Bond Head** National Gallery of Canada/artist N. Cook. **Hearne** PAC/HBC/artist Franklin Arbuckle, C-4280. **Hébert** Courtesy of General Publishing/Ulf Andersen photo. **Helmcken** PAC C-36104. **Henday** PAC/artist Franklin Arbuckle, C-22276. **Hepburn** PAC/SHF PA-50388. **Herzberg** PAC/NFB/Chris Lund photo, PA-128062. **Hewitt** PAC/SHF PA-50277. **Hill** Courtesy of B.C. Fiedler Management. **Hillier** University of Toronto Archives. **Hincks** PAC C-17563. **Hind** Courtesy of Winnipeg Free Press. **Hirsch** Courtesy of Stratford Festival/David Street photo. **Hoffman** PAC PA-116800. **Hoodless** PAC C-85284. **Houde** PAC/Arthur Roy photo, PA-47186. **Houston** Courtesy of McClelland and Stewart/NSL. **C.D. Howe** PAC C-68669. **G. Howe** PAC/Hockey Hall of Fame, PA-50540. **J. Howe** PAC C-44304. **Hudson** PAC C-2061. **M. Hughes** Adrienne Hughes photo. **S. Hughes** PAC C-2468. **Hull** PAC/Hockey Hall of Fame, PA-50502. **Hunter** Courtesy of CBC/Anne Grieves photo. **Iberville** PAC/artist C.W. Jefferys, C-70248. **Innis** PAC C-19695. **Irwin** PAC C-23092. **A.Y. Jackson** Courtesy of Dr. Naomi Jackson Groves. **R. Jackson** SHF. **Jefferys** Courtesy of National Gallery of Canada. Illustrations by C.W. Jefferys: Brûlé, By, Cabot, Champlain, Cook, Fraser, Frontenac, Grant, Iberville, Jolliet, Lescarbot, Salaberry, Selkirk, and Simcoe. **Jenkins** CP. **Jewett** Courtesy of NDP/Photo Features Ltd. **E. Johnson** Constantine Zottas. **P. Johnson** PAC C-14141. **Jolliet** PAC/artist C.W. Jefferys, C-70269. **Julien** Courtesy of CBC Photo Library, Montreal. **Juliette** Courtesy of Mrs. J. Cavazzi. **C. Kain** Archives of the Canadian Rockies, Banff/Byron Harmon photo. **K. Kain** Courtesy of National Ballet of Canada/Andrew Oxenham photo. **Kane** PAC C-261. **Karsh** PAC/NFB/Chris Lund photo, PA-129375. **Keefer** PAC PA-11852. **F. Kelsey** Colin Gillies. **H. Kelsey** Courtesy of Confederation Life/artist Rex Woods. **Kelso** PAC C-85881. **Kennedy** Courtesy of Betty Kennedy. **Kenojuak** Courtesy of West Baffin Eskimo Co-operative/Tessa Macintosh photo. **Khan** Courtesy of Sharif Khan. **Knudson** PAC/SHF PA-50407. **Konihowski** Athlete Information Bureau. **Korman** Courtesy of Scholastic-TAB Publications Ltd. **Krieghoff** Self-portrait, National Gallery of Canada. **Kurelek** PAC PA-12962. **Lacombe** Courtesy of RCMP/artist Frederic Remington. **Lafleur** PAC PA-112331. **La Fontaine** PAC C-5961. **Lalonde** PAC PA-100311. **Larsen** PAC C-70771. **La Salle** PAC/artist J.N. Marchand, C-17560. **Laskin** CP. **Laurence** Courtesy of University of Toronto/Robert Lansdale photo. **Laurier** PAC C-16748. **Laval** PAC/artist Frank Craig, C-10621. **La Vérendrye** PAC/artist A.H. Hider, C-6896. **Layton** Courtesy of McClelland and Stewart/Sherry Collins photo. **Leacock** PAC PA-110154. **D. Lee** Paul Orenstein photo. **J. Léger** PAC PA-121653. **P.E. Léger** Ken Bell photo. **Le Loutre** PAC C-1226. **Lemelin** Photo La Presse, Montreal. **Lemieux** Rose Zgodzinski. **Lesage** PAC/Duncan Cameron photo, PA-108147. **Lescarbot** PAC/artist C.W. Jefferys, C-106968. **Lévesque** PAC PA-117514. **Lewis** Courtesy of NDP/Photo Features Ltd. **Leyrac** Courtesy of CBC Photo Library, Montreal/Francis J. Menten photo. **Lifeson** Courtesy of Anthem Records of Canada/photo by Dimo Safari for Safari Images Ltd. **Lightfoot** Courtesy of Early Morning Productions. **Lismer** Courtesy of Art Gallery of Ontario. **Little** Graham Pilsworth. **Longboat** Dagmar Stegelmann. **Longden** PAC/SHF PA-50410. **Loring** Rose Zgodzinski. **Lougheed** Courtesy of Government of Alberta. **McAskill** PAC C-18686. **McBride** PAC C-6907. **McCarthy** PAC PA-25698. **McClelland** Courtesy of McClelland and Stewart. **McClung** Glenbow NA-1514-3. **McClure** PAC C-87256. **McConachie** PAC C-61893. **McCrae** PAC C-46284. **McCulloch** Public Archives of Nova Scotia. **McCurdy** University of Toronto Archives. **F. MacDonald** PAC C-6862. **J.A. Macdonald** Oil sketch by Robert Harris, private collection, Toronto. **J.E.H. MacDonald** Courtesy of National Gallery of Canada. **MacEwan** Provincial Archives of Alberta PA-168012. **McGarrigle** Courtesy of Jane McGarrigle/Randy Saharuni photo. **McGee** PAC C-16749. **McGill** Courtesy of RCMP. **McGillivray** PAC/artist Sir Martin Shee, C-167. **Ada Mackenzie** PAC/SHF PA-50296. **Sir Alexander Mackenzie** National Gallery of Canada/artist Sir Thomas Lawrence. **Alexander Mackenzie** PAC C-3890. **Bob and Doug McKenzie** Courtesy of Janice Polley. **W.L. Mackenzie** PAC/artist John W.L. Forster, C-11095. **W.L. Mackenzie King** PAC C-52832. **McLarnin** PAC/SHF PA-50295. **McLauchlan** Courtesy of Finkelstein Management Company. **MacLennan** Courtesy of Macmillan of Canada/Peter Paterson photo. **Macleod** Courtesy of RCMP. **McLuhan** Courtesy of CBC/Robert C. Ragsdale photo. **MacMillan** PAC C-16994. **Allan MacNab** PAC C-3615. **Archie MacNab** PAC C-22273.

McNaughton PAC C-33103. From *McNaughton*, Vol. 2 by John A. Swettenham. Reprinted by permission of McGraw-Hill Ryerson Limited. **Macphail** NFB. **Magnussen** Constantine Zottas. **Maillet** Courtesy of Antonine Maillet/Guy Dubois photo. **Mair** PAC PA-25944. **Maisonneuve** Courtesy of Confederation Life/artist Don Anderson. **Mance** PAC C-14360. **Maquinna** PABC 7931. **Marie de l'Incarnation** PAC/artist C.W. Jefferys, C-73422. **Marshall** Courtesy of CBC. **C.B. Martin** Courtesy of Law Society of Upper Canada. **Massey** PAC C-30795. **Maynard** Self-portrait, PABC 92057. **Meares** PABC 3591. **Meighen** PAC PA-26987. **Merritt** Archives of Ontario S-657. **Messer** artist David Shaw. **Michener** CP/Bill Corbett photo. **Middleton** PAC PA-12197. **Milne** PAC C-57194. **Miner** Courtesy of Jack Miner Foundation. **J. Mitchell** Graham Pilsworth. **W.O. Mitchell** Courtesy of University of Toronto/Robert Lansdale photo. **Moberly** PABC 3507. **Monck** Dagmar Stegelmann. **Montcalm** PAC/artist A.H. Hider, C-21457. **Montgomery** PAC C-66946. **Moodie** PAC C-7043. **Morenz** PAC C-29495. **Morrice** Self-portrait, courtesy of National Gallery of Canada. **F. Mowat** Courtesy of McClelland and Stewart/Ray Webber photo. **O. Mowat** Portrait by Robert Harris, courtesy of Government of Ontario Art Collection. **Mulroney** Courtesy of Progressive Conservative Party of Canada. **Munro** Courtesy of *The Review*, Imperial Oil Ltd./Barry Dursley photo. **Murphy** Glenbow NC-6-3152. **A. Murray** Constantine Zottas. **J.W. Murray** Courtesy of Fitzhenry & Whiteside/artist Rob McPhail. **M. Murray** CP. **Mynarski** Vlasta van Kampen. **Naismith** PAC C-80002. **Nattrass** Athlete Information Bureau. **Neatby** Saskatchewan Archives Board S-B 1182. **E. Nelligan** PAC C-88566. **K. Nelligan** Courtesy of Mr. and Mrs. P. Nelligan/Brigitte Lacombe photo. **Nelson** PAC C-28190. **Nicholas** Courtesy of Cindy Nicholas/Peter Mykusz photo. **Norquay** PAC C-12882. **Notman** PAC C-1153. **Nowlan** Courtesy of University of New Brunswick Public Relations Office/Kathleen Flanagan photo. **O'Donoghue** Courtesy of Canadian Labour Congress, PAC C-43281. **Oliver** PAC/artist Henri Julien, C-11436. **Ondaatje** Courtesy of Michael Ondaatje/Rolf Kalman photo. **Onderdonk** PABC 2917. **Orr** SHF. **Osler** Courtesy of the Canadian Medical Association. **Page** PAC/SHF PA-50447. **Palliser** Glenbow NA-808-1. **Papineau** PAC C-5414. **Pearson** PAC/Don McKague photo, PA-117612. **Peckford** Courtesy of Premier's Office, Government of Newfoundland. **Peguis** Courtesy of Peguis Publishers, Winnipeg. **Pellan** Courtesy of National Gallery of Canada/Philip Pocock photo. **Penfield** PAC/NFB/Chris Lund photo, PA-128398. **Peterson** Courtesy of Oscar Peterson/Regal Recordings/Horvath photo. **Piapot** PAC C-3864. **Pickford** Courtesy of McClelland and Stewart/NSL/Famous Players. **Pinsent** Courtesy of CBC/Norman Chamberlin photo. **Pitseolak** Courtesy of West Baffin Eskimo Co-operative/James Manning photo. **Plante** PAC C-29951. **Podborski** Athlete Information Bureau. **Pontiac** PAC C-11250. **Potts** Courtesy of RCMP. **Poundmaker** Saskatchewan Archives Board R-A 2872(1). **E.J. Pratt** Courtesy of Victoria University Library/Marcel Ray photo. **Purdy** Courtesy of McClelland and Stewart. **Radisson** Vlasta van Kampen. **Rae** Courtesy of Hudson's Bay Company. **Raffi** Courtesy of Troubadour Records/Peter Patterson photo. **Reaney** Courtesy of the University of Western Ontario. **Richard** PAC/Hockey Hall of Fame, PA-48850. **Richler** Courtesy of McClelland and Stewart. **Riel** Glenbow NA-504-3. **Rijnhart** From S.C. Rijnhart, *With the Tibetans in Tent and Temple* (Fleming H. Revell, 1901). **Roberts** PAC C-25611. **Robertson** Graham Pilsworth. **Robinson** Metropolitan Toronto Library Board. **Robson** PAC C-36107. **Roddick** Courtesy of Canadian Medical Association. **Rosenfeld** PAC/SHF. **Ross** Courtesy of McClelland and Stewart/Leiva photo. **Roy** Courtesy of McClelland and Stewart/John Reeves photo. **Ryan** PAC PA-117515. **Ryerson** PAC C-14235. **St. Laurent** PAC PA-125907. **Sainte-Marie** Courtesy of CBC/Fred Phipps photo. **Salaberry** PAC/artist C.W. Jefferys, C-70238. **Sauvé** Courtesy of Speaker's Office/Proulx Brothers photo. **Schreyer** Courtesy of Governor General's Office/Cavouk photo. **Schubert** PABC 7106. **Schultz** PAC PA-33253. **B.A. Scott** PAC/SHF PA-49893. **T. Scott** Metropolitan Toronto Library Board. **Secord** PAC/artist Lorne Smith, C-11053. **Selkirk** PAC/artist C.W. Jefferys, C-16750. **Selye** PAC/NFB/Chris Lund photo, PA-116671. **Service** Courtesy of McClelland and Stewart. **Seton** PAC C-9485. **Shadd** Courtesy of Colin A. Thomson, from his book *Blacks in Deep Snow* (Toronto: Dent, 1979). **Shawnawdithit** Provincial Archives of Newfoundland and Labrador A17-110. **Shearer** *Motion Picture Magazine*, February 1930. **Sifton** PAC PA-28125. **Simcoe** PAC/artist C.W. Jefferys, C-73667. **Simonds** Courtesy of Canadian War Museum/PAC. **Simpson** Notman Photographic Archives, McCord Museum, McGill University. **Sinclair** Courtesy of CBC/Fred Phipps photo. **Skreslet** Courtesy of Programmed Communications, Montreal. **Skvorecky** Courtesy of University of Toronto/Robert Lansdale photo. **Smallwood** PAC PA-113253. **G. Smith** Metropolitan Toronto Library Board. **Snively** Courtesy of Toronto General Hospital. **Somerville** PAC/SHF PA-50307. **Stanfield** Courtesy of Progressive Conservative Party of Canada. **Steele** Courtesy of RCMP. **Stefansson** PAC C-9439. **Steinhauer** Glenbow NA-352-4. **Stephen** PAC C-16322. **Stephenson** Department of National Defence/Hamish Hamilton Ltd. **Stowe** PAC C-9480. **Strachan** Metropolitan Toronto Library Board. **Strathcona** PAC C-3693. **Streit** PAC/SHF PA-50472. **Suzuki** Courtesy of CBC/Fred Phipps photo. **Swan** PAC PA-51546. **Taché** PAC PA-74103. **Takashima** Courtesy of Shizuye Takashima. **Talon** Courtesy of Confederation Life/artist Rex Woods. **Tanguay** Colin Gillies. **Tanner** Sports Hall of Fame. **Tarte** PAC/artist Henri Julien, C-13537. **Taschereau** PAC C-23565. **Angella Taylor** Athlete Information Bureau. **Cyclone Taylor** PAC/Hockey Hall of Fame, PA-49401. **Tecumseh** PAC/artist Lorne Smith, C-11052. **Tekakwitha** PAC C-4765. **Tennant** Courtesy of the National Ballet of Canada/Andrew Oxenham photo. **J. Thompson** PAC C-698. **Tom Thomson** Courtesy of Tom Thomson Memorial Gallery of Fine Art, Owen Sound. **Three Persons** Glenbow NA-778-7. **Tilley** PAC PA-25549. **Traill** PAC PA-117832. **Tremblay** Courtesy of John C. Goodwin et Associés. **Trout** Courtesy of Perth County Archives. **Trudeau** PAC/Duncan Cameron photo, PA-116412. **Tupper** PAC PA-25584. **Turnbull** Colin Gillies. **Tyson** Courtesy of CBC. **Uniacke** Public Archives of Nova Scotia. **Vancouver** Courtesy of Confederation Life/artist J.D. Kelly. **Van Horne** Notman Photographic

Archives, McCord Museum, McGill University. **Vanier** PAC C-63531. **Varley** Self-portrait, National Gallery of Canada. **Vaudreuil** PAC/artist Henri Beau, C-10614. **Verchères** PAC/artist C.W. Jefferys, C-10687. **Verigin** PABC 24169. **Vigneault** Courtesy of Les Productions Nordet/photo Birgit. **Walsh** Courtesy of RCMP. **Walters** Vlasta van Kampen. **Walton** PAC/SHF PA-50308. **Ware** Glenbow NA-263-1. **Watson** Courtesy of Mr. William Watson. **Wayne & Shuster** Courtesy of CBC/Harold White photo. **Weinzweig** Courtesy of CBC/Fred Phipps photo. **Whitton** PAC/Apex Photos, PA-121982. **Wiebe** Courtesy of Rudy Wiebe/Jorge Frascara photo. **Willan** PAC C-16995. **P. Williams** PAC/SHF PA-50465. **Willson** Martha Staigys. **E. Wilson** Courtesy of Eric Wilson/David Nicholas photo, *Atlantic Insight*. **Wolfe** PAC/artist Benjamin West, C-12248. **Wise Wood** Glenbow NA-2715-4. **Rex Woods** Illustrations of Kelsey and Talon. **Woodsworth** PAC C-55449. **Workman** PAC C-52307. **G. Young** PAC/SHF PA-50309. **Zurakowski** PAC C-61731.

Index

The following abbreviations are used in the index:

CC Companion of the Order of Canada
OC Officer of the Order of Canada
CM Member of the Order of Canada
VC Victoria Cross
CV Cross of Valour

Where a page number is given in italics, that means that the person does not have an individual biography. Information about this person will be found in someone else's biography on the page indicated.